COLERIDGE'S WRITINGS
General Editor: John Beer

Volume 2: On Humanity

COLERIDGE'S WRITINGS

Myriad-minded in his intellectual interests, Coleridge often passed quickly from one subject to another, so that the range and mass of the materials he left can be bewildering to later readers. *Coleridge's Writings* is a series addressed to those who wish to have a guide to his important statements on particular subjects. Each volume presents his writings in a major field of human knowledge or thought, tracing the development of his ideas. Connections are also made with relevant writings in the period, suggesting the extent to which Coleridge was either summing up, contributing to or reacting against current developments. Each volume is produced by a specialist in the field; the general editor is John Beer, Professor of English Literature at Cambridge, who has published various studies of Coleridge's thought and poetry.

Coleridge's Writings

Volume 2

On Humanity

Edited by

ANYA TAYLOR

Professor of English, John Jay College of Criminal Justice
The City University of New York

St. Martin's Press

Selection and editorial matter © Anya Taylor 1994
Foreword © John Beer 1994

All rights reserved. No reproduction, copy or transmission of
this publication may be made without written permission.

No paragraph of this publication may be reproduced, copied or
transmitted save with written permission or in accordance with
the provisions of the Copyright, Designs and Patents Act 1988,
or under the terms of any licence permitting limited copying
issued by the Copyright Licensing Agency, 90 Tottenham Court
Road, London W1P 9HE.

Any person who does any unauthorised act in relation to this
publication may be liable to criminal prosecution and civil
claims for damages.

First published in Great Britain 1994 by
THE MACMILLAN PRESS LTD
Houndmills, Basingstoke, Hampshire RG21 2XS
and London
Companies and representatives
throughout the world

A catalogue record for this book is available
from the British Library.

ISBN 0–333–54851–5

Printed in Great Britain by
Antony Rowe Ltd
Chippenham, Wiltshire

First published in the United States of America 1994 by
Scholarly and Reference Division,
ST. MARTIN'S PRESS, INC.,
175 Fifth Avenue,
New York, N.Y. 10010

ISBN 0–312–12129–6

Library of Congress Cataloging-in-Publication Data
(Revised for volume 2)
Coleridge, Samuel Taylor, 1772–1834.
Coleridge's writings.

Vol. 2 published: New York : St. Martin's Press.
Includes bibliographical references and indexes.
Contents: v. 1 On politics and society / edited by
John Morrow — v. 2 On humanity / edited by Anya
Taylor.
I. Anya Taylor. II. Morrow, John, Ph. D.
PR4472.M67 1994   821'.7   90–8673
ISBN 0–691–06887–9 (v. 1 : alk. paper)
ISBN 0–691–01503–1 (v. 1 : pbk. : alk. paper)
ISBN 0–312–12129–6 (v. 2)

Contents

Foreword by John Beer		vii
Preface		ix
List of Abbreviations		xi
Coleridge's Life		xiii

	Introduction	1

1	**Enquiries into the Nature of Man**	16
	(a) General Definitions of Man	16
	(b) Fluctuating Terms for Subjectivity: The Continuum	
	of Consciousness	23
	(i) The Body and Dreams	24
	(ii) Consciousness and Self-consciousness	30
	(iii) Inferred Continuities: Spirit and Soul	39
	(c) Persons	52

2	**Questions of Species and Gender**	55
	(a) The Challenge of Evolution	55
	(i) Human Beings and Animals	55
	(ii) Human Beings and the 'Laws of Nature'	66
	(iii) Early man	77
	(b) Women	82

3	**The Difficulty of Sustaining Humanity**	98
	(a) Lapses from Human Independence	98
	(i) Dependency on Drugs and Alcohol	103
	(ii) Dependency on the Will of the Group	115
	(iii) Economic Dependency	117
	(b) Mistaking Persons for Things	119
	(i) Slavery	122
	(ii) Terror and Militarism	131
	(iii) Industry and Trade	134
	(c) Human Evil	139

4 Transmitting Humanity   156
  (a) Marriage   156
  (b) Child-rearing   180
  (c) Education   200

5 The Humanity of Human Beings   218
  (a) Distinctive Faculties   218
    (i) Reason and Understanding   221
    (ii) Imagination and Fancy   227
    (iii) Conscience and Will   228
  (b) Distinctive Activities   229
    (i) Language   233
    (ii) Creative Arts   235
  (c) Distinctive Emotions   244
    (i) Love   245
    (ii) Guilt   255
    (iii) Yearning for Immortality   257

Notes   264
Select Bibliography   273
Index   276

Foreword

The appearance of hitherto unpublished material in the present century has brought out more fully the range and complexity of Coleridge's intelligence and knowledge. The *Notebooks* and *Collected Works*, both now well on the way to completion, together with the *Collected Letters*, have made it increasingly evident that this was the most extraordinary English mind of the time. The specialist or more general student who wishes to know what Coleridge had to say on a particular subject may, however, find the sheer mass of materials bewildering, since in his less formal writings Coleridge passed quickly from one subject to another. *Coleridge's Writings* is a series addressed to such readers. In each volume a particular area of Coleridge's interest is explored, with an attempt to present his most significant statements and to show the development of his thought on the subject in question.

His emphasis changed over the years. In the 1790s he involved himself with contemporary politics but became disillusioned with the prospects for immediate action; he then turned to think more intensively about criticism, religion, and the processes of the human mind. Further issues were always interwoven, however, such as the nature of language and what it is to be human; it is the latter that provides the basis for the present volume. Coleridge constantly returned to a fundamental assertion that mechanistic views of the world, whether in politics, philosophy or religion, led to the treatment of people in society as things rather than as persons, resulting in evils such as slavery and the exploitation of cheap labour. He was also concerned by the existence of abuses such as those connected with alcoholism, his critique being complicated by his own long struggle with drug addiction. Most intricate of all were his studies of human love, which he believed to provide the key to an understanding of the humanity of human beings, yet knew to his cost to be capable of creating extreme misery. The intractability of some of the problems involved led him to a belief in the importance of re-education at both the social and the individual levels, a process in which an enlightened religion could play an important part. This did not hinder him from attacking very directly some of the more obvious social abuses of the time, such as the use of child labour in factories.

In this volume Anya Taylor traces the course of such investigations and conclusions in the various texts where they are to be found, bringing the relevant statements into thematic sequences where they will be seen to illuminate one another and to stand as parts of a long and complex inquiry and insistence. The collection she has assembled, which has no predecessor on such a scale, will lead to a deeper understanding of the unity in all Coleridge's thinking.

Further projected volumes will include Coleridge's writings on language, on criticism and on nature. There will be no attempt at exhaustive presentation of Coleridge's writings on any of the subjects to be dealt with; for such further purposes the collected editions will remain indispensable. The purpose of the volumes in this series is to complement those more comprehensive presentations by drawing attention to his key statements and assembling them, with apposite commentary, in a coherent and approachable form.

J.B.B.
General Editor

Preface

The Collected Works, which began appearing in 1969 and are now moving towards completion, present us as never before with the evidence for Coleridge's concern with issues still alive in our age. The volume of his commentary on the contemporary scene, on philosophy, on religion, on politics, is seen to outweigh by far his poetic production, reinforcing the reputation he gained among his contemporaries as a significant thinker. The notes and commentary point us at every turn to the wider world – to debates on the slave trade and child labour, to influences from Germany, to sources in Plotinus, to readings in zoology – and to parallel passages in Coleridge's own work that indicate the swerves of his enquiries.

The history of the years between 1789 and 1834 has thus become available through the eyes of one of the era's geniuses, a man who was at the centre of consciousness (and of conscience) in his time. Meanwhile, individual passages of prose have become newly visible as adventures in intensely wrought language.

In attempting to provide a means of entry to this many-faceted achievement the present volume – interdisciplinary because of the very nature of Coleridge's thought – draws from an assortment of public and private writing: letters, notebook entries, sermons, lectures, meditations. The selections come from every period and therefore show where his opinions changed importantly during his lifetime. Some belong to the period in the 1790s when he was radical in his politics and full of reforming zeal. Others belong to the period of close collaboration with Wordsworth, when he was particularly intent on psychological explorations and on teasing out the full implications of being human by way of close observation. A third group belongs to the period after his quarrel with Wordsworth and his subsequent spiritual crisis, when his main purpose was to ground his view of humanity in divine truth. In several sections of the book the extracts show him moving through all three phases in turn.

Another factor emerges, however. Although he might turn away from some of his opinions during his career, it was his more characteristic behaviour as he advanced to try to retain what he felt to be good in his previous positions. For this reason the writings of the third phase are particularly complex, since they contain layerings from the earlier ones – even at the risk of self-contradiction. One reason that his contemporaries were at once fascinated and baffled lay in the fact that knowledge of the three phases was not always available to them. Modern readers are in a happier condition, being able to turn to the volumes of the *Collected Works* for some of the unpublished texts involved. The extracts in the present volume are also supplemented there by further explanations and fuller contexts.

My greatest indebtedness is clearly to Kathleen Coburn and the individual editors of *The Collected Works*, as well as to the editor of the *Collected Letters*. I am also grateful to Princeton University Press and Oxford University Press for continuing to permit the use of texts from the relevant volumes, and to Mrs A. H. B. Coleridge, for permission to quote brief extracts from some as yet unpublished manuscript material. John Beer, the general editor of this series of volumes, has worked meticulously, tactfully and wisely to correct my errors, beautify my sentences and enlarge my understanding. I am grateful for the privilege of working with him. At Macmillan Press Valery Rose has transformed an often chaotic-looking manuscript into a coherent whole. In addition, I wish to thank the worldwide, remarkably loving community of Coleridgeans, especially friends who have helped me in many specific ways: Marilyn Gaull, Raimonda Modiano, Anthony John Harding, J. Robert Barth, Laurence Lockridge, Heather Jackson, and Richard Matlack; also, in my own interdisciplinary college, the stalwart core of friends who have kept me alert and helped me with specific problems: Elisabeth Gitter, Patricia Licklider, Anne Barbeau-Gardiner, Robert C. Pinckert and Robert Crozier; and the staff of the microcomputer lab who patiently helped me with a difficult text.

Most of all I wish to thank my companion of 30 years, Mark Taylor, who has been my best reader, jester and consoler; my mother, Adda B. Bozeman, and step-father, Arne Barkhuus, who have encouraged me by the example of their vigour and curiosity; and my sons, Andrew and Nicholas, who have grown to manhood while Coleridge kept his long residence in our home.

List of Abbreviations

Add. Ms.	Coleridge manuscript notebook, British Library (Add. Ms) as shown. See also *N* below.
AR	S. T. Coleridge, *Aids to Reflection*, ed. John Beer (1993), *CC* 9.
BL	S. T. Coleridge, *Biographia Literaria, or Biographical Sketches of My Literary Life and Opinions*, ed. James Engell and W. Jackson Bate (1983), *CC* 7.
C&S	S. T. Coleridge, *On the Constitution of the Church and State According to the Idea of Each*, ed. John Colmer (1976), *CC* 10.
CC	*Collected Works of Samuel Taylor Coleridge*, gen. ed. Kathleen Coburn (Princeton, N.J., 1969–).
CL	*Collected Letters of Samuel Taylor Coleridge*, ed. Earl Leslie Griggs, 6 vols (Oxford, 1956–71).
CM	S. T. Coleridge, *Marginalia*, ed. George Whalley and Heather Jackson (1980–), *CC* 12.
CN	*Notebooks of Samuel Taylor Coleridge*, ed. Kathleen Coburn (New York and Princeton, N.J., 1957–).
EOT	*Essays on his Times*, ed. David V. Erdman, 3 vols (1978), *CC* 3.
Friend	S. T. Coleridge, *The Friend*, ed. Barbara E. Rooke, 2 vols (1969), *CC* 4.
Lects 1795	S. T. Coleridge, *Lectures 1795: On Politics and Religion*, ed. Lewis Patton and Peter Mann (1971) *CC* 1.
Lects 1808–19	S. T. Coleridge, *Lectures 1808–1819: On Literature*, ed. Reginald A. Foakes, 2 vols (1990), *CC* 5.
Logic	S. T. Coleridge, *Logic*, ed. J. R. de J. Jackson (1981), *CC* 13.
LS	S. T. Coleridge, *Lay Sermons*, ed. R. J. White (1972), *CC* 6.
N	Numbered Coleridge notebook in British Library: see also Add. Ms. above.
Op Max ms	S. T. Coleridge, *Opus Maximum* manuscript, Victoria College, Toronto, Canada.
PL (1949)	S. T. Coleridge, *Philosophical Lectures*, ed. Kathleen Coburn (London, 1949).

PW (EHC)   *The Complete Poetical Works of Samuel Taylor Coleridge,*
             ed. E. H. Coleridge, 2 vols (Oxford, 1912).
TL   S. T. Coleridge, *Hints Towards the Formation of a More
             Comprehensive Theory of Life,* ed. Seth B. Watson (1848);
             forthcoming in *Shorter Works and Fragments* (*CC*).
TT   S. T. Coleridge, *Table Talk,* ed. Carl Woodring, 2 vols
             (1990), *CC* 14.

Coleridge's Life

The following outline records some crucial events in Coleridge's career, particularly in relation to his writings on humanity. Full chronologies are printed in the various volumes of the Princeton *Collected Coleridge*.

1772   Coleridge born (21 October).
1781   (Oct)   Death of Coleridge's father.
1782   (until 1791)   School at Christ's Hospital, London.
1791   (until late 1794)   At Jesus College, Cambridge.
1794   (June)   Welsh tour; meeting with Southey at Oxford initiates pantisocratic scheme.
1795   (Jan)   Bristol Lectures begun;
        (May–June)   'Six Lectures on Revealed Religion'.
        (Oct)   Marriage to Sara Fricker.
        (Dec)   *Conciones ad Populum; The Plot Discovered.*
1796   (March–May)   *The Watchman.*
        (June)   Visits William and Dorothy Wordsworth at Racedown in Dorset.
        (Sept)   Hartley Coleridge born.
1797   (Nov)   'The Ancient Mariner' begun.
1798   (March)   'The Ancient Mariner' completed.
        (spring)   Swiss cantons suppressed: 'Recantation' (later 'France: an Ode'); 'Fears in Solitude'.
        (May)   Berkeley Coleridge born.
        (Sept)   *Lyrical Ballads* published; to Germany with the Wordsworths.
1799   Attends lectures on literature, biblical criticism and physiology at Göttingen.
        (April)   News of death of Berkeley.
        (July)   Return to England.
        (autumn)   Friendship with Humphry Davy begins.
        (Oct–Nov)   Visits Lakes; meets Sara Hutchinson.
        (Nov)   In London writing for *Morning Post* to April 1800.
        (Dec)   'On the French Constitution'.
1800   (Sept)   Derwent Coleridge born.
1801   (Mar–Nov)   Severe domestic discord.
        (Nov)   In London writing for *Morning Post* to March 1802.

1802   (Sept–Nov) In London writing for the *Morning Post*.
        (Oct)   Verse-letter of April to Sara Hutchinson published
        in new form as 'Dejection'.
        (Dec)   Sara Coleridge born.
1803   (Summer)   Scottish tour with Wordsworths
1804   (Jan–Mar)   In London, writing for *The Courier*.
1804–6   In Malta and Sicily, first as under-secretary to Alexander
        Ball, British High Commissioner. Drafts 'Observations on
        Egypt'.
1805   (Jan)   Acting Public Secretary in Malta.
1806   (Jan)   In Rome: meets Washington Allston, the Hum-
        boldts, L. Tieck, and Schlegel.
        (Aug)   Return to England.
        (Nov)   Keswick, determined on separation from Mrs C.
1807   (Mar)   Slave trade abolished.
1808   (Jan–June)   First literary lectures in London.
        (July)   Review of Clarkson, *History of the Abolition of the
        Slave Trade*.
        (Nov)   First prospectus of *The Friend*.
1809   (June)   First number of *The Friend*.
1810   (Mar)   Last number of *The Friend*; Sara Hutchinson leaves
        Grasmere for Wales.
        (Oct)   To London; quarrel with Wordsworth.
1812   Second edition of *The Friend*.
1813   *Remorse* opens at Drury Lane.
1813–14   In Bath and Bristol; spiritual crisis; lectures on Shake-
        speare, education, French Revolution and Napoleon.
        (Sept to Dec)   'Letters to Mr Justice Fletcher' in *The
        Courier*.
1815   (June)   Waterloo.
        (July–Sept)   Dictating *Biographia Literaria*.
1816   (April)   Accepted as house-mate by Gillmans at Highgate.
        (May)   'Christabel', 'Kubla Khan' and 'The Pains of Sleep'
        published.
        (Dec)   *The Statesman's Manual*.
1817   (Jan)   *A Lay Sermon*.
        (Jul)   *Biographia Literaria* and *Sibylline Leaves*.
        (Nov)   *Zapolya*.
1818   (Jan)   'Treatise on Method' in *Encyclopaedia Metropolitana*.
        (April)   Pamphlets supporting Peel against child labour.
        (Nov)   New edition ('*rifaccimento*') of *The Friend*.

1818–19 (Dec–Mar)   Lectures on the history of philosophy and on literature.
1820–2   Troubles with Hartley Coleridge at Oriel College.
1825   *Aids to Reflection* published by 1 June.
         Work on *Church and State* begun.
1828   *Poetical Works* (3 vols).
1829   (Dec)   *Church and State* (second edition, 1830).
1834   (25 July)   Death of Coleridge.

For Mark, Andrew, and Nicholas

Introduction

During the past century, Samuel Taylor Coleridge has been increasingly recognised as an important and original thinker about the nature of humanity, and of human freedom.

Despite his manifold concerns, these were themes that he returned to constantly: he divided the kinds of philosophy prevalent since Plato into those that promote or demean human freedom; he rejected the empirical philosophy of the Enlightenment in so far as its materialism limited human spiritual aspirations; he discovered and promoted the elements in contemporary German philosophy that were congenial to his own Platonic, neoplatonic and Christian thinking, introducing them into England (and into America by way of his admirers there) and showing in the process how they were sometimes indebted to earlier writers in the English tradition; he also enlarged upon their distinctions between reason and understanding and between imagination and fancy in support of his conviction that religion answers to a yearning inherent in the human spirit. Fifty years before *The Origin of Species*, he was considering the evidences of an ascending order in the animal creation and seeking to establish differences between human beings and animals that would avoid total confusion; he called attention to the dangerous consequences of materialist philosophies in the contemporary mistreatment of individual human beings by trade, industry, colonialism and warfare; he drew finer distinctions between the functions and powers within the mind, drawing on psychology, religion and ethics for his examples; and he supported the revolutionary idea that parents and educators should seek to draw out and guide the mental powers of the child in free growth. Yet he was equally insistent that human weakness was an ever-present psychological reality, evil a real power and human beings in need of divine mercy. The results of his inquiries join to form a coherent, inclusive and original philosophy of human freedom, the features of which are newly visible in the many volumes of the *Collected Works*.

Coleridge's political, social, literary and religious investigations into human nature arose from, and often in reaction to, the many 'treatises', 'essays', 'observations' and 'enquiries' on man, human nature and the human mind that were required reading for educated

1

men and women of the eighteenth century. Representative works such as John Locke's *Essay Concerning Human Understanding* (1690), George Berkeley's *Treatise Concerning the Principles of Human Knowledge* (1710), David Hartley's *Observations on Man* (1749), David Hume's *Treatise of Human Nature* (1739) and *Enquiry Concerning Human Understanding* (1758), Alexander Pope's *Essay on Man* (1734), Thomas Reid's *Inquiry into the Human Mind* (1764) and *Essays on the Intellectual Powers of Man* (1785), Dugald Stewart's *Elements of the Philosophy of the Human Mind* (1792), Etienne Bonnot de Condillac's *Essay on the Origin of Human Knowledge* (1746), Claude Adrien Helvetius's *Treatise on Man* (1773), J.-J. Rousseau's *Discourse on the Origins and Foundations of Human Inequality* (1755), and Immanuel Kant's *Anthropology* (1798) display the recurrent fascination with human psychology, human behaviour and the development of human institutions and indicate the wide range of eighteenth-century enquiry into psychology, ethics, ethnography, zoology, medicine, criminology, education, politics and religion, as these areas contributed to an understanding of human nature and its possible progress towards enlightenment.

Saturated with these readings since his boyhood, Coleridge subjected eighteenth-century generalities about human nature to scrutiny, often criticising them for demeaning the potential nobility of the human being. His criticism of Locke, the source in his view of many subsequent eighteenth-century errors, focused on the theory of the mind's blankness at birth, showing in numerous ways how this theory promoted bondage rather than the freedom proclaimed in Locke's liberating political tracts. He saw a contradiction between Locke's famous sentence about the mind – 'Let us suppose the mind to be, as we say, white paper, void of all characters, without any ideas: – How comes it to be furnished?'[1] – and his revolutionary belief that 'the natural liberty of man is to be free from any superior power on earth, and not to be under the will or legislative authority of man, but to have only the law of nature for his rule'.[2] If there was a natural law that men automatically followed, how could they be 'void of characters'?

Coleridge's criticisms of Locke focused on proving that the mind is more complex and active than Locke allowed. To Josiah Wedgwood he wrote a long and thorough critique of Locke's psychology, stressing that such a theory of mind was 'a complete Whirl-dance of Confusion with the words we, Soul, Mind, Consciousness, & Ideas'; for Locke 'the mind is only the Thought-Box', at once 'the Ware-house, the Wares, and the Ware-house-man', a confusion that elim-inates any effective personal agent.[3] The variety of his criticisms can be glimpsed in a notebook entry of November 1813:

> Locke & his Followers always attack the supporters of Innate Ideas, as maintaining a monstrous Tenet contrary to all Experi-ence – Now more than a 100,000 Genera of Living Animals have been already discovered – & this in all probability is not the 20th part of the real Number / A German Philosopher reasoning by analogy of the excess of Plants over Minerals states the result at seven Million – Now in all these innate Ideas do exist – for every other possible explanation of Instinct, i.e. constructive Artificial Instinct, as that of the Spider, the Silk-worm, &c, has [been] dem-onstrated insufficient . . . Grant then that Men's destination is Religion, & Morality, in reference to Immortality – & we shall immediately perceive, of what kind *his* appropriate innate Ideas must be – even those, to wit, which & which alone have ever been contended for – Right & Wrong – Amenability – Infinity – & God.[4]

With astonishing speed Coleridge leapt from the empiricists' denial of innate ideas to the recent German discoveries of zoological species imbued with instincts particular to their natures, and so to the pos-sibility that human beings were therefore also imbued with in-stincts particular to their own distinct kind, instincts, that is, that prepare them for a future life. He was delighted to ground his proposed refutation of Locke in the very empiricism that Locke advocated, and to challenge the atheism of Locke's French and Eng-lish followers by referring to the new German zoological research. But this was only one refutation among many; Coleridge took on the whole previous century for diminishing the imaginative power of human beings even as it advocated individual political rights. David Hume was even more dangerous than Locke, because of his argu-ments against personal identity, against heroic motives in history, against miracles, faith and the soul. Hume, in turn, had had a com-plex influence on the French sceptics, who, Coleridge believed, had undermined human worth.

Eighteenth-century literary predecessors had also erred in follow-ing or absorbing the assumptions of the philosophers that human beings are passive, discontinuous or bestial. Jonathan Swift's Yahoos were not the only debased creatures in the fourth book of *Gulliver's*

Travels. Coleridge argued that even the Houyhnhnms show 'a true Yahooism in the constant denial of the existence of Love, as not identical with friendship, and yet always distinct and very often divided from "lust" . . . a finer imagination would have been evinced if the author had shown the effects of the possession of reason and the moral sense on the outward form and gestures of the horses. In short, critics in general complain of the Yahoos; I complain of the Houyhnhnms.' If indeed these horses had reason and conscience, these higher qualities would transform their animal bodies into 'loveliness and dignity', reversing the process by which human beings who lack reason and moral sense became 'the most loathsome and hateful of all animals', their understanding manifested as 'malignant cunning', their free will as 'obstinacy and unteachableness' – as any madhouse or highway brothel would attest.[5] Coleridge's response to Swift's tale is an example of his extension of literary commentary to a wider study of human nature. Swift, that 'soul of Rabelais dwelling in a dry place', did not enquire deeply enough into the true nature of human beings and was, like the eighteenth-century philosopher at his most limited, in Coleridge's view, 'the contemptuous Calculator, who has left nothing omitted in his scheme of probabilities, except the might of the human mind',[6] the very Lilliputian and Laputan whom Swift himself satirises.

But despite their limitations eighteenth-century studies of human nature introduced new measurements of what is human and what is not, fixing the questionable boundaries of humanity at wild men, at idiots, at primitive peoples, at rustics, even at children. As Alan Bewell has claimed for Wordsworth, Coleridge, too, 'was writing at exactly that moment when the immense field of moral philosophy – the "science of man" – as Hume termed it, was about to break up into the modern disciplines of anthropology, sociology, psychology, philosophical ethics, economics, history, and political science'.[7] These studies, fortified by reports from the field of missionaries, colonial administrators and travellers, provoked questions about the universality of human cultural institutions, about the origins and development of language, family, religion and the state, which were often rendered imaginatively, as by Locke and Rousseau. Coleridge read these reports and speculations and integrated them into his own theories of human development. Like Wordsworth, he was interested in watching marginal individuals for evidence of natural language, natural affection, natural sociability and natural system-building. While he was eager to refute Hobbes's view that man was by nature savage and warlike, motivated solely by fear,[8] he was careful not to sentimentalise the ignorant mountain man, and knew enough about children to see that Locke was wrong to align them with idiots. The margin that most concerned him, however, was the wavering one between human beings and animals. Alert to what A. O. Lovejoy has called 'the *rapprochement* of man and ape' in the eighteenth century,[9] Coleridge struggled to preserve some area of separation. His attention to this juncture provoked some original lines of thought, anticipating the mid-nineteenth-century responses to Charles Darwin's theory of evolution. In small but significant ways, as in his metaphors for human degradation, and in large and daring speculations about the discontinuities in nature, as in his *Theory of Life*, he investigated the gap, or what he often calls the 'chasm', between human beings and animals. Whether he was examining human understanding, love or instinct, he attempted to locate a point at which the capacity could be called 'distinctly human', at which it lifted above the similar but slightly different capacity of the animal, seeking to prove that human beings would not suffer the hopeless mortality of the beasts. This continuing purpose gave a new resonance to his use of the words 'human', 'humanity' and 'human nature', so often repeated by his eighteenth-century predecessors, since he used the terms with a consciousness of human beings as richer, denser, more complex, mysterious and potentially noble creatures. Conversely, his purpose gave additional resonance to his terms of disapprobation: 'brutalised', 'bestial', 'imbrutement', 'be-thinged', and other, often witty, variants of these, for people who have slipped off the bottom of the human scale.

The subtlety of Coleridge's thinking about the differences between human beings and animals can be observed twisting and turning in a notebook entry written some time between 1811 and 1816. This entry is remarkable for its Coleridgean ability to incorporate contradictory views: despite his usual view of human beings as 'ever greater than [their] circumstances' (to quote an 1814 letter[10]) he investigated here the power of environment to impede free choice, concluding, nevertheless, that in some ways people choose their own forms of disintegration, that 'the stimulability determines the existence & character of the Stimulus . . . the temptability constitutes the temptation'. Once people recognise that their own personal nature attracts certain temptations, they can then work to transform that nature, 'to beget each in himself a new man'. The entry reads:

The individuality of Man, how wonderful. No one merely man, as every Tyger is simply Tyger – little more than numerically distinguishable – but this man, with *these* faculties, *these* tendencies, this peculiar character – His Wishes, Hopes, Actions, Fortunes, spring out of his own nature – Quisque suae fortunae faber – But on the other hand, however, this very nature appears conditioned & determined by an outward Nature, that comprehends his own – What each individual *turns out*, (Homo Phainomenon) depends, as it seems, on the narrow Circumstances & Inclosure of his Infancy, Childhood, & Youth – & afterwards on the larger Hedge-girdle of the State, in which he is a Citizen born – & inasmuch as this again receives a stamp & signature from the Zone, Climate, Soil, Character of Country, mountainous or champaign, inland or maritime, intersected with navigable streams or purely pastoral or woodland, he seems to be influenced & determined (caused to be what he is, qualis sit = qualified, *bethinged*) by Universal Nature, its elements & relations. – Beyond this ring-fence he cannot stray, of these circummurations he can seldom overleap the lowest & innermost, and the outermost is his apparent horizon, & insurmountable – from this Skein of necessities he cannot disentangle himself, which surrounds with subtlest intertwine the slenderest fibres of his Being, while it binds the whole frame with chains of adamant –. And yet again, the more steadily he contemplates this fact, the more deeply he meditates on these workings, the more clearly it dawns upon him that this conspiration of influences is no mere outward nor contingent Thing, that rather this necessity *is* himself, that that without which or divided from which his Being can not be even *thought*, must therefore in all its directions and labyrinthine folds belong to his Being, and evolve out of his essences. Abstract from these – and what remains? A general Term, after all the conceptions, notices, and experiences represented by it, had been removed – an Ens logicum [logical Entity] which instead of a *thought* represents only the act and process of Thinking, or rather the form & condition, under which it is possible to think or conceive at all. The more he reflects, the more evident he finds it, that the stimulability determines the existence & character of the Stimulus, the Organ the object, . . . and the Volitions beget the instruments of Action – the temptability constitutes the temptation, and the Man the Motives. – What then remains! O the noblest of all – to know that so it is, and in the warm & genial Light of this knowlege to beget each in himself a new man . . .[11]

In search of whatever it is that constitutes 'this man, with *these* faculties, *these* tendencies, this peculiar character', making choices within a 'Skein of necessities' – 'necessity' that '*is* himself' – Coleridge distinguishes the infinitely various pattern of human life from the sameness of the tiger's instinctive and invariable approach to its environment.

One of Coleridge's major contributions to modern thought is his multiplication of the forms of consciousness, using names from numerous traditions to identify psychological and spiritual forces. He tried to capture the density of personal being, a 'me-ness' that he seemed to experience with an almost preternatural intensity. Self, spirit, soul, self-consciousness, the phantom I, the substantial I, the person, the shadow: these were approaches to a characteristically scintillating experience of 'the slenderest fibres of his Being', the 'Wishes, Hopes, Actions, Fortunes [that] spring out of his own nature'.

To find these hidden dimensions of human nature (which the practice of the empiricists in fact supported) Coleridge leapt backward over the preceding century to glory in the humanists and platonists of the Renaissance. As Charles and Mary Lamb were to popularise stories from Shakespeare and the Jacobean dramatists, Keats to forage through Spenser and Shelley to find models for his dramatic and philosophical writings in Renaissance writings, so Coleridge also rediscovered the riches of that period. Not least among its attractions for him were its flexible and ecstatic theories of mind and soul. His schemes of human nature often bear a close resemblance to Marsilio Ficino's *Platonic Theology concerning the Immortality of the Soul* (1469–74) and to Pico della Mirandola's *Oration on the Dignity of Man* (1487), writings which supported a complicated, active, spiritual view of human nature, attributing to man a potentially angelic aspect and, in Pico's case, arguing that man could choose his own nature. 'Even as runaway youths who after long travels & various adventures return at length to their Father's Mansion', he learned from them to go back to Plato, Plotinus, Proclus and Iamblichus, great 'psychologists' who show us, like 'enchanted islands' or a 'stationary rainbow',[12] human consciousness in its true multiplicity, inward power and spiritual vitality, 'rendering the mind lofty and generous and able by splendid Imaginations that receive the beauty of forms by the Proportions of Science'. As early as 1790 the Platonists nourished the mind and imagination of the young Coleridge: Charles Lamb lovingly remembered him rhapsodising in the courtyard of Christ's Hospital over Plotinus and Jamblichus, marvelled at by passers-by as a 'young [Pico della] Mirandula'. It is remarkable how frequently throughout his life, even in his passionately Christian effusions as he approached death, Coleridge called on these neoplatonists for help against philosophies that would simplify, mechanise and render inert the upswelling fountains of human imagination. In his *Philosophical Lectures* of 1818–19, for instance, he traced in the writings and paintings of Sir Joshua Reynolds signs of the artist's love of Platonism, and looked forward to a new burgeoning of inspiration:

> And now I am happy to see and feel that men are craving for a better diet than the wretched trash they have been fed with for the last century; that they will be taught that what is sound must come out of themselves, and that they cannot find good with their eyes or with their ears or with their hands, that they will not discover them in the crucible or bring them out of a machine, but must look into the living soul which God has made His image, in order to learn, even in fragments, what that power is by which we are to execute the delegated power entrusted to us by Him.[13]

Further help against a reductive view of human nature was given by certain late eighteenth- and early nineteenth-century German philosophers – some of whom were also indebted to the same neoplatonists and mystics, including Boehme and Bruno, who had helped Coleridge. Their titles show the inheritance and continued challenge of eighteenth-century speculations about human nature and man: Immanuel Kant, *Anthropologie* (1798); Johann A. H. Reimarus, *Über die Gründe der menschlichen Erkenntniss und natürlichen Religion* (1787); Friedrich von Schelling, *Philosophische Untersuchungen über das Wesen der menschlichen Freyheit* (1809) and *Vom Ich als Prinzip der Philosophie* (1795); Johan Nicolas Tetens, *Philosophische Versuche über die menschliche Natur und ihre Entwickelung* (1777). For them, as for Coleridge, the Renaissance platonists brought assertions and images of inward power when rational arguments, using the limited terminology of empiricism, failed to break out from the circle of sense experience and proofs. Coleridge recalls that in the midst of his struggle to overthrow the mechanistic and atheistic theories of his English empirical predecessors, Kant took possession of him 'as with a giant's hand', teaching him not only to examine reason but also to assume a conscience.[14] Kant's categorical imperative, his transcendental unity of apperception and his system of ideal categories, along with his belief that God, Immortality and Freedom were concepts insusceptible to rational proof but nevertheless necessary for human functioning, provided Coleridge with new equipment for his thinking and a new direction for his arguments: engaging with the same categories he attempted, using empirical methods, to show them as grounded in human nature itself.

Whereas Coleridge was openly grateful to Kant, he was not always precise about his indebtedness to others. He has been frequently criticised for taking over long sections from Schelling's work to fill up pages in *Biographia Literaria* and to furnish summaries of arguments that he might later discard. Elsewhere he gave Schelling full credit for contributions such as his enrichment of the creativity of the subject and his layering of self-consciousness. As Walter Jackson Bate and James Engell have carefully documented in their notes and commentaries on the *Biographia Literaria*, Kant, Schelling, Jacobi and their German contemporaries contributed a vision of the multiple, active powers in the mind, both psychological and spiritual, which supported Coleridge's view of the mind's complex and incalculable activity, culminating in his incisive formulation, 'We learn all things indeed by *occasion* of experience; but the very facts so learned force us inward on the antecedents, that must be pre-supposed in order to render experience itself possible.'[15] As early as 1794, when he was 21, Coleridge had blasted his sceptical predecessors for recognising no 'home-born Feeling', no '*center* of the Ball that, rolling on thro' Life collects and assimilates every congenial Affection'.[16] Even during his youth, in other words, he had been looking for an inwardly generated self or soul (as a Christian, he always used this mystical word) to elevate man above his circumstances and give the inward self a measure of self-determination.

Such inward power was demonstrated for Coleridge in poetry (the most human of the arts), in the human voices that join to create the intricate texts of the Bible, in the creation of distinctly human institutions such as marriage and religion. It even appeared in the negative forces of human evil and human madness. Evil actions, for example, could serve, paradoxically, as demonstrations of Freedom. 'Christianity exclusively has asserted the positive being of Evil or

Sin – & thence exclusively the Freedom of the Creature', he wrote in a notebook entry of 12 December 1812.[17] Madness, too, commonly thought of as bound and compulsive, might be the result of our desires for freedom:

> We all love to be a little mad, when we are certain that there is no Witness or Noticer of our Madness. Two Master-feelings are gratified – *freedom* & *Dependence* – who can be himself, who does not at times prove to himself that he is *free*? Who does not the same moment yearn to feel himself dependent?[18]

Equally paradoxically, as Laurence Lockridge has pointed out, the assertion of free will might separate the human being increasingly from freedom.[19]

Study of the particular ways in which each person chooses among the impulses to freedom and the compulsions of his or her surrounding environment – the 'Hedge-girdle' of family, state and terrain – gave life to Coleridge's theories of personality. In observing other people, he again viewed the difficult choices that daily formed each person's unique nature as a process very different from the repetitive patterns of animal behaviour. Freedom, individuality, self-determination: these watchwords of eighteenth-century political theory were investigated closely as they applied to each person's development of character and conscience. For him 'Humanity' was very often written as 'Biography'.

For Coleridge, to study biographies was to study life in action. Gregarious and fluently communicative, he was a centre of intellectual life at Christ's Hospital, in Bristol, in Göttingen, in London – even, during a brief stay, in Rome. He knew many of the great men and women of his day – indeed, his friendship and encouragement helped to make some of them great. He could not participate in the reclusiveness of his friends William and Dorothy Wordsworth in Goslar but went to the university town of Göttingen; his subsequent attempts to join them in their Grasmere solitude were in the end equally unsuccessful and may have contributed to his opium addiction. London, by contrast, led to a merry round of dinners and taverns which he rarely refused, adapting nightly to a wide variety of people from different classes and political parties. In later life he was rarely so happy as when visited at Highgate by those who sought him out.

Although he looked for principles, he did not follow Samuel

Johnson in relishing generalities or types. With a precision of observation that came close to 'numbering the streaks of the tulip',[20] he saw Hazlitt, De Quincey, Pitt, Napoleon, Fox and others both as they appeared on the surface and as the individual 'soul' of each showed through the surface, forming a coherent if fractured whole. As a man intent on freedom of will, he studied the choices that people made to become finished selves; he usually described them as agents of their own destiny – unless victimhood was their distinct choice. In this he differed markedly from his early friend William Godwin, whose views on determinism and environment, applied to a fictional victim in *Caleb Williams* and invested in theory in his *Enquiry on Political Justice*, he repudiated very early, having seen in Godwin's poor relationship to his children and wives, for example, the reciprocal enactments of false philosophy.

His exclamation of wonder, 'O human nature! Ever greater than thy circumstances!',[21] expresses his amazement at the strength, autonomy and wholeness of individual lives. When he wrote about the wholeness of a life, he was more concerned with its freedom to choose its nature than with environmental factors. Even as he acknowledged the part played by economic conditions or class in the brutalising of uneducated labourers and the small-mindedness of uneducated women, he still looked at their opportunities for choice. In the case of his friend Thomas Poole, for instance, he saw how a country person, worried more about things than ideas, might narrow his vision and cling to his prejudices; where some readers might attribute this outlook to class, Coleridge ascribed it to a series of individual decisions.

By 'nature' human beings yearn for the invisible, hunger for immortality, need a God: religion was, as we have seen, a distinctively human 'instinct' in Coleridge's theory of human nature, constructed largely by himself from hints in Kant. His analogical argument for the religious nature of human beings, which is also a modified ontological proof of human immortality, is indeed not unlike Kant's view in 'Dialectic of Pure Practical Reason' in *The Critique of Practical Reason*; for Coleridge it stands as an ultimate proof of human freedom from the bondage of the mortal body. Along with the given freedom to choose one's own character and to be one's own person even when encircled by walls over which it is difficult to leap, the human being also achieves freedom when he or she chooses to have faith in the future life that the very fact of aspiration seems to promise.

Coleridge was at one and the same time more grand and more precise than his eighteenth-century predecessors. He was more grand in attempting to include aspects of the human that were not exclusively empirical, to reconcile contradictory elements without ignoring perplexity, to head off the powerful new evidence that human beings might be in fact, not just in metaphor, descended from animals and at the same time to incorporate the exacting methods of very recent sciences; he was more precise in ensuring that while his criticism homed in on generalities, it was yet tested by real experiences. Exercising the vigour of a young man clearing away the fathers to make room for himself, he grappled boldly with (and sometimes overstated) the errors of his predecessors, voicing his objections to the formulations of Locke;[22] to David Hume's denial of personal identity, of cause and effect, and of the coherence of experience; and to the scepticism of Condillac and other French writers, stressing their stylish lack of principle and hinting in francophobic asides at what he supposed to be their underlying atheism.

Above all, he tried to overturn eighteenth-century assumptions (seen from his point of view as monolithic) by drawing on the visionary writings of the Neoplatonists who, together with St Augustine, helped him to reinstate faith in a soul: for 'all that is truly human must proceed from within'.[23]

Although Locke's psychology came to appear inadequate to Coleridge, Locke's political assertion of individual rights in the *Two Treatises on Government* (1690) was the basis of his early politics, particularly in his early lectures against Pitt's two bills;[24] 'liberty', 'equality through education', 'benevolence' and denunciations of despotism were rallying cries that continued to inform his underlying thinking about individual worth, modified later by a Burkean obligation to the state, and reliance on a national church or clerisy to nurture the development of individual persons. Locke's advocacy of religious tolerance, based on the view that no knowledge was certain, that the impressions that ultimately formed opinions were themselves in flux, and that, in the absence of absolute truths or absolute structures, individuals had the right freely to choose their leaders and their forms of governments, led Coleridge not only to many of his important philosophical positions concerning the role of choices in individual growth but also to a search for more transcendent spiritual illumination than that available to the senses alone. Influenced by Lockean claims for self-determination, his early plans for pantisocracy aimed to cultivate the best in each human being in an ideal society – marred only by recognition of the danger that debased values would be reintroduced by people, particularly older women, whose materialistic and petty values had been inculcated by a barren education.

His campaign against Napoleon, which ran week after week, first in *The Morning Post* and then in *The Courier*, and took more permanent shape in his essays in *The Friend*, was a manifestation of his anger at the betrayal of these principles of individual freedom. His early belief in individual rights for all men regardless of class or colour (evident in his fulminations against the aristocracy and against slavery) continued with later outrage at the treatment of working children and the labouring poor by the very industrialists who had learned their doctrines of free enterprise from the theory of individual rights.

Eighteenth-century developments in biology, including early hints of evolutionary theory in Edward Tyson and Erasmus Darwin, in geology – especially Hutton's theory of the earth as layered and ancient – and in anthropology, based largely at that time on reports from missionaries and traders among the native American, Caribbean and African tribes, also enriched Coleridge's thinking about human nature, so frequent a topic with predecessors whose heroes – Candide, Zadig, Rasselas, Robinson Crusoe, Gulliver – had often searched for the variety of human experience only to see a generalised type of their own humanity in its most negative form. Indeed, as Rousseau pointed out in the Second Discourse, when they tried to decide who was human and who bestial, the subjects of their enquiry might be wondering the same about them. Coleridge's readings in science inspired new approaches – especially since he was not so amused as Swift or Voltaire by man's possible resemblances to the animals, new ways of distinguishing between them, of marking the borders of what is 'human' (an enquiry made vivid by Shakespeare's Caliban in *The Tempest*). Sir Humphry Davy called Coleridge the poet of science, and admired his insight into nature – even if his interest in finding an advantageous place for human beings in the assorted hierarchies of the new biology, of the new geology and of the new chemistry sometimes led him to scientific assertions that were tendentious rather than dispassionate.

Coleridge's divergence from the 200-year tradition of arguing about human nature – whether it was Hamlet's 'What a piece of work is a Man!' or Hobbes's description of the life of Man if left in a state of war as 'nasty, brutish, and short', or Swift's King of

Brobdingnag's assertion that Europeans must be 'the most pernicious race of little odious vermin that nature ever suffered to crawl
upon the surface of the earth' – is more than a matter of his opinions:
it is also a matter of *method*. At its best that method is a precise, open,
attentive process of discovery and self-correction, not blinded by
preconceptions. Coleridge does far more than add epigraphs or
judgements on the quality of human nature; he lives his quest. His
teasing out of layers of continuous being and discontinuous vision
in his own consciousness makes him a founding psychologist. He is
empirical, despite his anger at mere empiricism. 'But what are my
metaphysics', he asks in *The Friend*, 'but the referring of the Mind
to its own Consciousness for Truths indispensible to its own happiness?'[25] In his notebooks and letters he explored this consciousness as none of his predecessors had done, testing on his pulses
their generalities against his own. He was particularly provoked by
Hume's 'bundle theory' of the self, expressed in the *Treatise of
Human Nature:*

> But self or person is not any one impression, but that to which our
> several impressions and ideas are suppos'd to have a reference. If
> any impression gives rise to the idea of self, that impression must
> continue invariably the same, thro' the whole course of our lives;
> since self is suppos'd to exist after that manner. But there is no
> impression constant and invariable. Pain and pleasure, grief and
> joy, passions and sensations succeed each other, and never exist
> at the same time. It cannot, therefore, be from any of these impres-
> sions or from any other, that the idea of self is deriv'd; and
> consequently there is no such idea.[26]

Coleridge mused on this passage and the material following it in a
notebook entry of December 1804:

> How opposite to nature & the fact to talk of the one *moment* of
> Hume; of our whole being an aggregate of successive single sen-
> sations. Who ever *felt* a *single* sensation? Is not every one at the
> same moment conscious that there co-exist a thousand others in a
> darker shade, or less light; even as when I fix my attention on a
> white house on a grey bare Hill or rather long ridge that runs out
> of sight each way . . . the pretended single sensation is it any thing
> more than the *Light*-point in every picture either of nature or of a
> good painter; & again subordinately in every component part of

the picture? And what is a moment? Succession with *interspace*? Absurdity! It is evidently only the Licht-punct, the *Sparkle* in the indivisible undivided Duration.[27]

Goaded by Hume, Coleridge examined closely the many-layered act of perception, connecting his mental activities to perception in nature and in art. Like an impressionist painter, or like a writer such as Virginia Woolf, he encompassed in language the torrent of perceptions vivid at any moment to the consciousness – which is not pulverised by them but rather affirmed in its complexity.

Attending to eighteenth-century generalities about the benevolence or malevolence of human beings, Coleridge examined failures of character within himself which led him to resemble an assortment of beasts. His thinking was specific, personal, varied, contradictory, immediate, often funny, sometimes terrifying. He enacted what it is to be inside a human nature, to have a human consciousness, to suffer from its tyranny, or to find it subjected to that of the body. Because of the daily testing of his hypotheses, Coleridge's thought about humanity – its essential nature, its response to circumstance, its perversion of what it should be, its occasional triumph, its tentative and shifting choices toward self-definition, its cultural variations – was more than a compendium of generalities about 'the omne scibile of human Nature – *what* we *are* & how we *become* what we are',[28] more even than an 'Anthropology' on the lines of Kant's counterstatement to his own critiques. It was a life-work and a life in action.

1

Enquiries into the Nature of Man

(a) GENERAL DEFINITIONS OF MAN

Disillusionment with politics in the late 1790s led Coleridge to conclude that the most important task for his generation was to investigate more deeply the nature of man: 'What we are, and what we are capable of becoming'.[1] His pronouncements on the subject often followed the traditional tripartite scheme of man's being, as animal, as intellectual and as religious.[2] As early as 1796 and continuing into his late work on the Logos, he planned ambitious schemes that would arrange human accomplishments under similar categories.[3] For a long time he believed that Wordsworth's great philosophical poem would be constructed according to a similar scheme, agreed, he claimed, during their earlier discussions.[4]

The impulse to categorise could take various forms: in examining the Decalogue Coleridge perceived 'three great Sections', comprising in the first four commandments 'the Duties of man, as a moral & rational Individual'; in the next three 'his Duties, as a *social* being'; and in the last, 'his Duties, as a *citizen* or member of a *State*'.[5] In later life, his use of these categories increasingly emphasised the bestiality of the first level, the potential devilishness of the second, and the necessity of the third category to give meaning to the whole.[6] Although he sought a 'harmony of the whole Animal triplex – Body, Soul, and Spirit',[7] it was not easy to find.

In addition to these and other carefully organised arrangements of man's nature, Coleridge also set up a revolutionary approach to 'the vast Terra Incognita of Knowledge', drawing his terminology from a less rationalistic tradition, partly platonic and neoplatonic, partly occult, partly experiential, in order to preserve the mysterious 'xyz' of the mind from an excessively rationalistic analysis which, he feared, might diminish its potency and free agency. Aware that the early Greeks had kept in suspension a fluctuating variety of terms for mind, soul and spirit – located in various areas of the body – and perceiving that the study of subjectivity (sparked to some extent by the otherwise dangerous Hume[8]) was still in its infancy, Coleridge was eager to keep available as many various names for powers of mind as possible, even if their spheres of operation might seem at times to overlap.

Along a spectrum of 'intervening sympathies'[9] between matter and mind, he made subtle distinctions among terms such as consciousness, self, I,

16

agent, subject, person, spirit and soul, with the first six governing various aspects of temporal awareness, integrity and action, while spirit and soul described a disembodied, non-individual, progressive continuity beyond physical activity and existence. Sometimes, however, he used consciousness, self, I, subject, agent and person interchangeably, inasmuch as these secular, psychological terms are intertwined with the body in the complex 'mawwallop'[10] of mind and matter, will and action, at 'the Boundary between the material & spiritual World'.[11] Even the spirit was linked by equal signs to I and Self,[12] as he explored the inward and outward manifestations of psychological life and the 'infinite gradations of consciousness'.[13]

As early as 1796 Coleridge prepares to arrange a course based on the nature of man as animal, intellectual and religious being, combining his knowledge of much eighteenth-century anthropological and psychological research with a recognition of religion as a category often forgotten.[14]

On my return I would commence a School for 8 young men at 100 guineas each – proposing to *perfect* them in the following studies in order as follows –
1. Man as Animal: including the complete knowledge of Anatomy, Chemistry, Mechanics & Optics. –
2. Man as an *Intellectual* Being: including the ancient Metaphysics, the systems of Locke & Hartley, – of the Scotch Philosophers – & the new Kantian S[ystem –]
3. Man as a Religious Being: including an historic summary of all Religions & the arguments for and against Natural & Revealed Religion. Then proceeding from the individual to the aggregate of Individuals & disregarding all chronology except that of mind I should perfect them 1. in the History of Savage Tribes. 2. of semi-barbarous nations. 3. of nations emerging from semi-barbarism. 4. of civilized states. 5. of luxurious states. 6. of revolutionary states. – 7. – of Colonies. – During these studies I should intermix the knowlege of languages and instruct my scholars in Belles Lettres & the principles of composition. – Now seriously – do you think that one of my Scholars thus perfected would make a better Senator than perhaps any one Member in either of our Houses? –
Bright Bubbles of the aye-ebullient brain!
Gracious Heaven! that a scheme so big with advantage to this Kingdom, therefore to Europe, therefore to the World should be demolishable by one monosyllable from a Bookseller's Mouth!
No! –

In 1798 and 1803 he sets out to his brother George and to Godwin his current intellectual concerns and his plans for a great work.[15]

I have for some time past withdrawn myself almost totally from the consideration of *immediate* causes, which are infinitely complex & uncertain, to muse on fundamental & general causes – the "causae causarum". – I devote myself to such works as encroach not on the antisocial passions – in poetry, to elevate the imagination & set the affections in right tune by the beauty of the inanimate impregnated, as with a living soul, by the presence of Life – in prose, to the seeking with patience & a slow, very slow mind "Quid sumus, et quidnam victuri gignimur["] – What our faculties are & what they are capable of becoming.

When this Book is fairly off my hands, I shall, if I live & have sufficient health, set seriously to work – in arranging what I have already written, and in pushing forward my Studies, & my Investigations relative to the omne scibile of human Nature – *what* we *are*, & *how* we *become* what we are; so as to solve the two grand Problems, how, being acted upon, we shall act; how, acting, we shall be acted upon. But between me & this work there may be Death.

Seven years later, Coleridge continues to plan a vast study of human nature, based on the mysterious and obscure powers that the eighteenth-century empiricists overlooked.[16]

If it please God, I shall shortly publish, as a Supplement to the first Volume of the Friend, a work of considerable size & very great Labor – the toil of many years – entitled, The Mysteries of Religion grounded in or relative to the Mysteries of Human Nature: or the foundations of morality laid in the primary Faculties of Man.

In various notebook entries he indicates what these phenomena and powers might be.[17]

Time, Space, Duration, Action, Active, Passion, Passive, Activeness, Passiveness, Reaction, Causation, Affinity – here assemble all the Mysteries – known, all is known – unknown, say rather, merely known, all is unintelligible / and yet Locke & the stupid adorers of ~~this~~ that *Fetisch* Earth-clod, take all these for granted –

I do not like that presumptuous Philosophy which in its rage of explanation allows no xyz, no symbol representative of the vast Terra Incognita of Knowledge, for the Facts and Agencies of Mind and matter reserved for future Explorers / while the ultimate grounds of all must remain inexplorable or Man must cease to be progressive. Our Ignorance with all the intermediates of obscurity is the *condition* of our ever-increasing Knowledge.

Notwithstanding the arguments of Spinoza, and Descartes, and other advocates of the *Material system*, (or, in more appropriate language, the *Atheistical system*!) it is admitted by all men, not prejudiced, not biased by sceptical prepossessions, that *mind* is distinct from *matter*. The mind of man, however, is involved in inscrutable darkness, (as the profoundest metaphysicians well know) and is to be estimated (if at all) alone by an inductive process; that is, by its *effects*. Without entering on the question, whether an extremely circumscribed portion of the mental process, surpassing instinct, may, or may not, be extended to quadrupeds, it is universally acknowledged, that the mind of man, alone, regulates all the voluntary actions of his corporeal frame. Mind, therefore, may be regarded as a distinct genus, in the scale ascending above brutes, and including the whole of intellectual existences; advancing from *thought*, (that mysterious thing!) in its lowest form, through all the gradations of sentient and rational beings, till it arrives at a Bacon, a Newton, and then, when unincumbered by matter, extending its illimitable sway through Seraph and Archangel, till we are lost in the GREAT INFINITE!

In a letter of 1814 reminding Wordsworth of the subjects that he had agreed to treat in 'The Recluse', Coleridge reveals what he might have included in a long philosophical work of his own.[18]

I supposed you first to have meditated the faculties of Man in the abstract, in their correspondence with his Sphere of action, and first, in the Feeling, Touch, and Taste, then in the Eye, & last in the Ear, to have laid a solid and immoveable foundation for the Edifice by removing the sandy Sophisms of Locke, and the Mechanic Dogmatists, and demonstrating that the Senses were living growths and developments of the Mind & Spirit in a much juster as well as higher sense, than the mind can be said to be formed by the Senses –. Next, I understood that you would take the Human Race in the concrete, have exploded the absurd notion of Pope's Essay on Man, Darwin, and all the countless Believers – even (strange to say) among Xtians of Man's having progressed from an Ouran Outang state – so contrary to all History, to all Religion, nay, to all Possibility – to have affirmed a Fall in some sense, as a fact, the possibility of which cannot be understood from the nature of the Will, but the reality of which is attested by Experience & Conscience – Fallen men contemplated in the different ages of the World, and in the different states – Savage – Barbarous – Civilised – the lonely Cot, or Borderer's Wigwam – the Village – the Manufacturing Town – Sea-port – City – Universities – and not disguising the sore evils, under which the whole Creation groans, to point out however a manifest Scheme of Redemption from this Slavery, of Reconciliation from this Enmity with Nature – what are the Obstacles, the *Antichrist* that must be & already is – and to conclude by a grand didactic swell on the necessary identity of a true Philosophy with true Religion, agreeing in the results and differing only as the analytic and synthetic process, as discursive from intuitive, the former chiefly useful as perfecting the latter – in short, the necessity of a general revolution in the modes of developing & disciplining the human mind by the substitution of Life, and Intelligence (considered in it's different powers from the Plant up to that state in which the difference of Degree becomes a new kind (man, self-consciousness) but yet not by essential opposition) for the philosophy of mechanism which in everything that is most worthy of the human Intellect strikes *Death*, and cheats itself by mistaking clear Images for distinct conceptions, and which idly demands Conceptions where Intuitions alone are possible or adequate to the majesty of the Truth. – In short, Facts elevated into Theory – Theory into Laws – & Laws into living & intelligent Powers – true Idealism necessarily perfecting itself in Realism, & Realism refining itself into Idealism. –

Such or something like this was the Plan, I had supposed that you were engaged on –.

In The Friend *and in late notebooks Coleridge continues to assess human nature, recognising that any person's opinion is likely to be a function of his position – in prison or on the road, for example. God has created man in his own image, and although the Fiend subverts it, human needs ultimately bear witness to that inner identity.*[19]

And here I fully coincide with Frederic H. Jacobi, that the only true spirit of Tolerance consists in our conscientious toleration of each other's intolerance. Whatever pretends to be more than this, is either the unthinking cant of fashion, or the soul-palsying narcotic of moral and religious indifference. All of us without exception, in the same mode though not in the same degree, are necessarily subjected to the risk of mistaking positive opinions for certainty and clear insight. From this yoke we cannot free ourselves, but by ceasing to be men; and this too not in order to transcend but to sink below our human nature. For if in one point of view it be the mulct of our fall, and of the corruption of our will; it is equally true, that contemplated from another point, it is the price and consequence of our progressiveness. To him who is compelled to pace to and fro within the high walls and in the narrow court-yard of a prison, all objects may appear clear and distinct. It is the traveller journeying onward, full of heart and hope, with an ever-varying horizon, on the boundless plain, that is liable to mistake clouds for mountains, and the mirage of drouth for an expanse of refreshing waters.

But God created Man in his own Image: to be the Image of his own Eternity and Infinity created he Man. He gave us Reason and with Reason Ideas of its own formation and underived from material Nature, self-consciousness, Principles, and above all, the Law of Conscience, which in the power of an holy and omnipotent Being *commands* us to attribute Reality – among the numerous Ideas mathematical or philosophical, which the Reason by the necessity of its own excellence, creates for itself – to those, (and those only) without which the Conscience would be baseless and contradictory; namely, to the Ideas of Soul, the Free Will, Immortality, and God. To God as the Reality of the Conscience and the Source of all Obligation; to Free Will, as the power of the human being to maintain the Obedience, which God through the Conscience has commanded, against all the might of Nature; and to the immortality of the Soul as a State in which the weal and woe of man shall be proportioned to his moral Worth.

With this Faith all Nature,

> all the mighty World
> Of Eye and Ear

presents itself to us, now as the Aggregate *Materials* of Duty, and now as a Vision of the Most High revealing to us the mode, and time, and particular instance of applying and realizing that universal Rule, pre-established in the Heart of our Reason: as

> The lovely shapes and sounds intelligible
> Of that Eternal Language, which our God
> Utters: Who from Eternity doth teach
> Himself in all, and all things in Himself!

The Four States

(1) The Man, i.e. the Spiritual Man, the Finite Rational, the Image of the Absolute.
(2) The Beast, the Finite Irrational.
(3) The Fallen Man, the Spirit sunk into & partaking of the Bestial = the Will by self-determination become a *Nature*, and thus at once corrupting the innocent nature as an alien ingredient and corrupted *thro'* it. Briefly, state the 3rd is The Natural Man.
(4) The Fiend, the Spirit creating itself to evil. The Mystery of Evil, a Spirit *inverted*, and not as in N° 3 simply corrupted and adulterated by combination with the inferior.

But there is yet another contra-distinctive Property (several such indeed, and not one but will find a place in this great argument) but there is one in particular necessary to the completion of the evidence from the preceding, and this is the Individuality conformed with the Sociality of Man – he is neither a solitary nor a gregarious; but the identity of the states, of which these are shadows & resemblances. Man is a federative Being. There are needs and desires which belong to Man as the Kind, as a Race, as a Community, as a family, as an Individual – and to the last, as a temporal Denizen, and as a permanent Being – needs respecting his Circumstances, and needs & aspirations respecting the very principle of Individuality in him – his spiritual needs & desires – and it is a necessary consequence of this intenser Individuality that Man is by constitution a *religious* Creature.

(b) FLUCTUATING TERMS FOR SUBJECTIVITY: THE CONTINUUM OF CONSCIOUSNESS

Coleridge's terms consciousness, self-consciousness, subject, ego, I and self have seemed to many observers to foreshadow Freudian and Jungian psychology. As Richard Haven observes, 'we so often find in Coleridge startling anticipations of later writers whose primary concern has been the study and analysis of human consciousness. Coleridge . . . was a born psychologist trying to write as a metaphysician.'[20] Haven suggests that the absence of a subtle vocabulary for psychological activity forced Coleridge to use an existing metaphysical vocabulary to describe it.

Coleridge used 'consciousness' and 'self-consciousness' almost interchangeably to describe a continuous core of awareness, and the awareness of that awareness. From observing his empirical 'I', he determined that 'the act of self-consciousness is for us the source and principle of all our possible knowledge'.[21] The 'fullness of human intelligence' may be an expression translated from Schelling, but it is admirably applicable to his precise inspection of the mind in action, which he compared to the pulsive movement of a water insect.[22] In his notebooks he watched his own spontaneous consciousness gathering wayward memories, impressions and dreams and so enriched his understanding of the 'laws of association'.[23] Observing his own child, he noted an awareness already of the act of thinking, corresponding to a screen, dim presence, or shadow in the layers of his own mind. This early and spontaneous self-interrogation received a theoretical overlay from his reading of German philosophers. Coleridge sometimes identified the basic power of the mind with his 'primary imagination' – a power that permits the perception of experience as wholes (and that necessarily precedes and grounds the 'secondary' imagination).

Self, often synonymous with 'I', describes a level of organised integrity of body, senses and will higher than consciousness. Despite its rootedness in the body, it calls the body 'mine, not I'. It sometimes abets the aggrandising natural being when it becomes egotism, or, worse, 'He-goatism'.[24] Stephen Bygrave, describing the passive 'egoism' and active 'egotism' of the self, notes in contemporary society the 'cluster of first usages of egotism and its cognates between 1780–1830, the period we designate "Romantic" '.[25] Laurence Lockridge observes that Coleridge uses the word 'self' 'more insistently than any previous writer'. In Bygrave's formulation, 'If self-consciousness is that which enables the self to be, then egotism enables it to do, the soul's activity.'[27] The possible drawbacks of such a consciousness of self are the involution and reflexivity that Coleridge associated with Hamlet, and with similarly contorted paralyses of will in himself. Circling is pleasurable until it becomes an eddy,[28] in danger of drawing the consciousness downward into a numbing vortex.

To focus on Coleridge's proto-modern awareness of a self shadowed by its own watching and glimpsing its own unguarded subconscious urges in dream or reverie is, however, like concentrating on the crypt when making an architectural study of a cathedral, for it ignores the elements of the human being that were of greatest importance to Coleridge, those that permit free agency.

This larger self makes daily choices that should lead it to freedom of moral being, progressively disconnecting itself from nature. It aspires to be a 'Spirit', for the spirit lives – and communicates with other spirits – in the element of 'Freedom'.[29] Although Coleridge borrowed many formulations about Spirit from Schelling, he also drew from his wide reading in occult and mystical sources, using ghost-lore to describe the phantoms in his dreams, the multiplying population of his inner life. The word 'Soul' he almost always divorced from the temporal world,[30] imagining it as an exile from a far-distant place, a ship wrecked on a desert isle, an *it*, doomed perhaps to suffer in eternity – a ghostly touch for which words failed him.[31]

Along some such spectrum, from neutral awareness through active choosing and on to liberation from the body, Coleridge modified his vocabulary of subjective interior powers. He would shift the emphasis slightly toward one function or another, from knowledge of the past, to unity in the present, to action, and to continuity in the future. The welter of terms from many different traditions suggests the flux of psychological information at the time, along with the persistence of and need for additional terms to describe areas of mental activity (intuited, spiritual, supernatural, unforeseen, inspired) that had often been jettisoned in eighteenth-century essays on the mind and its senses, but which he was determined to restore.

(i) The Body and Dreams

In noting his fearful dreams (some of which are opium-induced hallucinations, others part of the withdrawal symptoms when he tries to rid himself of the habit) Coleridge is particularly interested in the connection of the mind with body, sometimes showing the nocturnal Ego mocking the daytime Ego.[32]

Friday Night, Nov. 28, 1800, or rather Saturday Morning – a most frightful Dream of a Woman whose features were blended with darkness catching holding of my right eye & attempting to pull it out – I caught hold of her arm fast – a horrid feel – Wordsworth cried out aloud to me hearing my scream – heard his cry & thought it cruel he did not come / but did not wake till his cry was repeated a third time – the Woman's name Ebon Ebon Thalud – When ~~my~~ I awoke, my right eyelid swelled –

A day of Storm / at dinner an explosion of Temper from the Sisters / a dead Sleep after Dinner / the Rhubarb had its usual enfeebling-narcotic effect / I slept again with dreams of sorrow &

pain, tho' not of downright Fright & prostration / I was worsted but not conquered – in sorrows and in sadness & in sore & angry Struggles – but not trampled down / but this will all come again, if I do not take care.

Nov. 10th, ½ past 2 o'clock, Morning. Awoke after long struggles & with faint screaming from a persecuting Dream. The Tale of the Dream began in two *Images* – in two Sons of a Nobleman, desperately fond of shooting – brought out by the Footman to resign their Property, & to be made believe that they had none / they were far too cunning for that / as they struggled & resisted their cruel Wrongers, & my Interest for them, I suppose, increased, I became they – the duality vanished – Boyer & Christ's Hospital became concerned – yet still the former Story was kept up – & I was conjuring him, as he met me in the Streets, to have pity on a Nobleman's Orphan, when I was carried back to bed, & was struggling up against an unknown impediment, some woman on the other side about to relieve me – when a noise of one of the Doors, strongly associated with Mrs. Coleridge's coming in to awake me, awaked me – the first thing, I became conscious of, was a faint double scream, that I uttered. – Drizzle. The Sky uncouthly marbled with white vapours, & large black Clouds, their surface of a fine wooly grain.

On his way to Malta in 1804, Coleridge describes in vivid detail the physical sufferings resulting from his condition and resolves to try the experiment of a month without stimulants.[33]

Pain without gloom & anxious Horror, & from causes communicable openly to all, rheumatism, &c O it is a sport! – but the Obscure, or the disgustful – the dull quasi finger-pressure on the Liver, the endless Flatulence, the frightful constipation when the dead Filth *impales* the lower Gut – to weep & sweat & moan & scream for the parturience of an excrement with such pangs & such convulsions as a woman with an Infant heir of Immortality / for Sleep a pandemonium of all the shames & miseries of the past Life from early childhood all huddled together, & bronzed with one stormy Light of Terror & Self-torture / O this is hard, hard, hard! – O dear God! give me strength of Soul to make one thorough Trial – if I land at

Malta / spite of all horrors to go through one month of unstimulated Nature – yielding to nothing but manifest Danger of Life! – O great God! Grant me grace truly to look into myself, & to begin the serious work of Self-amendment – accounting to Conscience for the Hours of every Day. Let me live in *Truth* – manifesting that alone which *is*, even as it *is*, & striving to be that which only Reason shews to be lovely – that which my Imagination would delight to manifest! – I am loving & kind-hearted & cannot do wrong with impunity, but o! I am very, very weak – from my infancy have been so – & I exist for the moment!

The vicious circle of suffering and renewed recourse to drugs.[34]

To Fear – most men affected by belief of *reality* attached to the wild-weed spectres of infantine nervousness – but I affected by them simply, & of themselves – / but for the last years I own & mourn a more deleterious Action of *Fear* – fear of horrors in *Sleep*, driving me to dreadful remedies & stimuli, when awake, not for the present Sensation, but to purchase daily a wretched Reprieve from the torments of each night's Daemons / selling myself to the Devil to avoid the Devil's own Visitations, & thereby becoming his *Subject*.

An analysis of dreams and their significance in 1818.[35]

Language of Dreams. – The language of the Dream = Night is)(that of Waking = the Day. It is a language of Images and Sensations, the various dialects of which are far less different from each other, than the various <Day->Languages of Nations. Proved even by the Dream Books of different Countries & ages.
2. The images either direct, as when a Letter reminds me of itself, or symbolic – as Darkness for Calamity. Again, either anticipation or reminiscence.
3. These latter either grounded on some analogy, as to see a friend passing over a broad & deep water = Death, or seemingly arbitrary, as in the signification of Colors, different animals &c.
4. Frequently ironical: as if the fortunes of the Ego diurnus appeared exceedingly droll and ridiculous to the Ego nocturnus – Dung = Gold &c. So in Nature, Man, Baboon, Horse, Ass. Cats' Love & Rage &c.
5. Probably, a still deeper Dream, or 'Υπερονειρος, of which there

remains only an imageless but profound Presentiment or Boding (See Lay-Sermon, Notes – 1ˢᵗ.)

6. The Prophets, and the Laws of Moses, the most majestic Instances. –

7. Prophetic combinations, *if* there be such, = the instincts previous to the use and to the organ. Bull-calf *buts* – and to the preparation of organs in a lower class for the higher – as rudiments of eyes useless to A but perfected in B. –

8. Beasts of Concord and Independence ending in the Elephant – Beasts of Discord and Dependence – the Lion.
Man and the beasts drawn into his Circle – Dog, Ox. Man – a mystery in this.

9. The Conscience – the Unity of Day and Night – Qʸ. Are ~~theirre~~ two Consciences, the earthly and the Spiritual? –

10. The sensuous Nature a Lexicon raisonné of Words, treating of, not being, <αυτα τα πραγματα> [the things themselves] spiritual things – Our Fall at once implied and produced a resistance, this a more or less confused Echo, and this a secondary Echo &c – And thus deeming the Echo to be the Words, the Words became Things – <Ειδωλολατρεῖα> [idolatry] On this principle is the system of Emanuel Swedenborg grounded: and may be true, tho' the particular Translations ~~may~~ should be found arbitrary or fantastic.

10[a]. Let them be compared with the views that might be presented by the physiologic Ideas of Reil, Bichat, Autenrieth, & the better disciples of the Natur-philosophy. – First, the Cerebral System –)(the Ganglionic, and at once ÷ and ⌢ the Sympathic and its vocal nerves. The importance of the Gastric and especially the hepatic – and ~~its~~ the paramouncy of the Ganglionic over the Cerebral in Sleep. The Liver, and lower Abdomen – the Engastrimuthi [ventriloquists], and the prophetic Power of *diseased* Life in the ancient Oracles, hard by Streams & Caverns of deleterious influences – these numerous in early Paganism, then decreased & with them the Oracles. Plutarch knew but of 3 or 4 remaining. – <Curious Phrase of Sᵗ Basil, that Ezra totum το βιβλιον *eructavit* [vomited up the whole book].>

11. Liver – &c. The passions of the Day as often originate in the Dream, as the Images of the Dream in the Day. Guilt, Falsehood, traced to the Gastric Life. See my *Pains* of Sleep, & a curious Passage in G. Fox's Journal.

12. The good side of this – i.e. ganglionic – System. As all Passions, and Feelings, so Love roots therein. The process of the action of Inspiration in the Prophets, as well as in the Sibyls. – The autobiographies of the New-born – the Durchbruch [Breakthrough] of the

Herrnhüter [Moravians] – &c. Whatever part be the source of the Disease, into that must the medicine first enter. In this way only can it be Specific.

We are nigh to waking when we dream, we dream.

In a note of January 1805 Coleridge examines his own senses to analyse the variety and full significance of experience through touch.[36]

The imperfection of the organs by which we seem to unite ourselves with external things – the tongue, the palate, the Hand – which latter becoming more *organic* is less passionate / now take an organ as ~~in~~ the highest exponent of passion with the least possible machinery of power, that is, the most Feeling, ~~and~~ the least Touch, & no Grasp / it can only suit a universal idea / ~~constantly~~sequently dim – & one by the dimness / ~~of its~~ however complex it may or may not be. Observe that in certain excited states of feeling the knees, ancle, sides & soles of the feet, become organic / Query – the nipple in a woman's breast, does that ever become the seat of a particular feeling, as one would guess by its dormancy & sudden awakings –

Touch – double touch /[1] Touch with the sense of immediate power [2]with retentive power – [3]retentive power extinguishing the sense of touch, or making it mere feeling – & the gradations preceding ~~these~~is extinction / [4]retentive power simply, as when I hold a thing with my Teeth / [5]with feeling not Touch in one part of the machinery, both in the other, as when I press a bit of sugar with my Tongue against my Palate / [6]with feeling & even touch but not ~~enjoyment~~ specific stim*ulari* (esse sub stimulo) as when I hold a quill or bit of fruit by my lips – 1. mem. vi/Riley. inacts of Es*sex*. 2. The Lips, or the thumb and forefinger in a slight pressure. 3. The Hand grasping firmly an inanimate Body – that is the one extreme of this third Class – the other would be a Lover's Hand grasping the soft white hand of his mistress / Here the retentive power and nisus modify but not extinguish the Touch – it tells the story still & the mind listens to it. –

The changing relations between body and mind.[37]

[R]emark the seeming identity of body and mind in infants, and thence the loveliness of the former; the commencing separation in boyhood, and the struggle of equilibrium in youth : thence onward the body is first simply indifferent; then demanding the translucency of the mind not to be worse than indifferent; and finally all that presents the body as body becoming almost of an excremental nature.

By 1830 the relationship can seem more like one of alienation.[38]

The regenerate Man contemplates his animal Self as an hostile Alien, an evil ground *out* of which he is to grow & growing to loosen and extricate his roots preparatively to a final transplantation into a divine ground – . He no longer endures to think of it, as *him*, but as his *Nature*, tho' with sincerest humiliation and groans that can have no *utterance*, no outward expression, he knows it to be *his*, and cries out to be delivered from "the body of this Death".

In notes of 1807 and 1808 Coleridge describes his experiences of the body's tyranny, coupled with a sense of the paradoxical increase in psychological awareness involved in his opium-taking.[39]

To lie in ease yet dull anxiety for hours, afraid to think a thought, lest some thought of Anguish should shoot a pain athwart my body, afraid even to turn my body, lest the very bodily motion should introduce a train of painful Thoughts –

Need we wonder at Plato's opinions concerning the Body, at least, need that man wonder whom a *pernicious Drug* shall make capable of conceiving & bringing forth Thoughts, hidden in him before, which shall call forth the deepest feelings of his best, greatest, & sanest Contemporaries? and this proved to him by actual experience? – But can subtle strings set in greater tension do this? – Or is it not, that the dire poison for a delusive time has made the body, <i.e. the *organization*, not the articulation (or instruments of motion)> the unknown somewhat, a fitter Instrument for the all-powerful Soul. – As the

Instrument, so will be the Manifestation, the Epiphany, of the Soul.
– How greatly does this both exalt soul & body – What a grand
exposition of Sᵗ Paul's 15ᵗʰ Chapter of the Corinthians –. We are finite
– an instrument we must have – but it may be a glorified Instrument
– the Soul varies only as its Instrument varies – & yet that by the
action of the Soul, or Arbitrement! – Infinite incomprehensible Mystery, yet absolute Truth! It seems, as if the Soul or Arbitrement were
a Spring, as a steel Spring, struggling up against an indefinite weight,
and increasing or diminishing its powers apparently, as the weight
increases or diminishes – this is comprehensible! But in what way
this indestructible uncrushable Spring (Stahl-feder, as the Germans
more happily have it, avoiding the equivoque of this with *Fountain*)
in what way it of itself acts toward t the increase or diminution of the
superincumbent weight – this is the mystery! – this that which has
caused the grand controversies of Protestants & Catholics, & afterwards, of Calvinists & Arminians – finally, this is that which forms
the Boundary between the material & spiritual World – & by its very
incomprehensibility gives the condition of Hope & Faith.

(ii) Consciousness and Self-consciousness

Throughout life, but particularly during the years of intimacy with
Wordsworth, Coleridge was fond of observing the layers of consciousness
unfolding in any moment of awareness, trying to identify thinking as 'a pure
act and energy'.

*Quoting from Wordsworth's 'Lines written . . . above Tintern Abbey' Coleridge
proceeds to analyse the ways in which, while the encounter between mind and object
can become a battle for supremacy, the feeling is unaffected – and if anything
enhanced.*[40]

> – and the deep power of Joy
> We see into the *Life* of Things –

i.e. – By deep feeling we make our *Ideas dim* – & this is what we mean
by our Life – ourselves. I think of the Wall – it is before me, a distinct
Image – here. I necessarily think of the *Idea* & the Thinking I as two
distinct & opposite Things. Now <let me> think of *myself* – of the
thinking Being – the Idea becomes dim whatever it be – so dim that

I know not what it is – but the Feeling is deep & steady – and this I call *I* – the identifying the Percipient & the Perceived –.

Hartley Coleridge, aged four, gives a vivid demonstration of thinking in action.[41]

March 17, 1801. Tuesday – Hartley looking out of my study window fixed his eyes steadily & for some time on the opposite prospect, & then said – Will yon Mountains *always* be? – I shewed him the whole magnificent Prospect in a Looking Glass, and held it up, so that the whole was like a Canopy or Ceiling over his head, & he struggled to express himself concerning the Difference between the Thing & the Image almost with convulsive Effort. – I think never before saw such an Abstract of *Thinking* as a pure act & energy, of *Thinking* as distinguished from *Thoughts*.

The essential deadness of the object is compared with the extraordinary vivacity and immediacy of the mind that registers that object.[42]

Nothing affects me much at the moment it happens – it either stupifies me, and I perhaps look at a merry-make & dance the hay of Flies, or listen entirely to the loud Click of the great Clock / or I am simply indifferent, not without some sense of philosophic Self-complacency. – For a Thing at the moment is but a Thing of the moment / it must be taken up into the mind, diffuse itself thro' the whole multitude of Shapes & Thoughts, not one of which it leaves untinged – between each w^ch & it some new Thought is not engendered / this a work of Time / but the Body feels it quicker with me –

The role of human communication in objectivising grief; and the endless links of memory from the past that sorrow may evoke.[43]

One excellent use of communication of Sorrows to a Friend is this: that in relating what ails us we ourselves first know exactly what the real Grief is – & see it for itself, in its own form & limits – Unspoken Grief is a misty medley, of which the real affliction only plays the first fiddle – blows the Horn, to a scattered mob of obscure feelings &c. Perhaps, at certain moments a single almost insignificant Sorrow may, by association, bring together all the little relicts of pain & discomfort, bodily & mental, that we have endured even from Infancy. –

The interplay of active and passive powers in mental acts.[44]

In every voluntary movement we first counteract gravitation, in order to avail ourselves of it. It must exist, that there may be a something to be counteracted, and which by its re-action, aids the force that is exerted to resist it. Let us consider, what we do when we leap. We first resist the gravitating power by an act purely voluntary, and then by another act, voluntary in part, we yield to it in order to light on the spot, which we had previously proposed to ourselves. Now let a man watch his mind while he is composing; or, to take a still more common case, while he is trying to recollect a name; and he will find the process completely analogous. Most of my readers will have observed a small water-insect on the surface of rivulets, which throws a cinque-spotted shadow fringed with prismatic colours on the sunny bottom of the brook; and will have noticed, how the little animal *wins* its way up against the stream, by alternate pulses of active and passive motion, now resisting the current, and now yielding to it in order to gather strength and a momentary *fulcrum* for a further propulsion. This is no unapt emblem of the mind's self-experience in the act of thinking.

The active power of contracting consciousness so as to extract the sense of life from perceived objects; and the power of sorrow, sickness, and other such forces to expand it in its passive state.[45]

Important remark just suggests itself – 13 Nov[r.] 1809 – That it is by a negation and voluntary Act of *no*-thinking that we think of earth, air, water &c as dead – It is necessary for our limited powers of Consciousness that we should be brought to this negative state, & that should pass into Custom – but likewise necessary that at times we should awake & step forward – & this is effected by Poetry & Religion / –. The Extenders of Consciousness – Sorrow, Sickness, Poetry, Religion – . – <The truth is, we stop in the sense of Life just when we are not *forced* to go on – and then adopt a permission of our feelings for a precept of our Reason – >

The intimate relationship between Conscience and Reason.[46]

Above all things it is incumbent on me who lay such a stress on Conscience, & attach such a sacredness to it, to shew that it is no

Socratic Daimon which I mean, but the dictate of universal Reason, accompanied with a feeling of free Agency – that it is *Light* – that an erring Conscience is no Conscience, and as absurd as an erring Reason – i.e. not Reason / –

The importance of consciousness in maintaining a balance between identity and ever-varying variety.[47]

Suffice it, that one great Principle is common to all, a principle which probably is the condition of all consciousness, without which we should feel & imagine only by discontinuous Moments, & be plants or animals instead of men – I mean, that ~~balance~~ ever-varying Balance – or Balancing – of Images, Notions, or Feelings (for I avoid the vague word, Idea) conceived as in opposition to each other – in short, the perception of ~~Likeness & Difference~~ Identity & Contrariety – the least degree of which constitutes *Likeness* – the greatest, absolute Difference – but the infinite gradations between these two from all the Play & all the Interest of our Intellectual & Moral Being, till it lead us to a Feeling & an Object more aweful, than it seems to me compatible with even the present Subject to ~~p~~ utter aloud, tho' most desirous to suggest it – for there alone a⊞re all things at once ~~once~~ different and the same – there alone, as the principle of all things, does distinction exist unaided by division / Will, and Reason, Succession of Time & unmoving Eternity, infinite Change and ineffable Rest. –

The symmetrical roles of consciousness in examining our past selves and seeing our future selves in others.[48]

That *much-suggesting* ~~Feeling~~ Mood, with which we look back on our own youth with a feeling strictly analogous to that with which we regard our offspring: as if the line on each side of the central point representing the Present, <Say, Janus capable of both> were different only by an arbitrary relation like that of Right & Left as depended on the accident of my turning N. or S. on a plain, where all was the same.

Past Self		children, Sons &c
in Childhood youth &c		Future Self in others

Speculating in note-books of 1809 and 1813–15, and drawing in the Biographia *on Schelling's complex philosophical writings,[49] Coleridge argues from the reality of self-consciousness to the reality of spirit, and so to a higher form not only of knowing, but also of being.*

The Doctors of Self-love are misled by the wrong use of words – we love ourselves – now this impossible for a finite and created Being, in the *absolute* meaning of SELF; and and in its secondary & figurative meaning Self signifies only a less degree of distance, a narrowness of moral view, & a determination of value by distance – Hence the body is in this sense our self, ~~& our~~ because the sensations have been habitually appropriated to it in too great a proportion – but this is not a necessity of our Nature – there is a state possible even in this Life, in which we may truly say – My self loves, freely constituting its secondary or objective Love in what it *wills* to love, commands what it wills, and wills what it commands. The difference between Self-lo~~ving~~e, and Self, that loves, consists in the Objects of the former as *given* to it according to the Laws of the Senses – while ~~the Objects of~~ the latter determines ~~its~~ the Objects according to the Law in the spirit – The first loves because it *must*, the second because it *should* – and the guilt of the first is not in any <objective imaginable comprehensible> *action* but in that action by which it abandoned its power of true Agency, and willed its own *Fall* – this is indeed a mystery – How *can* it be otherwise? – For if the will be unconditional, it must be inexplicable / for ~~all expl~~ to understand~~ing~~ a thing is to see what the conditions of it were, & causes –. But whatever is in the Will, is the Will, & must therefore be equally inexplicable / –

The I = Self = Spirit is definable as ~~that~~ a Subject whose only possible Predicate is itself – Ergo, a Subject which is its own Object, i.e., a Subject-Object. But Object quoad Object is necessarily dead, inert, self-capable of no Action but only the Object of the action. The Spirit therefore cannot *be* an Object, ~~but~~ it is *a being* it – (nicht seyn, sondern werden). It becomes an Object thro' its own act –

But whatever is ipso termino and in its essence finite, is essentially an object. / The Subject therefore, as in toto the anti-thesis of Object, cannot be aboriginally, or of its own nature, finite. Is it then infinite? – But it is Spirit or Self, only as far as it becomes an object for itself – Ergo, it can neither be infinite without being at the same time finite, nor can it be finite (for itself) without being at the same time infinite

– It is ~~neither~~ therefore neither the one nor the other, alone, but in it subsists the primary Union of Finity & Infinity – and this is its third characteristic, or form of development. In this absolute Co-presence of the Infinite and the Finite lies the essence of an Individual Nature, of ~~a~~ the Self (der Ichheit) – This follows likewise out of the very possibility (or sole conditions) of Self-consciousness, thro' which alone the Spirit is what it is. For are we originally infinite, it is not to be comprehended how finite Representations and a succession of finite Representations can have arisen in us – and on the other hand, are we originally finite, it is inexplicable how an Idea of Infinitelyy [*sic*] together with the Faculty of abstracting from the Finite, could have come in thus. –

Further! the Spirit is whatever it is by an act of its own – Therefore, there must be from the very beginning in it Actions in antithesis, or (*formaliter*) opposite modes of Action, the one aboriginally infinite, the other aboriginally finite – & both distinguishable in their reciprocal Bearing on each other, and essential co-adunation/~~in This I know the while I can comprehend~~ The condition of knowing this; that I combine both at once in one Action — which Act is what we call Intuition, ~~or immediate Beholding~~, or ~~direct~~ immediate Presence. This Intuition, or simple direct Beholding, is not yet Consciousness, but yet the indispensable Condition of all Consciousness as I retire back from it to a former Intuition as its ground, & sally forth over and beyond it, Consciousness commences – In this act of Consciousness first can we distinguish the two Activities, the one positive, the other negative, the one *fills*, the other bounds, a Sphere. The one is represented as Activity tending outward (ad-extrant) the other as introitive. Whatever in the strict sense of the word *is*, all that possesses actual Being, *is* only in consequence of the *Direction upon itself*, or act of Introition / the symbol of this in the lifeless object which *is* not, but only exists (i.e. is not for itself but merely exists for another) ~~by~~ is the power of attraction, and in the ~~material~~ System of the Universe by the centripetal Tendency of the Mundane Bodies – The Spirit then is no other than this activity ~~self-bounded~~ and this limitation, both conceived as co-instantaneous. It is Power self-bounded by retroition on itself, and *is* only for itself – . – But in Self-limitation is implied the co-existence of Activity & Passivity – The Spirit is at once active & passive, and as this is a condition sine quâ non of our Consciousness, this union, ~~of Activity~~ this absolute Oneness of the Active & Passive must be another characteristic of an individual Nature – i.e. a new development of the original Self-predication / Passivity = negative Action. Absolute Passive p̶r̶ is absolute Nothing = nihil *privativum*. In us it is it *aliquid negativum*.

Hence we may now deduce a strict Demonstration of Idealism. – All, that is finite, is conceivable only as a balance or unition of opposite Activit~~y~~ies – b̶u̶t̶ These can only be conceived the one, as ad-extrant, the other as intröitive, or as exition and retröition – but <the latter, or> the Direction in on itself is the essential character of Spirit – the two powers therefore can o̶r̶ only be, & o̶f̶ consequently can only be united, in a Spirit – N̶o̶w̶ Ergo etc. Again, an Intuition, or p̶e̶r̶c̶e̶i̶v̶e̶d̶ b̶e̶h̶e̶l̶d̶ Present Beholding, combines actively, Activity & Passivity, <but any object is act. + pass. combined –> therefore the Object or Presence beheld, is the Spirit itself in this combination – But the Spirit merged in an Intuition cannot at the same <time> distinguish it from itself – Hence the absolute Identity of the Thing and the Perception, of the present Beholding and of the Presence beheld – & a compleat Confutation of physical or spiritual Influx, intermediate Images, &c – <Hence in all Languages Vision & a Vision – Thought & a Thought – Fancy & a Fancy, &c –>

However, we yet do distinguish our Self from the Object, tho' not in the primary Intuition – Visio visa – now this is impossible without an act of abstraction – we abstract from our own product – the Spirit snatches it<self> loose from its own self-immersion, and self-actualizing distinguishes itself from its Self-realization – But this is absolutely impossible otherwise than by a free Act –

THESIS VI

This principle, and so characterised manifests itself in the Sᴜᴍ or I ᴀᴍ; which I shall hereafter indiscriminately express by the words spirit, self and self-consciousness. In this, and in this alone, object and subject, being and knowing, are identical, each involving and supposing the other. In other words, it is a subject which becomes a subject by the act of constructing itself objectively to itself; but which never is an object except for itself, and only so far as by the very same act it becomes a subject. It may be described therefore as a perpetual self-duplication of one and the same power into object and subject, which presuppose each other, and can exist only as antitheses.

Sᴄʜᴏʟɪᴜᴍ. If a man be asked how he *knows* that he is? he can only answer, sum quia sum. But if (the absoluteness of this certainty having been admitted) he be again asked, how he, the individual person, came to be, then in relation to the ground of his *existence*, not to the ground of his *knowledge* of that existence, he might reply, sum quia deus est, or still more philosophically, sum quia in deo sum.

But if we elevate our conception to the absolute self, the great eternal I AM, then the principle of being, and of knowledge, of idea, and of reality; the ground of existence, and the ground of the knowledge of existence, are absolutely identical, Sum quia sum; I am, because I affirm myself to be; I affirm myself to be, because I am.

THESIS VII

If then I know myself only through myself, it is contradictory to require any other predicate of self, but that of self-consciousness. Only in the self-consciousness of a spirit is there the required identity of object and of representation; for herein consists the essence of a spirit, that it is self-representative. If therefore this be the one only immediate truth, in the certainty of which the reality of our collective knowledge is grounded, it must follow that the spirit in all the objects which it views, views only itself. If this could be proved, the immediate reality of all intuitive knowledge would be assured. It has been shown, that a spirit is that, which is its own object, yet not originally an object, but an absolute subject for which all, itself included, may become an object. It must therefore be an ACT; for every object is, as an *object*, dead, fixed, incapable in itself of any action, and necessarily finite. Again, the spirit (originally the identity of object and subject) must in some sense dissolve this identity, in order to be conscious of it: fit alter et idem. But this implies an act, and it follows therefore that intelligence or self-consciousness is impossible, except by and in a will. The self-conscious spirit therefore is a will; and freedom must be assumed as a *ground* of philosophy, and can never be deduced from it.

from THESIS X

. . . The principle of our knowing is sought within the sphere of our knowing. It must be something therefore, which can itself be known. It is asserted only, that the act of self-consciousness is for *us* the source and principle of all *our* possible knowledge. . . .

That the self-consciousness is the fixt point, to which for *us* all is morticed and annexed, needs no further proof. But that the self-consciousness may be the modification of a higher form of being, perhaps of a higher consciousness, and this again of a yet higher and so on in an infinite regressus; in short, that self-consciousness may be itself something explicable into something, which must lie beyond the possibility of our knowledge, because the whole synthesis of our intelligence is first formed in and through the self consciousness, does not at all concern us as transcendental philosophers. For to us the self-consciousness is not a kind of *being*, but a kind of *knowing*, and that too the highest and farthest that exists for *us*. It may however be shown, and has in part already been shown in pages 256–8 that even when the Objective is assumed as the first, we yet can never pass beyond the principle of self-consciousness. Should we attempt it, we must be driven back from ground to ground, each of which would cease to be a Ground the moment we pressed on it. We must be whirl'd down the gulph of an infinite series. But this would make our reason baffle the end and purpose of all reason, namely, unity and system. Or we must break off the series arbitrarily, and affirm an absolute something that is in and of itself at once cause and effect (*causa sui*), subject and object, or rather the absolute identity of both. But as this is inconceivable, except in a self-consciousness, it follows, that even as natural philosophers we must arrive at the same principle from which as transcendental philosophers we set out; that is, in a self-consciousness in which the principium essendi does not stand to the principium cognoscendi in the relation of cause to effect, but both the one and the other are co-inherent and identical. Thus the true system of natural philosophy places the sole reality of things in an ABSOLUTE, which is at once causa sui et effectus, πατὴρ αὐτοπάτωρ, υἱὸς ἑαυτοῦ [Father of himself, son of himself] – in the absolute identity of subject and object, which it calls nature, and which in its highest power is nothing else but self-conscious will or intelligence.

Coleridge makes one of his various divisions of people or minds into two kinds, one capable of originality, the other capable only of absorbing from others and therefore liable to deny the existence of the first kind.[50]

There are two Kinds of Heads in the world of Literature. The one I would call, SPRINGS: the other TANKS. The latter class habituated to receiving only, full or low, according to the state of it's Feeders, attach no distinct notion to living production as contra-distinguished from mechanical formation. If they find a fine passage in Thomson, they refer it to Milton; if in Milton to Euripides or Homer; and if in Homer, they take for granted it's pre-existence in the lost works of Linus or Musaeus. It would seem as if it was a part of their Creed, that all Thoughts are traditional, and that not only the Alphabet was revealed to Adam but all that was ever written in it that was worth writing. –

Four kinds of reading minds.[51]

4 Sorts of Readers. 1. Spunges that suck up every thing and, when pressed give it out in the same state, only perhaps somewhat dirtier –. 2. Sand Glasses – ~~that~~ or rather the upper Half of the Sand Glass, which in a brief hour assuredly lets out what it has received – & whose reading is only a profitless measurement & dozeing away of Time –. 3. Straining Bags, who get rid of whatever is good & pure, and retain the Dregs. – and this Straining-bag Class is again sub-divided into the Species of the Sensual, who retain evil for their ~~own~~ <base> gratification of their own base Imaginations, & the calumni-ous, who judge only by defects, & to whose envy a beauty is an eye-sore, a fervent praise ~~from~~ respecting an other a near-grievance, and the more virulent in its action because the miserable man does not dare confess the Truth to his own Heart –. 4 and lastly, the Great-Moguls Diamond Sieves – which is perhaps going farther for a Simile than its superior Dignity can repay, inasmuch as a common Cullender would have been equally symbolic / but imperial or culinary, these are the only good, & I fear ~~not~~ the least numerous, who assuredly retain the good, & while the superfluous or impure passes away & leaves no trace /

(iii) Inferred Continuities: Spirit and Soul

Coleridge related some of his thinking about consciousness to his idea of the soul or spirit – terms sometimes used interchangeably. The spirit, too, was seen to inhabit a light, free, intelligent sphere beyond nature, detached, finally, from the body that first gave it life.

Truth as recognition.[52]

At the annunciation of *principles*, of *ideas*, the soul of man awakes, and starts up, as an exile in a far distant land at the unexpected sounds of his native language, when after long years of absence, and almost of oblivion, he is suddenly addressed in his own mother-tongue. He weeps for joy, and embraces the speaker as his brother.

The discovery of the soul as an awakening from amnesia.[53]

If it were asked of me to justify the interest, which many good minds – what if I speak out, and say what I believe to be the truth – which the majority of the best and noblest minds feel in the great questions – Where am I? What and for what am I? What are the duties, which arise out of the relations of my Being to itself as heir of futurity, and to the World which is its present sphere of action and impression? – I would compare the human Soul to a ~~Man~~ Ship's Crew cast on an unknown Island (a fair Simile: for these questions could not suggest themselves unless the mind had previously felt convictions, that the present World was not its whole destiny and abiding Country) – What would be ~~his~~ their first business? Surely, to enquire <what the Island was? in what Latitude?> what ships visited that Island? when? and whither they went? – and what chance that they should take off first one, & then another? – and after this – to think, how they should maintain & employ themselves during their stay – & how best stock themselves for the expected voyage, & procure the means of inducing the Captain to take them to the Harbour, which they wished to go to? –

The moment, when the Soul begins to be sufficiently self-conscious, to ask concerning itself, & its relations, is the first moment of its *intellectual* arrival into the World – Its *Being* – enigmatic as it must seem – is posterior to its *Existence* –. Suppose the shipwrecked man stunned, & for many weeks in a state of Ideotcy or utter loss of Thought & Memory – & then gradually awakened /

The alienation created by failures of communication between spirits.[54]

The medium, by which spirits understand each other, is not the surrounding air; but the *freedom* which they possess in common, as the common ethereal element of their being, the tremulous reciprocations of which propagate themselves even to the inmost of the soul. Where the spirit of a man is not *filled* with the consciousness of freedom (were it only from its restlessness, as of one still struggling in bondage) all spiritual intercourse is interrupted, not only with others, but even with himself. No wonder then, that he remains incomprehensible to himself as well as to others. No wonder, that in the fearful desert of his consciousness, he wearies himself out with empty words, to which no friendly echo answers, either from his own heart, or the heart of a fellow being; or bewilders himself in the pursuit of *notional* phantoms, the mere refractions from unseen and distant truths through the distorting medium of his own unenlivened and stagnant understanding!

The groping life of the Soul.[55]

– Hence even in dreams of Sleep the Soul never *is*, because it either cannot or dare not be, any <ONE> THING; but lives in *approaches* – touched by the outgoing pre-existent Ghosts of many feelings – It feels for ever as a blind man with his protended Staff dimly thro' the medium of the ~~act~~ instrument by which it pushes off, & in the act of repulsion, O for the eloquence of Shakespeare, who alone could feel & yet know how to embody these conceptions, with as curious a felicity as the thoughts are subtle. As if the finger which I saw with eyes Had, as it were, another finger invisible – Touching me with a ghostly touch, even while I feared the real Touch from it. What if in certain cases Touch acted by itself, co-present with vision, yet not coalescing – then I should see the finger as at a distance, and yet feel a finger touching which was nothing but it & yet was not it / the two senses cannot co-exist without a sense of causation / the *touch* must be the effect of that Finger, I see, yet it's not yet near to me, <and therefore it is not it; & yet it is it. Why,> it is it in an imaginary preduplication. N.B. there is a passage in the second Part of Wallenstein, expressing not explaining the same feeling – The Spirits of great Events Stride on before the events – it is in one of the last two or 3 Scenes.

How few would read this Note – nay, *any one?* / and not think the writer mad or drunk!

The relation between Spirit and Will.[56]

If there be aught *Spiritual* in Man, the Will must be such.
If there be a Will, there must be a Spirituality in Man.
I suppose both positions granted. The Reader admits the reality of

the power, agency, or mode of Being expressed in the term, Spirit; and the actual existence of a Will. He sees clearly, that the idea of the former is necessary to the conceivability of the latter; and that, vice versâ, in asserting the *fact* of the latter he presumes and instances the truth of the former – just as in our common and received Systems of Natural Philosophy, the Being of imponderable Matter is assumed to render the Lode-stone intelligible, and the Fact of the Lode-stone adduced to prove the reality of imponderable Matter.

In short, I suppose the Reader, whom I now invite to the third and last Division of the work, already disposed to reject for himself and his human Brethren the insidious title of "Nature's noblest *Animal*," or to retort it as the unconscious Irony of the Epicurean Poet on the animalizing tendency of his own philosophy. I suppose him convinced, that there is more in man than can be rationally referred to the life of Nature and the mechanism of Organization; that he has a will not included in this mechanism; and that the Will is in an especial and pre-eminent sense the spiritual part of our Humanity.

Having read of a woman who, after a trance-like sleep, remembered all that had taken place around her, Coleridge considers the role of the body as interpreter.[57]

Could this Fact, if a fact, admit of another solution, but that of a Soul = Principium Individual[it]atis or substantial Person capable if not of existing separately from the body, yet of perceiving, remembering, and thinking independently of the bodily Organs of Sense, memory, & Thought – i.e. the Brain and the Senses? If the latter capability, that of *acting* I mean, were demonstrated positively by the fact, would not the former, that of separately existing, be proved *negatively* – i.e. by the impossibility of conceiving any cause or reason for the contrary? – And *then*, would it not follow that the Body is a moveable Dungeon with windows, and Sound holes – & that we might well exclaim with the great Apostle, Who shall deliver me from *the Body of this Death?* – But as always God brings good out of evil, and often mercifully converts the consequences of Evil to a remedy . . . the question will be – What on this supposition can be imagined to be the *uses* of the Body? *A Sheath?* an Interpreter in our communion with *lower natures!*

The difference between mind and 'I'.[58]

I now see that the I is Life in the form of mind – and look forward to the establishment of a twofold I – the accidental or phantom I, and the substantial personal I – the first being the transformation of the self finding of animal Life in its first dim participation of Mind – and this empirical I is doubtless possessed by the higher Order at least of the Animals, by the Dog, the Elephant, &c – of the substantial I I only anticipate the solution in the immanent Life in the communicative Logos – and which being communicated is the *Light* of Man, the Spirit which subsists subjectively by its unity with, and correlation to the Holy Spirit objectively. As a spirit of *Intelligence*, it is its' own Object, but this Object it perpetually construes as a Subject by the act of Self-renunciation constituting its' antithesis to the Objectivity of the Holy Spirit –

Corollary – The simplification of the definition of mind, as a pure *active* and proper *Perceptivity*: thus cleansing my system from the last adhesion of the Berkeleian Passivity . . . the Differency of Mind and the *I*.

The difference between living as self and living 'in spirit'.[59]

My soul. *My*? Yes! as long as Sin reigns, so long must this "my" have a tremendous force, a substantial meaning. Every Sin & thought of Sin sink us back in upon the swampy rotten ground of our *division* from God, make us participant and accomplices of the Hades, the only conceivable Contrary of God not indeed conceivable of itself, but only by means of the Coercion from the at once determining (and all determination ab alio is a confining) and the subliming Word & Spirit – i.e. Form and Energy – not conceivable as Hades, but by a Light cast back on its antecedent Ens non verè Ens by its commencing entity as Nature. Nature is Hades rendered intelligible by the energy, which combining herewith makes it no longer Hades: even as Number is brute Multëity raised into intelligibility, and made the possible Object of Mind, by Unity. But in proportion as the Captivity, the chain, is loosened, & we can *go forth*, we leave the *my* behind, forget it and so find it, our own I becoming an indivisible Breathing included in the Eternal *I Am*. But now I strive with my Soul, if by any means I may be emancipated, and live in Spirit – not as *a* Spirit, but Spirit.

In his early speculations Coleridge defies materialism and accepts the belief that he is a spirit, an 'I myself I', a body with a soul.[60]

– Well, true or false, Heaven is a less gloomy idea than Annihilation!
– Dr Beddoes, & Dr Darwin think that *Life* is utterly inexplicable, writing as Materialists – You, I understand, have adopted the idea that it is the result of organized matter acted on by external Stimuli.
– As likely as any other system; but you *assume* the thing to be proved – the *'capability* of being stimulated into sensation' *as a property* of organized matter – now 'the Capab.' &c is *my* definition of *animal Life* – Monro believes in a plastic immaterial Nature – all-pervading –

> And what if all of animated Nature
> Be but organic harps diversely fram'd
> That tremble into *thought* as o'er them sweeps
> Plastic & vast &c –

by the bye – that is my favourite of *my* poems – do *you* like it? Hunter that the *Blood* is the Life – which is saying nothing at all – for if the blood were *Life*, it could never be otherwise than Life – and to say, it is *alive*, is saying nothing – & Ferriar believes in a *Soul*, like an orthodox Churchman – so much for Physicians & Surgeons – Now as to the Metaphysicians, Plato says, it is *Harmony* – he might as well have said, a fiddle stick's end – but I love Plato – his dear *gorgeous* Nonsense! And *I, tho' last not least, I* do not know what to think about it – on the whole, I have rather made up my mind that I am a mere *apparition* – a naked Spirit! – And that Life is I myself I! which is a mighty clear account of it. Now I have written all this not to expose my ignorance (that is an accidental effect, not the final cause) but to shew you, that I want to see your Essay on Animal Vitality – of which Bowles, the Surgeon, spoke in high Terms – Yet *he* believes in a *body* & a *soul*.

The butterfly's metamorphosis as an image of unseen development toward freedom.[61]

I addressed a Butterfly <on a Pea-blossom> thus – Beautiful Psyche, Soul of a Blossom that art visiting & hovering o'er thy former friends whom thou hadst left –. Had I forgot the Caterpillar or did I dream like a mad metaphysician the Caterpillars hunger for Plants was

Self-love – recollection-feeling, & a lust that in its next state refined itself into Love? – 12 Dec. 1804.

Space as an image of soul.[62]

Yon long not unvaried ridge of Hills that runs out of sight each way, it is *spacious*, & the pleasure derivable from it is from its *running*, its *motion*, it assimilation to action / & here the scale is taken from my *Life*, & *Soul* – not from my body. Space <is one of> the Hebrew names for God / & it is the most perfect image of *Soul, pure Soul* – being indeed to us nothing but unresisted action. – Wherever action is resisted, limitation begins – & limitation is the first constituent of body – the more omnipresent it is in a given space, the more ~~it~~ that is *body* or matter // but thus all body necessarily presupposes soul, inasmuch as all resistance presupposes action / Magnitude therefore is the intimate *unison* blending, the most perfect union, thro' its whole sphere, in every minutest part of it, of action and resistance to action / it is spaciousness in which Space is *filled up*; & ~~feelingly stopped~~ <as we well say – i.e. transmitted by incorporate accession, not destroyed> ~~and~~ In all limited things, that is, in all *forms*, it is at least fantastically *stopped* / and thus from the positive *grasp* to the mountain, from the mountain to the Cloud, from the Cloud to the blue depth of Sky, ~~that~~ which, as on the top of Etna in a serene atmosphere, seems to go *behind* the Sun, all is *gradation*, that precludes division indeed, but not distinction.

In a letter to Thomas Clarkson of 1806 Coleridge describes some of the gradations of consciousness as he tries to answer the question, 'What is (that is, what can we congruously conceive of) the Soul?' and the implications of the communication between human beings.[63]

There are infinite gradations of consciousness:
1. those who exist to themselves only in *moments*, and whose continuousness exists in higher minds. 2. those who are conscious of *a* continuousness, but not only not of their whole continuousness, but who do not make that consciousness of *a* continuousness an object of a secondary consciousness – i.e. who are not endued with reflex Faculties. 3. Those who tho' not conscious of the whole of their continuousness, are yet both conscious of *a* continuousness, & make

that the object of a reflex consciousness – And of this third Class the
Species are infinite; and the first or lowest, as far as we know, is Man,
or the human Soul. For Reflexion seems the first approach to, &
shadow of, the divine Permanency; the first effort of divine working
in us to bind the Past and Future with the Present, and thereby to let
in upon us some faint glimmering of that State in which Past, Present,
and Future are co-adunated in the adorable I AM. But this state &
growth of reflex consciousness (my Time will not permit me to
supply all the Links; but by a short meditation you will convince
yourself) is not conceivable without the action of kindred souls on
each other, i.e. the modification of each by each, and of each by the
Whole. A male & female Tyger is neither more or less whether you
suppose them only existing in their appropriate wilderness, or
whether you suppose a thousand Pairs. But Man is truly altered by
the co-existence of other men; his faculties cannot be developed in
himself alone, & only by himself. Therefore the human race not by a
bold metaphor, but in a sublime reality, approach to, & might become, one body whose Head is Christ (the Logos). Hence with a
certain degree of satisfaction to my own mind I can define the
human Soul to be that class of Being, as far as we are permitted to
know, the first and lowest of that Class, which is endued with a
reflex consciousness of it's own continuousness, and the great end
and purpose of all it's energies & sufferings is the growth of that
reflex consciousness: that class of Being too, in which the Individual
is capable of being itself contemplated as a Species of itself, namely,
by it's conscious continuousness moving on in an unbroken Line,
while at the same time the whole Species is capable of being regarded as one Individual. Now as the very idea of consciousness
implies a recollection of the last Links, and the growth of it an
extension of that retrospect, Immortality – or a recollection after the
Sleep and Change (probably and by strict analogy the growth) of
Death (for growth of body and the conditional causes of intellectual
growth are found all to take place during sleep, and Sleep is the
Term repeatedly and as it were fondly used by the inspired Writers
as the Exponent of Death, and without it the aweful and undoubtedly taught, Doctrine of the Resurrection has no possible meaning) –
the very idea of such a consciousness, permit me to repeat, implies a
recollection after the Sleep of Death of all material circumstances
that were at least immediately previous to it. A spacious field here
opens itself for moral reflection, both for Faith, and for Consolation,
when we consider the growth of consciousness (and of what kind

our's is, our *conscience* sufficiently reveals to us: for of what use or meaning could *Conscience* be to a Being, who in any state of it's Existence should become to itself utterly lost, and entirely new?) as the end of our earthly Being – when we reflect too, how habits of Vice of all Kinds tend to retard this growth, and how all our sufferings tend to extend & open it out, and how all our Virtues & virtuous and loving Affections tend to bind it, and as it were to inclose the fleeting Retrospect as within a wall! – And again, what sublime motives to Self-respect with humble Hope does not the Idea give, that each Soul is a Species in itself; and what Impulses to more than brotherly Love of our fellow-creatures, the Idea that all men form as it were, one Soul! –

Beset by maladies during the years 1813–14 he is particularly troubled by the suffering of his soul but notes how it has opened up a perception of the infinite.[64]

You have no conception of what my sufferings have been, forced to struggle and struggle in order not to desire a death for which I am not prepared. – I have scarcely known what sleep is, but like a leopard in its den have been drawn up and down the room by extreme pain, and restlessness, worse than pain itself.

O how I have prayed even to loud agony only to be able to pray! O how I have felt the impossibility of any real *good will* not born anew from the Word and the Spirit! O I have seen far, far deeper and clearer than I ever saw before the ground of pernicious errors! O I have seen, I have felt that the worst offences are those against our own souls! That our souls are infinite in depth, and therefore our sins are infinite, and redeemable only by an infinitely higher infinity; that of the Love of God in Christ Jesus. I have called my soul infinite, but O infinite in the depth of darkness, an infinite craving, an infinite capacity of pain and weakness, and excellent only as being passively capacious of the light from above. Should I recover I will – no – no may God grant me power to struggle to become *not another* but a *better man* –

Arguing against the absence of a personal agent in art, Coleridge invokes the writings of Byron and Southey, the inventing of watches and philosophies, and the historical paintings of Washington Allston (1779–1843), an American painter with whom he became friends in Rome in 1806. He stresses the need to distinguish the workings of the infinite spirit from the means by which its effects are produced.[65]

We will pass by the utter incompatibility of such a law (if law it may be called, which would itself be the slave of chances) with even that *appearance* of rationality forced upon us by the outward phænomena of human conduct, abstracted from our own consciousness. We will agree to forget this for the moment, in order to fix our attention on that subordination of final to efficient causes in the human being, which flows of necessity from the assumption, that the will, and with the will all acts of thought and attention, are parts and products of this blind mechanism instead of being distinct powers, whose function it is to controul, determine, and modify the phantasmal chaos of association. The soul becomes a mere ens logicum; for as a real separable being, it would be more worthless and ludicrous, than the Grimalkins in the Cat-harpsichord, described in the Spectator. For these did form a part of the process; but in Hartley's scheme the soul is present only to be pinched or *stroked*, while the very squeals or purring are produced by an agency wholly independent and alien. It involves all the difficulties, all the incomprehensibility (if it be not indeed, ὡς ἔμοιγε δοκεῖ, the absurdity) of intercommunion between substances that have no one property in common, without any of the convenient consequences that bribed the judgement to the admission of the *dualistic* hypothesis. Accordingly, this caput mortuum of the Hartleian process has been rejected by his followers, and the consciousness considered as a *result*, as a *tune*, the common product of the breeze and the harp: tho' this again is the mere remotion of one absurdity to make way for another, equally preposterous. For what is harmony but a mode of relation, the very *esse* of which is *percipi*? An ens rationale, which pre-supposes the power, that by perceiving creates it? The razor's edge becomes a saw to the armed vision; and the delicious melodies of Purcell or Cimarosa might be disjointed stammerings to a hearer, whose partition of time should be a thousand times subtler than ours. But this obstacle too let us imagine ourselves to have surmounted, and "at one bound high overleap all bound!" Yet according to this hypothesis the disquisition, to which I am at present soliciting the reader's attention, may be as truly said to be written by Saint Paul's church, as by *me*: for it is the mere motion of my muscles and nerves; and these again are set in motion from external causes equally passive, which external causes stand themselves in interdependent connection with every thing that exists or has existed. Thus the whole universe co-operates to produce the minutest stroke of every letter, save only that I myself, and I alone, have nothing to do with it, but merely the causeless and *effectless* beholding of it when it is done. Yet scarcely can it be called a beholding; for it is neither an act nor an effect; but an impossible creation of a *something–nothing* out of its very contrary! It is the mere quick-silver plating behind a looking-glass; and in this alone consists the poor worthless I! The sum total of my moral and intellectual intercourse dissolved into its elements are reduced to *extension, motion, degrees of velocity*, and those diminished *copies* of configurative motion, which form what we call notions, and notions of notions. . . .

The inventor of the watch did not in reality invent it; he only look'd on, while the blind causes, the only true artists, were unfolding themselves. So must it have been too with my friend ALLSTON, when he sketched his picture of the dead man revived by the bones of the prophet Elijah. So must it have been with Mr SOUTHEY and LORD BYRON, when the one *fancied* himself composing his "RODERICK," and the other his "CHILD HAROLD." The same must hold good of all systems of philosophy; of all arts, governments, wars by sea and by land; in short, of all things that ever have been or that ever will be produced. For according to this system it is not the affections and passions that are at work, in as far as they are *sensations* or *thoughts*. We only *fancy*, that we act from rational resolves, or prudent motives, or from impulses of anger, love, or generosity. In all these cases the real agent is a *something–nothing–every-thing*, which does all of which we know, and knows nothing of all that itself does.

The existence of an infinite spirit, of an intelligent and holy will, must on this system be mere articulated motions of the air. For as the function of the human understanding is no other than merely (to appear to itself) to combine and to apply the phænomena of the association; and as these derive all their reality from the primary sensations; and the sensations again all *their* reality from the impressions ab extra; a God not visible, audible, or tangible, can exist only in the sounds and letters that form his name and attributes. If in *ourselves* there be no such faculties as those of the will, and the scientific reason, we must either have an *innate* idea of them, which would overthrow the whole system; or we can have no idea at all. The process, by which Hume degraded the notion of cause and effect into a blind product of delusion and habit, into the mere sensation of *proceeding* life (nisus vitalis) associated with the images of the memory; this same process must be repeated to the equal degradation of every *fundamental* idea in ethics or theology.

In one of his Philosophical Lectures Coleridge argues, as previously in the Biographia, *that human beings are distinguished from animals by their power to create or originate acts. In addition to the creation of art, government and ideas, the person demonstrates his or her free agency in moral acts, thus asserting independence from nature and a hope for the continuity of consciousness. The person, not the dagger, commits the murder.*[66]

And if without thinking, if he is a dogmatic materialist . . . by a corrupt and ignorant hierarchy he will worship statues, and imagine the same power into those statues which the more philosophic materialist imagines in his composition of particles, which are called atoms. But this would be nothing, if it only left something in us to force a belief in God, which cannot be destroyed without destroying the basis of all truth. That is, it destroys the possibility of free agency, it destroys the great distinction between the mere human and the mere animals of nature, namely the powers of originating an act. All things are brought, even the powers of life are brought, into a common link of causes and effect that we observe in a machine, and all the powers of thought into those of life, being all reasoned away into modes of sensation, and the will itself into nothing but a current, a fancy determined by the accidental copulations of certain internal stimuli. With such a being, to talk of a difference between good and evil would be to blame a stone for being round or angular. The thought itself is repulsive. No, the man forfeits that high principle of nature, his free agency, which though it reveals itself principally in his moral conduct, yet is still at work in all departments of his being. It is by his bold denial of this, by an inward assertion, "I am not the creature of nature merely, nor a subject of nature, but I detach myself from her. I oppose myself as man to nature, and my destination is to conquer and subdue her, and my destination is to be lord of light, and fire, and the elements; and what my mind can comprehend, that I will make my eye to see, and what my eye can see, my mind shall instruct me to reach through the means of my hand, so that everywhere the lower part of my nature shall be taken up into the higher. And why? Because I am a free being. I can esteem, I can revere myself, and as such a being I dare look forward to permanence. As I have never yet called this body 'I', but only 'mine', even as I call my clothes so, I dare look forward to a continued consciousness, to a continued progression of my powers, for I am capable of the highest distinction, that of being the object of the approbation of the God of the Universe, which no mechanism can be. Nay further, I am the cause of the creation of the world. . . ." This I say is so sacred a privilege, that whatever dares to tell us that we are like the trees or like the streams, links in an inevitable chain, and that the assassin is no more worthy of abhorrence than the dagger with which he murders his benefactor, that man I say teaches treason against human nature and against the God of human nature.

The free agency of others thus becomes sacrosanct.[67]

Morality = Individuals in relation to their personal Integrity.

Religion = Persons in relation to the Absolute Person, as their common Ground. This morality respects persons under the view of their independence: Religion respects Persons under the view of their Dependence. The former contemplates the Individual as commencing his personality by detachment from Nature; the latter contemplates the same Individual, as completing and perpetuating his Personality by union with Deity.

The difference between moral doing and moral being.[68]

Assuredly much happier & more truly tranquil I have already found myself, and shall deem myself amply remunerated if in consequence of my exertions a Few only of those, who had formed their moral creed on Hume, Paley, and their Imitators, with or without a belief in the facts of mere historical Christianity, shall have learnt to value actions primarily as the language & natural effect of the state of the agent; if they shall consider what they *are* instead of *merely* what they *do*; so that the fig-tree may bring forth it's own fruit from it's own living principle, and not have the figs tied on to it's barren sprays by the hand of outward Prudence & Respect of Character. These indeed are aids & great ones to our frailty, & it behoves us to be grateful for them & to use them; but let not the confidence in the gardner or his manures render us careless as to the health & quality of the *seed*. "Would not the whole moral code remain the same on the principle of enlightened Selfishness, as on that of Conscience, or the unconditional obedience of the Will to the pure Reason?" has been asked more than once of me. My answer was: All possibly might remain the same, only not the men themselves for whom the moral Law was given. . . .

(c) PERSONS

One of the most complex terms in Coleridge's array of mental subdivisions is 'person', a term that in his time was developing its various legal, theological, physical, psychological and eventually deeply emotional meanings. It was applied to the body, to the voice inside the body, to the continuity of the consciousness over time, to responsibility for actions and properties, to autonomous boundaries around the person, to ownership and command of other persons, and to respect for other persons. The term came to accumulate honorific, and even holy, connotations. As a legal term, a 'person' was an agent (or even a group of agents acting as a decision-making corporation) with certain rights and responsibilities. As a psychological term, 'person' denoted a coherent identity of body and mind that remembers its past, is conscious of its present, and anticipates its future; it was thus capable of responsibility for its decisions, its deeds and its lifelong growth.

Two eighteenth-century developments which worked to undermine both the legal and the psychological meanings reinforced one another. The first was the industrial, commercial, and utilitarian *uses* of persons, who were thus treated as *things*; the second was Hume's 'bundle theory' of personality, the sceptical denial that persons had continuity or coherence from one moment to the next.

Coleridge deplored both developments, often repeating Kant's formulation that whereas things are means to an end, persons are ends in themselves, and his injunctions that persons must never be used as things.[69] Recognising, nevertheless, that (as Hume showed) personal identity is often fragmented and discontinuous, he also explored alternative ways of defining the person so as to take account of such inward multifariousness. These included defining the person as a divided subjectivity reflexively conscious of itself, as a dialogue of many voices, as a multiplicity in unity akin to a work of art, as an agent with intentions and responsibilities. Indirectly disputing Hume's denial of personal identity, and modifying Kant's rationalism by a more complex psychological insight, his work in this difficult area between philosophy and psychology will bear comparison with that of a number of late-twentieth-century philosophers such as A. J. Ayer, Derek Parfit, Bernard Williams and Peter J. McCormick.

When Coleridge spoke of 'the sacred distinction between persons and things'[70] he owed his assigning of religious significance to persons partly to the German philosopher Jacobi, but also to familiar religious doctrines, such as that of the three Persons of God, and (with a different emphasis) the Unitarian notion of Jesus as a Person. One benefit of such a concept was that it protected individual persons from being treated as things.

On the tendency to individualise things, whereas persons can be universalised.[71]

The distinction, on which depend all Morality, all true State-wisdom, all Law that deserves the name, is that of Person and

Things. It is this alone, which can supply a ground of Reason in the division of Professions and Trades, the Liberal and the Mechanic, Arts. As long as the legitimate deductions from, and necessary accomplishments of this distinction of personal interests, this interest *for* persons, from the interest in things, remain the acknowleged Rules of a Profession, so long the Profession is to be honored, however too large a number of Individual Members may in *fact* and the tenor of their actions sink into *Thing*-seekers. . . .

Mem. Things have no true individuality, their *plural* in mind as actually in the Greek Language govern a verb singular – thence the impulse to individualize them by *property*. Persons are essentially individual – thence the moral impulse & command to universalize, to reduce them to a *Unity* – . . .

A central statement in The Friend *of his belief in the need for the endowment of Reason to make human beings persons and not things – with the further implication that in the process not only free agency but human rights are guaranteed.*[72]

All voluntary actions, say they, having for their objects, good or evil, are *moral* actions. But all morality is grounded in the reason. Every man is born with the faculty of Reason: and whatever is without it, be the shape what it may, is not a man or PERSON, but a THING. Hence the sacred principle, recognized by all Laws, human and divine, the principle indeed, which is the *ground-work* of all law and justice, that a person can never become a thing, nor be treated as such without wrong. But the distinction between person and thing consists herein, that the latter may rightfully be used, altogether and merely, as a *means*; but the former must always be included in the *end*, and form a part of the final cause. We plant the tree and we cut it down, we breed the sheep and we kill it, wholly as *means* to our own *ends*. The wood-cutter and the hind are likewise employed as *means*, but on an agreement of reciprocal advantage, which includes them as well as their employer in the *end*. Again: as the faculty of Reason implies free-agency, morality (i.e. the dictate of Reason) gives to every rational being the right of acting as a free agent, and of finally determining his conduct by his own will, according to his own conscience: and this right is inalienable except by guilt, which is an act of self-forfeiture, and the consequences therefore to be considered as the criminal's own moral election. In respect of their Reason all men are equal. The measure of the Understanding and of all other faculties of man, is different in different persons: but Reason is not susceptible of degree. For since it merely decides whether any given thought or action is or is not in contradiction with the rest, there can be no reason better, or more *reason*, than another.

2

Questions of Species and Gender

(a) THE CHALLENGE OF EVOLUTION

(i) Human Beings and Animals

Coleridge's prose writings about animals differed markedly from his poetic depictions of them, partly because his increasing moral preoccupations took him away from the close empathising with the life in nature characteristic of earlier years. Whereas the three poems that prominently feature animals or birds – 'To a Young Ass, Its Mother Being Tethered Nearby'; 'The Rime of the Ancient Mariner'; and 'Christabel' – depict them as victims of oppressive or unthinking actions (even if also as related in various ways to 'Christian souls'), the prose writings concentrate increasingly on the distance or gap between human beings and animated nature.

Beginning with a metaphorical use of the words 'beasts', 'bestial' and 'brute', to describe human beings who have been deprived by a harsh economic system and a dislocating war of the basic necessities that would allow them to cultivate their nobler faculties, Coleridge learned to relocate animal metaphors such as those that Shakespeare used for his villains in the new science of zoology. His play with these debasing downward metaphors (which by implication and extension suggested metamorphoses of human beings into wolves, foxes, serpents) was checked and deepened as he studied current writings on animal behaviour such as Henry Smeathman's *Some Account of the Termites, which he found in Africa and other hot Climates* (1781), Pierre Huber's *Natural History of Ants*, and Reimarus's *On the Instincts of Animals*. During his stay in Germany in 1798–9 he attended the physiological lectures of J. F. Blumenbach, which included arguments against an 'identification of Man with the Brute, in Kind'.[1]

Other writers, however, were not certain that such a clear distinction could be drawn. As early as 1699, in his *Orang-Outang, sive Homo Sylvestris* ('Orang-utan, or Man of the Forests'), Edward Tyson had reluctantly noted some telling similarities. From then on, the gentle orang-utan became a recurrent threat to human uniqueness, discussed by J.-J. Rousseau in his *Discourse on the Origin and Foundations of Inequality* and by Lord Monboddo in *Of the Origin and Progress of Language*.[2] (See also Geoffrey Symcox in 'The Wild Man's Return'.[3]) Rudimentary evolutionary theories were developed in writings such as Buffon's *Histoire naturelle* (1749) and Maupertuis' *Lettre sur le progrès des sciences* (1751); as John G. Burk has pointed out,[4] 'Linnaeus'

Systema Naturae (1735) considered man as a quadruped animal, placing him in the same class as the ape and the sloth.' Even Erasmus Darwin, a naturalist poet whom Coleridge in many ways admired, seemed to anticipate in his *Zoonomia* (1794) the evolutionary theory that would later be identified with his grandson Charles. According to John Beer, 'The doctrine of evolution which seems implicit in all this is furthered by the idea (voiced also in *The Botanic Garden*) that the anthers and stigmata might mark the point at which the insect creation begins. Coleridge, on the other hand, was . . . drawn to argue that the difference between plant and anther marked, not a point of continuity, but a chasm which existed from the beginning of creation.'[5]

Coleridge fulminated against making the orang-utan an ancestor of humanity because that would introduce what was for him a fearful continuity with the amoral and the mindless. His revulsion, pronounced in a letter to Wordsworth[6] and in late notebooks, drove him to elaborate some of his most important conceptions: the difference between reason and understanding, the chasm introduced into biological nature by human spirit and will, the difference between degree and kind; he was also led to analyse in these terms distinctly human activities, institutions and feelings, such as literature, the family and love. The fear of full identification with the animals may be said to lie behind many of his constructions, as he sought to locate the point where some element unique to human beings entered the chain of animal life. When he recorded his son Hartley's nightmare of a blurring between species, he took it as evidence that such a loss of distinction was instinctively abhorrent even to a child.

The fact that human beings and animals shared physical bodies, senses and the lower forms of understanding engaged him constantly. He was fascinated by animal instincts, and frequently compared them with built-in human yearnings. He not only drew on Francis Hutcheson's use of the term 'instinct' to describe his notion of the innate moral sense but elaborated on its implications by using analogies with various animals that prepare 'by instinct' for future metamorphoses. While feeling a fellowship with animals as living, sensible and sympathising beings, he nevertheless believed that human beings must cultivate nobler faculties. When, in his 'Theory of Life', he envisaged a rising sequence of increasingly complex forms of life from the jelly fish to human beings, he presented it as one that had been divinely established, not as having evolved through time. Just before the entrance of human beings, moreover, he interjected into this rising sequence a discontinuity, a new departure, the breathing in of a new spirit. The words 'chasm' and 'gap' appeared frequently to designate the depth and impassability of this difference, however narrow. Many of his meditations can be seen as attempts to rebut in advance theories – which were already beginning to circulate in his time – based on the assumption of a continuous evolution from the animals to the human.

The modern use of the term 'humane' in connection with protection of animals against human exploitation in laboratories and forests shows how far we have moved from Coleridge's anxiety about this separation. In his time the animal kingdom was not yet endangered by the development of human civilisation: the much greater fear was that if people were not shown to be different they would be treated like animals and brutalised – a fear to be realised with horrible vividness in Zola's naturalistic descriptions of Parisian crowds as herds or, with more complex meanings, in Kafka's *Metamorphosis*, where labour practices, family greed and loss of a sense of personal significance lead to an emblematic presentation of the debasement that Coleridge dreaded.

Coleridge writes to Sara Hutchinson in 1802 about young Hartley's fear of the blurring of the species when he meets a neighbour whose behaviour calls in question the boundaries between human beings and animals.[7]

Dear Hartley – ! – I picked up a parcel of old Books at Wilkinson's which he gave me / among them is an old System of Philosophy by some FANTASTIC or other, with a large Print of Sun, Moon, & Stars, Birds, Beasts, & Fishes – with Adam & Eve, rising out of a Chaos! – Derwent immediately recognized the Horse & Cow – Hos! Cu! – & then putting his finger to Eve's Bosom, said – *Ma*! – *Ma*! PAP! – *Ma* – pap! – i.e. his Mother's or Mary's bosom / into which he puts his little Hand when he is petting. But I asked Hartley what he thought of it – & he said – [']it is *very* curious! A Sea not in a World, but a World rising out of a Sea! (these were his own unprompted words, & entirely his own idea) – There they all are – Adam & all! – Well! I dare say, they stared at one another finely!' – This strikes me as a most happy image of the Creation – Yesterday, *crazy* Peter Crosthwaite (not the Museum Peter) came in to Mr Jackson – (and Mrs Wilson & Hartley only were at home) – Hartley soon found out that he was crazy, turned pale & trembled – & Mrs W. snatched him up & brought him in to us / as soon as he came in, he cried aloud in an agony, nor could we appease him for near a quarter of an hour – When I talked to him how foolish it was. Well! says he, you know, I am always frightened at things that are not like other things. But, Hartley! said I – you would not be frightened if you were to see a number of new Beasts or Birds or Fishes in a Shew – Yes – said he! when I was a little Boy, I was frightened at the Monkey & the Dromedary in London (*so he was, poor fellow! God knows*) – but now I am not frightened at them, *because they are like themselves.* What do you mean, Hartley? – "Don't ask me so many questions, Papa! I can't bear it. I mean, that I am frightened at men that are not like men / a Monkey is a monkey – & God made the Dromedary – but Peter is a crazy man – he has had a chain upon him!" – Poor fellow! when he recovered, he spent the whole afternoon in whirling about the Kitchen, & telling Mrs Wilson wild Stories of his own extempore composition about mad men & mad animals – all frightful: for tho' he cannot endure the least approximation to a sorrowful Story from another Person, all his own are most fantastically tragical. – O dear Sara! – how dearly I love you! Dear Mary! Heaven bless you & send back our dear Friends to you! S. T. Coleridge.

The superior skills shown in some instinctive behaviour, without the intervention of reason, are typical of the animal creation.[8]

Fear in animals awakens instincts of Skill – but in man blunders of direct Destruction, as is seen in instances of Women or Ladies rather catching *fire* – Why? – Ecclesiasticus. It withdraws the aids of REASON – Quære. Is or can any Animal be afraid to the extent that *Man* is? I suspect not. – from the want of the agglomerative faculty of Reason, arising out of the comparing power – and in such cases producing perpetual bewilderment.

Compare the Madness of Animals with the madnesses of Man.

Singing as a distinctively human art.[9]

Man the only animal who can *sing*; music is is his Invention, if not God's Gift by Inspiration / for unlike painting, it is not an imitative Art – To man alone it is given to make not only the air articulated, and the articulated Breath a symbol of the articulations & actualities of his Heart & Spirit, but to render his gestures, his postures, & all his outward Habiliments symbolical – Are these gifts of God? And dare we despise them, or neglect them?

The implications of ascribing reasoning power to animals.[10]

But a moment's steady self-reflection will shew us, that in the simple determination "Black is not White" – or, "that two straight Lines cannot include a space" – all the powers are implied, that distinguish Man from Animals – first, the power of *reflection* – 2d. of *comparison* – 3d. and therefore of *suspension* of the mind – 4th ergo of a controlling Will, and the power of acting from *Notions*, instead of mere

Images exciting appetites, from *Motives*, not mere dark *instincts*. – Was it an insignificant thing to weigh the Planets, and determine all their courses, and prophecy every possible relation of the Heavens a thousand years hence? Yet all this mighty Pile of Science is nothing but a *linking* together of the truths of the same kind as, *the whole is greater than it's part:* – or, if A and B = C, then A = B – or 3 + 4 = 7, therefore 7 + 5 = 12, and so forth. X is to be found either in A or B or C or D: It is not found in A, B, or C, – therefore it is to be found in D. – What can be simpler? Apply this to an animal – a Dog misses his master where four roads meet – he has come up one, smells to two of the others, and then with his head aloft darts forward to the third road without any examination. – If this was done by a conclusion, the Dog would have *Reason* – how comes he then never to shew it in his *ordinary* habits? Why does this story excite either wonder or incredulity? – If the Story be a fact, and not a fiction, I should say – the Breeze brought his Master's scent down the 4th Road, to the Dog's nose, and that *therefore* he did not put it down to the Road, as in the two former instances. So aweful and almost miraculous does the simple act of concluding, that *take* 3 from 4, *there remains one*, appear to us when attributed to the most sagacious of all animals.

Even if there exist on another planet beings that seem to fill the interspace between human beings and the highest animals the chasm between them will remain.[11]

The different gradations in which the Past or Memory in the power of Imagination modifies the Present Impression, ~~would~~ appear to me a good ground-work for a Theory concerning the Understanding & Souls of Brutes, and their relation to that of man – The probability that there is in some other systems or Planets Beings that form the intermediate links between man & the most intellectual brute animals of this Planet / in some Planet it must be, in which the uppermost Creature is so greatly superior to man, that the *softenings down* of man into the brute creation of this Planet may be no softening down, no transition of his own / may not do away that chasm, which Reason requires for self-esteem, & sense of distinct difference of kind. And here notice the bad effects on the moral and intellectual character of the belief of mere difference of degree. <Such *may* be; but there is no reason to suppose it – because between Rational & Irrational there must be a chasm, but all *chasm*; – between two Kinds is infinite.>

The brutalisation of the poorest classes through heavy labour and lack of education and its likely consequences.[12]

To unenlightened minds, there are terrible charms in the idea of Retribution, however savagely it be inculcated. The Groans of the Oppressors make fearful yet pleasant music to the ear of him, whose mind is darkness, and into whose soul the iron has entered.

This class, at present, is comparatively small – Yet soon to form an overwhelming majority, unless great and immediate efforts are used to lessen the intolerable grievances of our poorer brethren, and infuse into their sorely wounded hearts the healing qualities of knowledge. For can we wonder that men should want humanity, who want all the circumstances of life that humanize? Can we wonder that with the ignorance of Brutes they should unite their ferocity? peace and comfort be with these! But let us shudder to hear from men of dissimilar opportunities sentiments of similar revengefulness. The purifying alchemy of Education may transmute the fierceness of an ignorant man into virtuous energy – but what remedy shall we apply to him, whom Plenty has not softened, whom Knowledge has not taught Benevolence? This is one among the many fatal effects which result from the want of fixed principles.

Wherein am I made worse by my ennobled neighbour? Do the childish titles of Aristocracy detract from my domestic comforts, or prevent my intellectual acquisitions? But those institutions of Society which should condemn me to the necessity of twelve hours daily toil, would make my *soul* a slave, and sink the *rational* being in the mere animal. It is a mockery of our fellow creatures' wrongs to call them equal in rights, when by the bitter compulsion of their wants we make them inferior to us in all that can soften the heart, or dignify the understanding. Let us not say that this is the work of time – that it is impracticable at present, unless we each in our individual capacities do strenuously and perseveringly endeavour to diffuse among our domestics those comforts and that illumination which far beyond all political ordinances are the true equalizers of men.

Caliban as an exemplum of the infrahuman through his lack of reason or a moral sense.[13]

Caliban, on the other hand, is all earth, all condensed and gross in feelings and images; he has the dawnings of understanding without reason or the moral sense, and in him, as in some brute animals, this advance to the intellectual faculties, without the moral sense, is marked by the appearance of vice. For it is in the primacy of the moral being only that man is truly human; in his intellectual powers he is certainly approached by the brutes, and, man's whole system duly considered, those powers cannot be considered other than means to an end, that is, to morality.

The differences between human beings and animals more often to the disadvantage of humans.[14]

These are all the Positives of the modern Socinian Creed, and even these it was not possible to extricate wholly from the points of Disbelief. But if it should be asked, why this resurrection, or re-creation is confined to the human animal, the answer must be – that more than this has not been revealed. And so far all Christians will join assent. But some have added, and in my opinion much to their credit, that they hope, it may be the case with the Brutes likewise, as they see no sufficient reason to the contrary. And truly, upon *their* scheme, I agree with them. For if Man be no other or nobler Creature *essentially*, than he is represented in their system, the meanest reptile, that maps out its path on the earth by lines of slime, must be of equal worth and respectability, not only in the sight of the Holy One, but by a strange contradiction even before Man's own reason. For re-move all the sources of Esteem and the Love founded on esteem, and whatever else presupposes a Will and, therein, a possible transcend-ence to the material world: Mankind, as far as my experience has extended, (and I am less than the least of many whom I could cite as having formed the very same Judgment) are *on the whole* distin-guished from the other Beasts incomparably more to their *disadvan-tage*, by Lying, Treachery, Ingratitude, Massacre, Thirst of Blood, and by Sensualities which both in sort and degree it would be libelling their Brother-beasts to call *bestial*, than to their advantage by a greater extent of Intellect. And what indeed, abstracted from the Free-will, could this intellect be but a more shewy instinct? of more various application indeed, but far less secure, useful, or adapted to its purposes, than the instinct of Birds, Insects, and the like.

Distinguishing the beast from the devil.[15]

As there is much Beast and some Devil in Man – so is there some Angel and some God in him. The Beast and the Devil may be conquered, but in this life never destroyed.

Hence in morals the double meaning of the *Beast* – commencing in nature it is a conquest *from* the Devil / Commencing in Man, a conquest *of* the Devil i.e. Man as either a conquest of the Beast from the Devil, or Conquest of the Devil's from God. But this is the infinite difference – that God raises the Beast into Man; but the Devil can never bring Man down onto the Beast but by transmuting him into himself. Man may sink into a Devil; but never become a Beast, and the appearance of the contrary is merely the occultation of his descending Humanity during transit.

In a long notebook entry Coleridge teases out further the distinctions between human beings and animals.[16]

The individuality of Man, how wonderful. No one merely man, as every Tyger is simply Tyger – little more than numerically distinguishable – but this man, with *these* faculties, *these* tendencies, theseis peculiar character – His Wishes, Hopes, Actions, Fortunes, spring out of his own nature – Quisque suæ fortunæ faber – But on the other hand, however, this very nature appears conditioned & determined by an outward Nature, that comprehends his own – What each individual *turns out*, (Homo Phainomenon) depends, as it seems, on the narrow Circumstances & Inclosure of his Infancy, Childhood, & Youth – & afterwards on the larger Hedge-girdle of the State, in which he is a Citizen born – & inasmuch as this again receives a stamp & signature from the Zone, Climate, Soil, Character of Country, mountainous or champaign, inland or maritime, intersected with navigable streams or nat purely pastoral or woodland, he seems to be [. . . .] influenced & determined (caused to be what he is, qualis sit = qualified, *bethinged*) by it Universal Nature, its elements & relations. – Beyond this ring-fence he cannot stray, of these circummurations he can seldom overleap the lowest & innermost, and the outermost is his apparent horizon, & uninsurmountable – from this knot Skein of necessities he cannot disentangle himself, which surrounds and with subtlest intertwine the slenderest fibres of his Being, ~~and~~ while it binds the whole frame with chains of adamant – . And yet again, the more steadily he contemplates this fact, the more de~~p~~eply he meditates on these workings, the more clearly it dawns upon him that this conspiration of influences is no mere outward nor contingent Thing, that rather this necessity *is* himself, that that without which or divided from which his Being can not be even *thought*, must therefore in all its directions and labyrinthine folds belong to his Being, and ~~enter into~~ evolve out of his essences. Abstract from these – and what remains? A general Term, after all the ~~notices~~ conceptions, notices, and experiences represented by it, had been removed – an Ens logicum which instead of a *thought* <or Conception> represents only the ~~condi~~ act and process of Thinking, or rather the form & condition, under which is it possible to think or conceive at all. The more he reflects, the more evident he finds it, that the stimulability determines the existence & character of the Stimulus, the Organ the object, ~~the Mind the Organ <inherent tendencies>~~ the ~~Volitions the Organs~~, Instincts, or the germinal Anticipations ~~striving to evolve~~ in the Swell of nascent evolution, the dark yet <pregnant> prophecies of the Future in the Present bud or blossom forth in the Organs, and the Volitions beget the instruments of Action – the temptability constitutes the temptation, and the Man the Motives. – What then remains! O the noblest of all – to *know* that so it is, and in the warm & genial Light of this knowledge to beget each in himself a new man, which comprehends the whole ~~in~~ of which this phænomenal Individual is but a component point, himself comprehended ~~only~~ in God – alone. –

The existence of human faculties also in the animals suggests by analogy that our organs of Spirit are formed for a corresponding world of Spirit.[17]

To what purpose are the *human* faculties given to the Animal, who by them becomes contra-distinguished as *man*? This an Atheist might ask, by the fair Logic of Analogy: until he shall have discovered plain & demonstrative proofs in other parts of Nature of permanent & constituent organization which is yet no means to any End. His ignorance of the End in this case or that is a necessary consequence of his Progressive Nature – & that too in the lowest Form: a certainty, which disqualifies his Babble about the Spleen &c from being even negative Proof. For if that, which he denies, be true, the occasion of his objection *must* exist. Are they for the *support* of the animal Body?

or for its enjoyment? – The Support? – O Heavens, how much better would one little Instinct have secured this! – The Support! – Alas! every Apple from the Tree of Knowledge expels the curious Taster from the animal Paradise! – For its pleasure! – Alas, every refinement is but a distillation of consuming Spirit out of the food-ful Corn! It is but fleaing the Body in a world of keen Blasts that demand a bear skin or Ass's Hide – And then too, this very bodily fullness of Enjoyment, to which our higher faculties are to be as *means*, actually preclude these *means* – and as long as we wallow in the full tumult of our Mahometan Eden, so long both Individuals & whole Tribes give evidence of their Humanity only by crimes which are at once beyond the powers & below the value, of Beasts – Otaheite, for instance. –

That no man can be truly happy without Truth, Virtue, & Beauty, & the Faith in God & Immortality as the Key-stone of the former; arise, from hence – that he can be only happy *in* them, that they are themselves the *Ends*, not the means –. But that the *Ends* re-act & recirculate thro' all the means, subliming and perfecting them, is but the beautiful necessity of a Law of Life, which never loses but always gains. The Organized does not lose Substance, but the Substance gains Organiz. – the Living does not lose organized Substance but this gains life – the Sentient does not lose living organized Substance but this gains sentience – thus too the Understanding – & thus the rational – & thus finally, the Spiritual – / all that ever was, is retained; but all glorified & partaking of the nature into which it is married. – add to this the convincing fact, that the things of *Sense* are always Things of Degrees – so much food, so much wealth, so much Enjoyment – but the actualities of the inner world are always Things of Kind – Virtue never dissatisfies because it is only so much Virtue – but because it is not yet *Virtue* – because a portion of Vice is counteracting it. – Hence, to Pleasure there is no satisfying boundary – while the Hermit in his Cell is happy if he be good. –

We are born in the mountains, in the Alps – and when we hire ourselves out to the Princes of the Lower Lands, sooner or later we feel an incurable Home-sickness – & every Tune that recalls our native Heights, brings on a relapse of the Sickness. – I seem to myself like a Butterfly who having foolishly torn or bedaubed his wings, is obliged to crawl like a Caterpillar with all the restless Instincts of the Butterfly.

Our Eye rests in an horizon – still moving indeed as we move – yet still there is an Horizon & there the Eye rests – but our Hands can only pluck the Fruit a yard from us – there is no Horizon for the *Hand* – and the Hand is the symbol of earthly realities, the Eye of our Hope & Faith. And what is Faith? – it is to the Spirit of Man the same Instinct, which impels the chrysalis of the horned fly to build its involucrum as long again as itself to make room for the Antennæ, which are to come, tho' they never yet have been – O the *Potential* works *in* us even as the Present mood works *on* us! –

Love with Virtue have almost an actual Present – tho' for moments and tho' for few – but in general, we have no present unless we are brutalized – the Present belongs to the two extremes, Beast & Angel – We in youth have Hope, the Rainbow of the Morning in the West – in age, we have recollections of Hope, the Evening Rainbow in the East! – In short, all the organs of Sense are framed for a corresponding World of Sense: and we have it. All the organs of Spirit are framed for a correspondent World of Spirit: & we cannot but believe it. The Infidel proves only that the latter organs are not yet developed in him –. The former are ~~our~~ their appointed Nurse; but the Nurse may *overlay* the Child. – How comes it that even Worldlings, who are not wholly Worldlings in their thoughts, as well as conduct, will contemplate the man of simple goodness & disinterestedness with the contradictory feeling of Pity and of Respect – "He is not made for this World" – O therein he utters a prophecy for himself. For he *pities* the Ideot; but does he respect him? does he feel awe & an inward Self-questioning in his Presence? No.

Christianity as peculiarly adapted to elevate human nature.[18]

Form and endeavour to strengthen into an habitual and instinct-like feeling, the sense of the utter incompatibility of Christianity with every thing wrong or unseemly, with whatever betrays or fosters the mind of flesh, the predominance of the *animal* within us, by having habitually present to the mind, the full and lively conviction of its perfect compatibility with whatever is innocent of its harmony, with whatever contra-distinguishes the HUMAN from the animal; of its sympathy and coalescence with the cultivation of the faculties, affections, and fruitions, which God hath made *peculiar* to *man*, either wholly or in their ordained *combination* with what is peculiar to humanity, the blurred, but not obliterated signatures of our original title deed, (and God said, man will we make in our own image.)

What? – shall Christianity exclude or alienate us from those powers, acquisitions, and attainments, which Christianity is so pre-eminently calculated to elevate an enliven and sanctify?

The uniqueness of human beings has its origin in the divine image.[19]

Whatever we do or know, that in kind is different from the brute creation, has its origin in a determination of the reason to have faith and trust in itself. This, its first act of faith is scarcely less than identical with its own being. . . .

. . . Man alone was created in the image of God: a position ground-less and inexplicable, if the reason in man do not differ from the understanding. For this the inferior animals, (many at least) possess *in degree*: and assuredly the divine image or idea is not a thing of degrees.

(ii) Human Beings and the 'Laws of Nature'

Coleridge's many changing responses to nature as such are examined in another volume in the present series. However, in so far as his late work defined 'human beings' as 'not nature', it is appropriate to include here some passages associated with these definitions.

His views about the relation of man to nature were extremely diverse. His own activity in nature, whether seabathing, fellwaking or stalking the deck of the *Speedwell* in high seas, aroused his energies, inspiring precise descriptions (which were sometimes accompanied by drawings) in poems, note-books and letters. But his complex attitude also included a revulsion against organic death and the submergence of human individuality in nature. He discovered increasingly that, in so far as it equated mental and physical phenomena and ascribed divinity to organisms, his own, like Wordsworth's early devotion to nature, led to pantheism. He found, too, that while phys-ical activity could stimulate his creative powers of observation and notation, his body (his own miniature nature) could also drag down his spirit: indi-gestion produced strange images in his dreams; his body's sicknesses and dependencies tainted his thoughts and indirectly, through his writings, influenced his readers. This fear, increased by old age and illness, showed itself in an increasing and Manichaean disdain for his own embodiment in the flesh.[20] Several entries describe his impatience with his rebellious body, the material nature he must live with if he was to live at all.

Writing in The Morning Post *in 1800, Coleridge argues against economists whose habit of applying to persons analogies from natural law ignores the realities of individual suffering.*[21]

I have often heard unthinking people exclaim, in observing differences of price in different parts of the country, What has become of Adam Smith's *level*? I, God knows, am no friend to those hardhearted comparisons of human actions with the laws of inanimate nature. Water will come to a level without pain or pleasure, and provisions and money will come to a level likewise; but, O God! what scenes of anguish must take place while they are coming to a *level*!

The theories in Natural Law that might makes right may lead to tyranny.[22]

But nature dictates plainly enough another code of right, namely, that the nobler and stronger should possess more than the weaker and more pusillanimous. Where the power is, there lies the substantial right. The whole realm of animals, nay the human race itself as collected in independent states and nations, demonstrate, that the stronger has a right to control the weaker for his own advantage. Assuredly, they have the genuine notion of right, and follow the law of nature, though truly not that which is held valid in our governments. But the minds of our youths are preached away from them by declamations on the beauty and fitness of letting themselves be mastered, till by these verbal conjurations the noblest nature is tamed and cowed, like a young lion born and bred in a cage. Should a man with full untamed force but once step forward, he would break all your spells and conjurations, trample your contra-natural laws under his feet, vault into the seat of supreme power, and in a splendid style make the right of nature be valid among you.

It would have been well for mankind, if such had always been the language of sophistry! A selfishness, that excludes partnership, all men have an interest in repelling.

Although Coleridge believes himself to be separate from nature, he recognises that his soul is subject to nature through the body.[23]

<N.B. Nature used here as the *Mundus sensibilis*.>
Important thought that Death, judged of by *corporeal* analogies, certainly implies discerption or dissolution of Parts; but Pain & Pleasure do not – nay, they seem inconceivable except under the idea of concentration. Therefore the influence of the Body on the Soul will not prove the common destiny of Both. – I feel myself not the Slave of Nature, in the sense in which animals are. Not only my Thoughts, Affections extend to Objects transnatural, as Truth, Virtue, God; not only do my Powers extend vastly beyond all those, which I could have derived from the Instruments & Organs, with which Nature has furnished me, but N̶ I can do what Nature per se cannot – I engraft, I raise a heavy bodies above the clouds, and guide my course over Ocean & thro' Air – I alone am Lord of Fire & of Light – Other creatures but their *Almsfolk* – and of all the so called Elements, Water, Earth, Air, & all their Compounds (to speak in the ever [?enduring/endearing] Language of <the> *Senses*, to which nothing can be revealed but as compact, or fluid, or aerial, or luciform) I not merely subserved myself of them, but I employ them. – Ergo, there is in me or rather *I* am præternatural, i.e. supersensuous – but what is not nature, why should it perish with Nature? Why lose the faculty of Vision, because my spectacles are broken? – Now to this it will be objected & very forcibly too – but this Soul or Self is acted upon by Nature thro' the body – and Water or Caloric diffused thro' or collected in the brain will derange the faculties of the Soul by deranging the organization of the Brain – the Sword can not touch the Soul but by rending the flesh will rend the feelings – Therefore, the Violence of Nature may in destroying the Body mediately destroy the Soul. –

The relationship between the Will and Nature.[24]

I have already given one definition of Nature. Another, and differing from the former in words only, is this: Whatever is representable in the forms of Time and Space, is Nature. But whatever is comprehended in Time and Space, is included in the Mechanism of Cause and Effect. And conversely, whatever, by whatever means, has its principle in itself, so far as to *originate* its actions, cannot be contemplated in any of the forms of Space and Time – it must, therefore, be considered as *Spirit* or *Spiritual* by a mind in that stage of its Development which is here supposed, and which we have agreed to understand under the name of Morality, or the Moral State: for in this stage we are concerned only with the forming of *negative* conceptions, *negative* convictions; and by *spiritual* I do not pretend to determine *what* the Will *is*, but what it is *not* – namely, that it is not Nature. And as no man who admits a Will at all, (for we may safely presume, that no man not meaning to speak figuratively, would call the shifting Current of a stream the WILL – of the River), will suppose it *below* Nature, we may safely add, that it is supernatural; and this without the least pretence to any positive Notion or Insight.

This sense of the word [origin] is implied even in its metaphorical or figurative use. Thus we may say of a *River* that it *originates* in such or such a *fountain*; but the water of a *Canal* is *derived* from such or such a River. The Power which we call Nature, may be thus defined: A Power subject to the Law of Continuity (*Lex Continui. In Natura non datur Saltus.*) which law the human understanding, by a necessity arising out of its own constitution, can *conceive* only under the form of Cause and Effect. That this *form* (or law) of Cause and Effect is (relatively to the World *without*, or to Things as they subsist independently of our perceptions) only a form or mode of *thinking*; that it is a law inherent in the Understanding itself (just as the symmetry of the miscellaneous objects seen by the kaleidoscope inheres in (*i.e.* results from) the mechanism of the kaleidoscope itself) – this becomes evident as soon as we attempt to apply the pre-conception directly to any operation of Nature. For in this case we are forced to represent the cause as being at the same instant the effect, and vice versa the effect as being the cause – a relation which we seek to express by the terms Action and Re-action; but for which the term Reciprocal Action or the law of Reciprocity (*germanice* Wechselwirkung) would be both more accurate and more expressive.

These are truths which can scarcely be too frequently impressed on the Mind that is in earnest in the wish to *reflect* aright. Nature is a Line in constant and continuous evolution. Its *beginning* is lost in the Super-natural: and *for our understanding*, therefore, it must appear as a continuous line without beginning or end. But where there

is no discontinuity there can be no origination and every appearance
of origination in *Nature* is but a shadow of our own casting. It is a
reflection from our own *Will* or spirit. Herein, indeed, the Will consists. This is the essential character by which WILL is *opposed* to Nature, as *Spirit*, and raised *above* Nature as *self-determining* Spirit – this,
namely, that it is a power of *originating* an act or state.

*In his 'Hints towards the Formation of a more Comprehensive Theory of Life',
written in 1816 and partially adapted from Schelling, he celebrates the multiple
forms in the chain of life, but stops that progression short of the development of
individual consciousness, which 'begins a new series'. While rejecting mechanistic
theories of life and praising wholeness and organic form he is eager even here to
distinguish the soul from organisms.*[25]

Convinced – by revelation, by the consenting authority of all countries, and of all ages, by the imperative voice of my own conscience,
and by that wide chasm between man and the noblest animals of the
brute creation, which no perceivable or conceivable difference of
organization is sufficient to overbridge – that I have a rational and
responsible soul, I think far too reverentially of the same to degrade
it into an hypothesis, and cannot be blind to the contradiction I must
incur, if I assign that soul which I believe to constitute the peculiar
nature of man as the cause of functions and properties, which man
possesses in common with the oyster and the mushroom.

I define life as *the principle of individuation*, or the power which unites
a given *all* into a *whole* that is presupposed by all its parts. The link
that combines the two, and acts throughout both, will, of course, be
defined by the *tendency to individuation*.

. . . the unity will be more intense in proportion as it constitutes each
particular thing a whole of itself; and yet more, again, in proportion
to the number and interdependence of the parts, which it unites as a
whole. But a whole composed, *ab intra*, of different parts, so far
interdependent that each is reciprocally means and end, is an individual, and the individuality is most intense where the greatest
dependence of the parts on the whole is combined with the greatest
dependence of the whole on its parts; the first (namely, the depend-

ence of the parts on the whole) being absolute; the second (namely, the dependence of the whole on its parts) being proportional to the importance of the relation which the parts have to the whole, that is, as their action extends more or less beyond themselves. For this spirit of the whole is most expressed in that part which derives its importance as an End from its importance as a Mean, relatively to all the parts under the same copula.

Finally, of individuals, the living power will be most intense in that individual which, as a whole, has the greatest number of integral parts presupposed in it; when, moreover, these integral parts, together with a proportional increase of their interdependence, as *parts*, have themselves most the character of wholes in the sphere occupied by them.

In the lowest forms of the vegetable and animal world we perceive totality dawning into *individuation*, while in man, as the highest of the class, the individuality is not only perfected in its corporeal sense, but begins a new series beyond the appropriate limits of physiology. The tendency to individuation, more or less obscure, more or less obvious, constitutes the common character of all classes, as far as they maintain for themselves a distinction from the universal life of the planet; while the degrees, both of intensity and extension, to which this tendency is realized, form the species, and their ranks in the great scale of ascent and expansion.

It has been before noticed that the progress of Nature is more truly represented by the ladder, than by the suspended chain, and that she expands as by concentric circles. This is, indeed, involved in the very conception of individuation, whether it be applied to the different species or to the individuals. In what manner the evident interspace is reconciled with the equally evident continuity of the life of Nature, is a problem that can be solved by those minds alone, which have intuitively learnt that the whole *actual* life of Nature originates in the existence, and consists in the perpetual reconciliation, and as perpetual resurgency of the primary contradiction, of which universal polarity is the result and the exponent.

For lo! in the next step of ascent the power of sensibility has assumed her due place and rank: her minority is at an end, and the complete and universal presence of a nervous system unites absolutely, by instanteity of time what, with the due allowances for the transitional process, had before been either lost in sameness, or perplexed by multiplicity, or compacted by a finer mechanism. But with this, all the analogies with which Nature had delighted us in the preceding step seem lost, and, with the single exception of that more than valuable, that estimable philanthropist, the dog, and, perhaps, of the horse and elephant, the analogies to ourselves, which we can discover in the quadrupeds or quadrumani, are of our vices, our follies, and our imperfections. The facts in confirmation of both the propositions are so numerous and so obvious, the advance of Nature, under the predominance of the third synthetic power, both in the intensity of life and in the intenseness and extension of individuality, is so undeniable, that we may leap forward at once to the highest realization and reconciliation of both her tendencies, that of the most perfect detachment with the greatest possible union, to that last work, in which Nature did not assist as handmaid under the eye of her sovereign Master, who made Man in his own image, by superadding self-consciousness with self-government, and breathed into him a living soul.

The class of *Vermes* deposit a calcareous stuff, as if it had torn loose from the earth a piece of the gross mass which it must still drag about with it. In the insect class this residuum has refined itself. In the fishes and amphibia it is driven back or inward, the organic power begins to be intuitive, and sensibility appears. In the birds the bones have become hollow; while, with apparent proportional recess, but, in truth, by the excitement of the opposite pole, their exterior presents an actual vegetation. The bones of the mammalia are filled up, and their coverings have become more simple. Man possesses the most perfect osseous structure, the least and most insignificant covering. The whole force of organic power has attained an inward and centripetal direction. He has the whole world in counterpoint to him, but he contains an entire world within himself. Now, for the first time at the apex of the living pyramid, it is Man and Nature, but Man himself is a syllepsis, a compendium of Nature – the Microcosm!

•   •   •

. . . In Man the centripetal and individualizing tendency of all Nature is itself concentred and individualized – he is a revelation of Nature! Henceforward, he is referred to himself, delivered up to his own charge; and he who stands the most on himself, and stands the firmest, is the truest, because the most individual, Man. In social and political life this acme is inter-dependence; in moral life it is independence; in intellectual life it is genius. Nor does the form of polarity, which has accompanied the law of individuation up its whole ascent, desert it here. As the height, so the depth. The intensities must be at once opposite and equal. As the liberty, so must be the reverence for law. As the independence, so must be the service and the submission to the Supreme Will! As the ideal genius and the originality, in the same proportion must be the resignation to the real world, the sympathy and the inter-communion with Nature. In the conciliating mid-point, or equator, does the Man live, and only by its equal presence in both its poles can that life be manifested!

The human instinct to contradistinguish ourselves from nature.[26]

In a self-conscious and thence reflecting being, no instinct can exist, without engendering the belief of an object corresponding to it, either present or future, real or capable of being realized: much less the instinct, in which humanity itself is grounded: that by which, in every act of conscious perception, we at once identify our being with that of the world without us, and yet place ourselves in contradistinction to that world.

In a late letter the 'contra-distinction' from nature becomes sharper, with mind and nature more like rival magicians.[27]

In Youth and early Manhood the Mind and Nature are, as it were, two rival Artists, both potent Magicians, and engaged, like the King's Daughter and the rebel Genie in the Arabian Nights' Enternts., in sharp conflict of Conjuration – each having for it's object to turn the other into Canvas to paint on, Clay to mould, or Cabinet to contain. For a while the Mind seems to have the better in the contest, and makes of Nature what it likes; takes her Lichens and Weather-stains for Types & Printer's Ink and prints Maps & Fac Similes of Arabic and Sanscrit Mss. on her rocks; composes Country-Dances on her moon-shiny Ripples, Fandangos on her Waves and Walzes on her Eddy-pools; transforms her Summer Gales into Harps and Harpers, Lovers' Sighs and sighing Lovers, and her Winter Blasts into Pindaric Odes, Christabels & Ancient Mariners set to music by Beethoven, and in the insolence of triumph conjures her Clouds into Whales and Walrusses with Palanquins on their Backs, and chaces the dodging Stars in a Sky-hunt! – But alas! alas! that Nature is a wary wily long-breathed old Witch, tough-lived as a Turtle and divisible as the Polyp, repullulative in a thousand Snips and Cuttings, integra et in toto! She is sure to get the better of Lady MIND in the long run, and to take her revenge too – transforms our To Day into a Canvass dead-colored to receive the full featureless Portrait of Yesterday; not alone turns the mimic Mind, the ci-devant Sculptress with all her kaleidoscopic freaks and symmetries! into clay, but *leaves* it such a *clay*, to cast dumps or bullets in; and lastly (to end with that which suggested the beginning –) she mocks the mind with it's own meta-phors, metamorphosing the Memory into a lignum vitae Escrutoire to keep unpaid Bills & Dun's Letters in, with Outlines that had never been filled up, MSS that never went farther than the Title-pages, and Proof-Sheets & Foul Copies of Watchmen, Friends, Aids to Reflec-tion & other *Stationary* Wares that have kissed the Publisher's Shelf with gluey Lips with all the tender intimacy of inosculation! – Finis! –

The implications for one's view of divine providence.[28]

Now as Freedom: Necessity:: Man to the irrational, organic, or inor-ganic creatures and by carrying the contra-distinguishing constitu-ents of Humanity into the necessary detail, I infer a correspondent difference in the law by which the divine conservative influences are communicated to Man and on this ground the rationality of Prayer – & Faith – and the corollary – that they must be *super*natural – hence the *alien*-ness of Time –. . . .

Definition. That is the state of Nature, or Natural State of every Creature, in which the circumstances present the most facilities and the fewest obstacles to the development of its' organization & char-acteristic tendencies and faculties – or more briefly, That is the state of Nature or natural State of every creature, in which its essential Characters can be most perfectly expressed.

Now then I return to my position – it is eminently distinctive of

Man, that his state of Nature is necessarily *ideal*, and instead of being the antecedent ground & condition of the developement of his characteristic form & faculties must be proposed as the *consequent* of such developement. In the inferior world, the natural state is required to the adequate realization of the Animal – here, it is the Creature's aim and proper business to realize his natural state. . . . and tho' it would be easy to imagine a nature or complexus of circumstances which would render the developement of our proper humanity impossible, it would not be easy to determine the circumstantial state which would most favour or least counteract this developement – and tho' we should succeed in discovering this state, it would apply only to a given stage in the process of humanization – and (more important still) this state itself would in its' most essential points be the product & result of this evolving Humanity. The vantage-ground for each individual is derived from preceding Individuals, i.e. not from a nature distinguished from the creature, but from the Creature self-distinguished from Nature. . . .

• • •

. . . for Man what is not won by himself, by himself will be lost – . . .

The Sum of the Reasoning is this: all Beings below Man are included in Nature. Collectively they form the Great Organismus of Living Nature: and singly they are the joint Product of the Nature within . . . and of the Nature without. . . .

Every creature below Man (Plant, Insect, or Animal) is the joint Product of the inherent and the circumstantial Nature. In all things received by them they are simply recipients, in all things done by them simply instruments: Machines of Nature's construction. As in sundry manufacture we speak of *feeding* the machine, and setting it at work, with no less propriety may it be said, that Nature feeds her Living Machines and sets them at work. Need I declare, that whatever is beneficent or lovely in the Nature, Law, Order, Beauty, Kindness, and kindly Delight, is produced by the Word of the Most High constraining and controlling Nature? and without which there were no Nature, but only the Dust, blank Multëity, below Thought even as the High & Holy One transcends it, blank chaos, and essential Unintelligibility . . . The Nest and the Hive are but seeming exceptions. Not the individual Creature, but the generic Nature working with them as with tools constructs the same every where according to the kind Benignant Word! sustaining Spirit!. . . . Contrariwise with

Man . . . Beyond, incomparably beyond any Animal, is Man the beneficiary of his Predecessors; but still so as not to predetermine or preclude his Freedom. The Bequests are not conveyed with his Blood – he is born naked of them, mute, ignorant. Even these must be Products of his own Act, he must win them by his Will. . . . the great comprehensive Distinction of Man is that he must act in order to receive.

Late notebook entries express an increasing aversion from the physical body.[29]

. . . God has permitted and enabled us to divide our personal Will from our corrupt and evil Nature. . . . And this therefore is the aweful aggravation of every personal transgression for the con- science of a Christian, that it tends to destroy the division between our person and our corrupt nature – to restore and reproduce the identity or indistinction of the "I" and the Nature. We *become* Evil and burrow in the Ground which God hath cursed (Gen. II). The personal Being ought to be as the Electricity by a mysterious Law attached to but not combined with the electrified Body. . . .

Whatever confoundeth the Man with the Animal, whatever *merges* the humanity in the animal nature, so as to make the latter float on the surface, or (to change the metaphor) whatever is a *Breaking-out* of the latent & subordinate Beast in us, is a *Defilement.* . . .

. . . and every particular defilement may be referred to some mode or habit of the different kinds of Animals – all of which are contained *potentially*, vi praeteritae actualitatis, in Man – the Crown and Co- rolla of all inferior life. Briefly, every defilement is a retrogressive metamorphosis, such as that by which the Petals of Flowers degen- erate into Calyx or leaves, leaves into thorns (= miniature stems) &c. Now the evil Will, the Will of the Ground, in its manifestation as Animal life reveals itself most nakedly in the Blood-thirst of the Tyger & other carnivorous Beasts of Prey. Man was forbidden to taste of the Blood. . . . Blood-thirsty he kills – and in the act attempts to quench the tygrine thirst – i.e. *in Will* he drinks it. But the Blood itself, taken separately, is the Life of the Ground unsanctified by the Organization – i.e. by the forming and actualizing Law. It is the potential actualized as potential. . . . The animal life appearing for itself, uncontained and unsubjected, is the defilement of the human *Spirit* – which whatever bird-limes, defiles, pollutes. Mem. The de- basing & obscuring *Passions* are all retrograde transactions from the

Man to the Characters of the Brute – i.e. what is the *character* of a Wolf or a Rhinoceros becomes by anticipation of mind a Passion in the Man.

(iii) Early Man

Between the orang-utan and the human being stands the ambiguous figure of early man. Coleridge's curiosity about approaches towards and fallings away from human nature led him to examine people who were in the process of lapsing from human nature, on the one hand, or arising into its full potentialities on the other. He studied the loss of distinctive human nature in civilised England through the brutalising effect of poverty, hunger or ignorance, but also, from his readings in geology, palaeontology and biology, envisaged the dawn of this distinctive nature in early man. By such features of their behaviour as their cultivation of ornaments, even scarifications, to show their difference from beasts, people on the margins between nature and civilisation seemed to demonstrate vividly the essential drives that developed into 'humanness'.

Eighteenth-century primitivism – the study of noble and ignoble natives from America, the South Pacific and Africa – posed basic questions: was early man violent and savage, or benevolent and innocent? Why was the social contract first required? How did the structures of government and culture first come into being? Were inequality, the love of property, fear inherent in human beings? The study of early man had begun with books of travel and missions to the new world, prompting observations such as those by Shakespeare in *The Tempest*, by Montaigne in 'Of Cannibals', and by Hobbes in *Leviathan*. The interest had continued in Locke's imaginary acorn-gatherers in the *Second Treatise on Government* (1690), in Defoe's *Life and Adventures of Robinson Crusoe* (1719), in Rousseau's visions of early man in the *Discourse on the Origin of Inequality* (1755), in Voltaire's portrayal of the monkeys and their native lovers in *Candide*, and in E. M. Itard's *Historical Account of the Discovery and Education of a Savage Man* (1820). As Edward Dudley and Maximillan E. Novak have shown, the Wild Man was a central eighteenth-century preoccupation – evident even in Mozart's Papageno.

Alan Bewell describes the intricacy of this early study of man: 'The Enlightenment representation of human origins was grounded in a twofold activity. First, one had to reconstruct the physical characteristics and social organization of the primitive world, a project supported by the anthropological reinterpretation of history, myth, and Scripture, by the state of other cultures and the observation of marginal individuals, and by Enlightenment geology. Then the philosopher placed himself imaginatively in this world, attempting to see it through the eyes of the first humans.'[30] Bewell concentrates on the influence of these early anthropological theories on Wordsworth's poems about idiots, solitaries, mad people, and leechgatherers; Coleridge also had tried to imagine the traumas faced by early human beings and the processes of their discovery of language, family bonding and self-defence. Less sympathetic than Wordsworth towards inarticulate and uncultivated people, he nevertheless explored the power of Obeah witch-craft, as he explained in the preface to 'The Three Graves'; other primitive theories of possession, magic and spell-casting left their marks on 'The Rime of the Ancient Mariner', 'Christabel', and 'Kubla Khan'.[31]

In notebooks of 1808 to 1810 Coleridge imagines the frightening lives of early people and contemplates writing a poem on the wild child of Aveyron as a living example of their bewildering entry into a new world.[32]

Lord of Light and Fire – what is the universal of Man in all, but especially in savage states – fantastic ornaments, and in general, the most frightful Deformities – slits, &c &c (here enumerate them from books of Travels) – What is the solution? – Man will not be a mere thing of Nature – he will be & will shew himself a power of himself – hence these violent disruptions of himself from all other creatures. What they are made, that *they* remain / they are Nature's & wholly Nature's.

A fine subject to be introduced in William's great poem is the Savage Boy of Aveyron in Itard's account – viz – his restless joy & blind conjunction of his Being with natural Scenery; and the manifest influence of Mountain, Rocks, Waterfalls, Torrents, & Thunderstorms – Moonlight Beams quivering on Water, &c on his whole frame – as instanced in his Behaviour in the Vale of Monmorency – his eager desires to escape, &c. How deserving this whole account of a pro-found psychological examination / & comparison with wild animals in confinement /
    The savage seems clearly a *man* / & his conduct nearer derange-ment than absolute Imbrutement.

The midnight-wild beasts staring at the Hunter's Torch / or when the Hunter sees the Tyger's eye glaring in the red light of his own Torch / –

In a notebook of 1803 he speculates on the origin of the taboo against incest.[33]

I cannot account for the great religious *Horror* reached to Incest, but by supposing that some one Tribe, or body of men, from some Caprice of Superstition, had confined marriages to Brother & Sister . . . and . . . that the consequences of this in a few Generations became so marked & so terrific, as to attract the attention of mankind then few in number comparatively, so as to be wisely regarded by them as proof of divine Vengeance on the Practice. . . . probably in the Temples of Egypt & of India the physical Fact was carefully pre-served – & from these the great Legislators of Antiquity, Moses, &c derived the wisdom & prudence of accumulated Experience. – This Horror having been once bottomed in the human race would easily be kept.

Looking back, perhaps, to Southey's 'Botany Bay Eclogues' of 1794, Coleridge considers in 1810 how hordes of savages in New Holland, Australia, might be treated.[34]

All right being founded exclusively in the moral Being, Men in a state that confessedly precludes the development & progression of *Humanity*, of which the moral Being is the evidence, cann have no *moral* claims, beyond those which we owe to all sentient nature, Birds, & Beieasts, encreased by the duties to our own moral feelings – thus it would be a greater crime to drive away wantonly a *herd* of New Holland *Savages* than *wantonly* to injure a flock of wildfowl, because we ourselves should be more injured – even as by wildfowl more than by killing a swarm of flies – / This I affirm of Tribes & hordes, without Government or any possible means of progression / The murder of each or any *Individual* among them is *murder*, because his Savagery does not *take away* the *posse* of a moral being – now this *Posse* is the essence of morality – and he who *murders*, i.e. kills wantonly, might perhaps have improved. But I speak of occupation of Territory: and I do affirm spite of the Howl & Whoop of Hypo-crites & Mock Cosmopolites, that if it be an absurdity to affirm, that two or 3 hundred naked bloody Savages have by the accident of pre-occupation a fair right of property in the whole of that immense Island or Continent, it must be likewise absurd to affirm, that the colonists of a civilized nation have not the same right to secure themselves & the <*rightful*> Objects of their Colonization, tho'

Coercion of those Savages, or even compelling them into a form
of civilization were a necessary means, provided 1. that in truth of
conscience the moral & good & personal Happiness of the Savages
themselves were a part of the End – 2. that the means be *appropriate*,
both *morally*, and *prudentially*. (N.B. I have said, *Savages* – not nations
under what we may deem less perfect forms of Government & civil
& religious Institution than our own /) – and if this be denied, I do
not see how we can justify the coercion of Children, or of Lunatics –
and at all events call upon the opponents to shew any other way,
which it has pleased Providence to appoint for the <extended>
cultivation of the human Race. Can they mention any one savage
Country christianized, even by the Apostles, even in the miraculous
Ages of the Church, till the Roman Arms & Colors had preceded
them? All the *cry out* against this system arises from the absurdity of
General Consequences, of which I have shewn in the *Friend* the gross
contradictions.

In his lecture 'On Poesy or Art' he imagines the origins of language and music.[35]

The primary art is writing; – primary, if we regard the purpose
abstracted from the different modes of realizing it, those steps of
progression of which the instances are still visible in the lower degrees of civilization. First, there is mere gesticulation; then rosaries
or *wampum*; then picture-language; then hieroglyphics, and finally
alphabetic letters. These all consist of a translation of man into nature, of a substitution of the visible for the audible.

The so called music of savage tribes as little deserves the name of
art for the understanding, as the ear warrants it for music. Its lowest
state is a mere expression of passion by sounds which the passion
itself necessitates; – the highest amounts to no more than a voluntary
reproduction of these sounds in the absence of the occasioning causes,
so as to give the pleasure of contrast, – for example, by the various
outcries of battle in the song of security and triumph.

In the Biographia *he disputes Wordsworth's claim (in the 1800 preface to the*
Lyrical Ballads) *that the language of primitive man is noble, simple and pure.*[36]

To this I reply; that a rustic's language, purified from all provincial-
ism and grossness, and so far re-constructed as to be made consistent

with the rules of grammar (which are in essence no other than the laws of universal logic, applied to Psychological materials) will not differ from the language of any other man of common-sense, however learned or refined he may be, except as far as the notions, which the rustic has to convey, are fewer and more indiscriminate. This will become still clearer, if we add the consideration (equally important though less obvious) that the rustic, from the more imperfect development of his faculties and from the lower state of their cultivation, aims almost solely to convey *insulated facts*, either those of his scanty experience or his traditional belief; while the educated man chiefly seeks to discover and express those *connections* of things, or those relative *bearings* of fact to fact, from which some more or less general law is deducible. For *facts* are valuable to a wise man, chiefly as they lead to the discovery of the indwelling *law*, which is the true *being* of things, the sole solution of their modes of existence, and in the knowledge of which consists our dignity and our power.

As little can I agree with the assertion, that from the objects with which the rustic hourly communicates, the best part of language is formed. For first, if to communicate with an object implies such an acquaintance with it, as renders it capable of being discriminately reflected on; the distinct knowledge of an uneducated rustic would furnish a very scanty vocabulary. The few things, and modes of action, requisite for his bodily conveniences, would alone be individualized; while all the rest of nature would be expressed by a small number of confused, general terms. Secondly, I deny that the words and combinations of words derived from the objects, with which the rustic is familiar, whether with distinct or confused knowledge, can be justly said to form the *best* part of language. It is more than probable, that many classes of the brute creation possess discriminating sounds, by which they can convey to each other notices of such objects as concern their food, shelter, or safety. Yet we hesitate to call the aggregate of such sounds a language, otherwise than metaphorically. . . .

The extreme difficulty, and often the impossibility, of finding words for the simplest moral and intellectual processes in the languages of uncivilized tribes has proved perhaps the weightiest obstacle to the progress of our most zealous and adroit missionaries. Yet these tribes are surrounded by the same nature, as our peasants are; but in still more impressive forms; and they are, moreover, obliged to *particularize* many more of them.

In the 1818 Friend *Coleridge traces the development of non-biblical peoples in the Near East.*[37]

Those, on the contrary, who wilfully chose a mode opposite to this method, who determined to shape their convictions and deduce their knowledge from without, by exclusive observation of outward and sensible things as the only realities, became, it appears, rapidly *civilized!* They built cities, invented musical instruments, were artificers in brass and in iron, and refined on the means of sensual gratification, and the conveniences of courtly intercourse. They became the great masters of the AGREEABLE, which fraternized readily with cruelty and rapacity: these being, indeed, but alternate moods of the same sensual selfishness. Thus, both before and after the flood, the vicious of mankind receded from all true cultivation, as they hurried towards civilization. Finally, as it was not in their power to make themselves wholly beasts, or to remain without a semblance of religion; and yet continuing faithful to their original maxim, and determined to receive nothing as true, but what they derived, or believed themselves to derive from their senses, or (in modern phrase) what they could prove *a posteriori*, – they became idolaters of the Heavens and the material elements. From the harmony of operation they concluded a certain unity of nature and design, but were incapable of finding in the facts any proof of a unity of person.

(b) WOMEN

Women posed difficulties for Coleridge in that they often seemed to incorporate animal nature to a greater extent than did men, to enact some of the ambiguities of early man in their 'primitive' moral nature, and, because they were more subject than men to the hedge-girdle of social conventions, to be less capable of leaping over the boundaries, more eager to enforce on others those social constructions. Coleridge wrote a great deal about individual women and about women in general – sometimes with remarkable sympathy, sometimes with the prejudices of his male contemporaries. He was horrified by the sufferings of women's bodies from the working of nature, and angry that women were prevented from the exercise of free choice by laws against their inheriting or owning property. He was keenly alive to the injustice involved when men owned or had the right to abuse their wives and daughters, and wondered how particular women, such as Dorothy Wordsworth, might have developed had they been more free to choose. He sometimes revealed conventional gender discriminations, on the other hand, whether he was making fun of fat, stupid and petty women or formulating general laws on the differences between men and women.

He was physically susceptible to female presences; even as an elderly sage he reacted tenderly whenever a pretty woman came near.[38] He veered between a yearning for companionship and assertions of superiority when that companion was necessarily uneducated, and smarted at his wife's public lack of respect for his failure to be a conventional wage-earner, husband and father, and at her obliviousness to his genius. While scorning her narrow moral values, he admired a number of women among the intelligentsia of London and fostered their careers.

He was torn, in short, in his views of women. The subject was of great importance to him, so much so that he planned to write a 'Novel on Men and Women' and a 'Treatise on Marriage', and to give a series of lectures on 'female Education from Infancy to Womanhood' – a subject which he claimed to have given 'more thought to than to any other' – in which he would explain 'the whole machinery of a school organized on rational principles from the earliest age to the completion of FEMALE EDUCATION, with a list of the books recommended, &c, so as to evolve gradually into utility and domestic happiness the powers and qualities of Womanhood'.[39] The contents of the novel, the treatise and the lectures can only be imagined, but they would surely have been complicated by his confused emotions toward his mother and his wife, and by the dividedness of his own impulses of lust, tender attraction, friendship, esteem and distant adoration. Sometimes he seems to have regarded women as inferior forms of humanity, less humorous, imaginative, intelligent, spontaneous, moral, in their essential nature; at other times he lamented the financial dependency, narrow social training, limited education, and lack of freedom that kept them from developing their full humanity; at still other times he praised particular women as representatives of humanity at its best.

In preparing for their venture to set up a community founded on new principles by the banks of the Susquehanna, the young Coleridge writes to Southey about the role of women. Can they care for babies and also work? Will they have benevolent values or will they pass on the errors of society – even, perhaps, teaching superstition?[40]

Surely every Eye but an Eye jaundiced by habit of peevish Scepticism must have seen, that the Mother's cares are repaid even to rapture by the Mother's endearments – and that the long helplessness of the Babe is the *means* of our superiority in the filial & maternal Affection & Duties to the same feelings in the Brute Creation – it is likewise among other causes the *means* of Society – that thing which makes Man a little lower than the Angels. – Mrs S. & Mrs F. go with us – they can at least prepare the Food of Simplicity for us – Let the married Women do only what is absolutely convenient and customary for pregnant Women or nurses – Let the Husbands do *all* the Rest – and what will that all be – ? Washing with a Machine and cleaning the House. One Hour's addition to our daily Labor – and

Pantisocracy in it's most perfect Sense is practicable. – That the greater part of our Female Companions should have the task of Maternal exertion at the same time is very *improbable* – but tho' it were to happen, An Infant is almost always sleeping – and during it's Slumbers the Mother may in the same Room perform the little offices of ironing Cloaths or making Shirts. – But the Hearts of the Women are not *all* with us. – I do believe that Edith & Sarah are exceptions – but do even they know the bill of fare for the Day – every duty that will be incumbent on them – ? –

Quere. Should not all, who mean to become members of our Community, be incessantly meliorating their Tempers and elevating their Understandings? Qu: Whether a very respectable Quantity of *acquired* knowledge (History, Politics, above all, *Metaphysics*, without which no man *can* reason but with women & children) be not a prerequisite to the improvement of the Head and Heart? Qu. Whether our Women have not been taught by us habitually to contemplate the littlenesses of indiv[id]ual Comforts, and a passion for the *Novelty* of the Scheme, rather than the generous enthusiasm of Benevolence? Are they saturated with the Divinity of Truth sufficiently to be always wakeful? In the present state of their minds whether it is not probable, that the *Mothers* will tinge the Mind of the Infants with prejudications? –

These Questions are meant *merely* as motives to you, Southey! to be strengthening the minds of the Women and stimulating them to literary Acquirements. – But, Southey! – there are *Children* going with us. Why did I never dare in my disputations with the Unconvinced to *hint* at this circumstance? Was it not, because I knew even to certainty of conviction, that it is subversive of *rational* Hopes of a permanent System? These children – the little Fricker for instance and *your* Brothers – Are they not already *deeply* tinged with the prejudices and errors of Society? Have they not learnt from their Schoolfellows *Fear* and *Selfishness* – of which the necessary offspring are Deceit, and desultory Hatred? *How* are we to prevent them from infecting the minds of *our* Children? By reforming their Judgments? – At so early age *can* they have *felt* the ill consequences of their Errors in a manner sufficiently vivid to make this reformation practicable? Reasoning is but *Words* unless where it derives force from the repeated experience of the person, to whom it is addressed. – *How* can we ensure their silence concerning *God* &c –? Is it possible, *they* should enter into our *motives* for this silence? If not we must produce their *obedience by Terror. Obedience*? *Terror*? The Repetition is sufficient –

. . . my Judgement is not asleep: nor can I suffer your Reason, Southey! to be entangled in the web, which your feelings have woven. Oxen and Horses possess not intellectual Appetites – nor the powers of acquiring them. We are therefore Justified in employing their Labor to our own Benefit – Mind hath a divine Right of Sovereignty over Body – But who shall dare to transfer this Reasoning from "from Man to Brute" to "from Man to Man["]! To be employed in the Toil of the Field while *We* are pursuing philosophical Studies – can Earldoms or Emperorships boast so huge an Inequality? Is there a human Being of so torpid a Nature, as that placed in our Society he would not feel it? – A *willing* Slave is the worst of Slaves – His *Soul* is a slave. – Besides, I must own myself incapable of perceiving even the temporary *convenience* of the proposed Innovation – The *Men* do not want assistance – at least, none that *Shad* can particularly give – And to the Women what assistance can little Sally, the *wife* of Shad, give – more than any other of our married women? Is she to have no domestic Cares of her own? No house? No husband to provide for? No Children? – *Because* Mr & Mrs Roberts are not likely to have Children, I see, *less* objection to their accompanying us. – Indeed – indeed – Southey! I am fearful that Lushington's prophecy may not be altogether vain – "Your System, Coleridge! appears strong to the head and lovely to the Heart – but depend upon it you will never give your *women* sufficient strength of mind, liberality of heart, or vigilance of Attention – *They* will spoil it!" . . .

I wish, Southey! in the stern severity of Judgment, that the two Mothers were *not* to go and that the children stayed with them – Are you wounded by my want of feeling? No! how highly must I think of your rectitude of Soul, that I should dare to say this to so affectionate a Son! *That* Mrs Fricker – we shall have her teaching the Infants *Christianity*, – I mean – that mongrel whelp that goes under it's name – teaching them by stealth in some ague-fit of Superstition! –

Drawing both on his own experience and on general observation he comments on injustices to women ranging from the pains of pregnancy to unfair divorce laws and labour conditions; from the scourging of women to their being denied the right to vote, whether on the 1791 constitution for France or in British elections.[41]

Yesterday Mrs Coleridge miscarried – but without danger and with little pain. From the first fortnight of Pregnancy she has been so very ill with the Fever, that she could afford no nourishment to the Thing which might have been a Newton or an Hartley – it had wasted & melted away. – I think the subject of Pregnancy the most obscure of all God's dispensations – it seems coercive against Immaterialism – it starts uneasy doubts respecting Immortality, & the pangs which the Woman suffers, seem inexplicable in the system of optimism – Other pains are only friendly admonitions that we are not acting as Nature requires – but here are pains most horrible in consequence of having obeyed Nature.

A few years ago, several books were published in defence of the Rights of Women. In, general, those works were too absurd to require any answer; – but with more reason might a book on that subject be written when women are run down with severity by the new Divorce Bill, now before the House of Lords. – All good men abhor the crime of adultery, and good women too abhor it; but is it equal justice to make the whole weight of punishment fall upon the weaker sex? Is not every guilty woman punished throughout life in her reception by society? But what punishment is inflicted upon the man beyond that which the courts of common law, or his own conscience, may inflict? Why is the man, the superior being, the protector of the other sex: why is he to escape when he uses his great endowments for wicked purposes, and betrays his trust? We shall not object to further punishment for the crime, even in the persons of women; but before we consent, a very severe punishment, indeed, must be decreed against the male seducer.

We were in hopes, that with the progressive refinement and increased tenderness of private and domestic feelings (in which we are doubtless superior to our ancestors, whatever the average of virtue may be), this unmanly practice of scourging females had gradually become obsolete, and placed among the *Inusitata* of the law dictionary. It is not only the female herself, who yet, if not already a miscreant, must needs (to use a far softer phrase than our feelings would prompt) be grievously injured in the first sources and primary impulses of female worth – for who will deny, that the infamy which would attend a young woman from having been stripped naked under the lash of a townsman, would be incomparably greater, and have burnt deeper in, than what would accrue from her having been detected in stealing half a dozen loaves? We are not shocked for the female only, but for the inflictor, and at the unmanliness of the punishment itself. Good God! how is it possible, that man, *born of woman*, could go through the office? O never let it be forgotten either by the farmers or dispensers of criminal law, that the stimulus of shame, like other powerful medicines, if administered in too large a dose, becomes a deadly narcotic poison to the moral patient! Never let it be forgotten, that every human being bears in himself that indelible something which belongs equally to the whole species, as well as that particular modification of it which individualizes him: that *the* woman is still *woman*, and however she may have debased herself, yet that we should still shew some respect, still feel some reverence, if not for her sake, yet in awe to that Being, who saw good to stamp in her his own image, and forbade it ever, in this life at least, to be utterly erased.

Is the House of Commons to be constructed on the principle of a resentation of interests, or of a delegation of Men? If on the former, we may perhaps see our way; if on the latter – then I say you can never stop short of universal suffrage – and women in that case have as good a right to vote as the men.

As to the right to tax being only commensurate with direct representation, it is a fable, falsely and treacherously brought forward by the Whigs, who knew its hollowness well enough. You may show its weakness in a moment by observing that not even the universal suffrage of the French or Benthamites avoids the difficulty; for although it may be allowed to be contrary to decorum that women should legislate, yet there can be no reason why women should not choose their representatives to legislate; and if it be said that they are merged in their husbands, let it be allowed, where the wife has no separate property; but where she has a distinct taxable estate, in which her husband has no interest, what right can her husband have to choose for her the person whose vote may affect her separate interests? Besides, at all events, a single unmarried adult woman of age, possessing a £1000 a year, has surely as good a right to vote, if Taxation without representation is tyranny, as any man in the kingdom.

Individual women are described with a keen, sometimes mocking eye: a young girl glimpsed in a boat in 1794 – and another begging vainly for food; an old woman in her cottage in 1796; four of the famous women writers of 1800 (Mrs Mary ('Perdita') Robinson, Miss Hays, Mrs Charlotte Smith and Mrs Inchbald); a fat woman on shipboard to Malta; and, probably, the Brent sisters (Charlotte and Mary).[42]

Gloucester is a nothing-to-be-said-about Town – the Women have almost all of them sharp Noses. As we walked last night on the Severn Banks, a most lovely Girl glided along in a Boat – there were at least 30 naked men bathing – she seemed mighty unconcerned – and they addressing her with not the most courtly gallantry, she snatched the Task of Repartee from her Brother who was in the Boat with her, and abused them with great perseverance & elocution. I stared – for she was elegantly dressed – and not a Prostitute. Doubtless, the citadel of her chastity is so impregnably strong, that it needs not the ornamental Out-works of Modesty.

It is *wrong*, Southey! for a little Girl with a half-famished sickly Baby in her arms to put her head in at the window of an Inn – "Pray give me a bit of Bread and Meat"! from a Party dining on Lamb, Green Pease, & Sallad – Why ? ? Because it is *impertinent* & *obtrusive*! – I am a Gentleman! – and wherefore should the clamorous Voice of Woe *intrude* upon mine Ear!?

I enquired my road at a Cottage – and on lifting up the latch beheld a tall old Hag, whose soul-gelding Ugliness would chill to eternal chastity a cantharidized Satyr – However an Angel of Light could not have been more civil –

I have inclosed a Poem which Mrs Robinson gave me for your Anthology – She is a woman of undoubted Genius. There was a poem of her's in this Morning's paper which both in metre and matter pleased me much – She overloads every thing; but I never knew a human Being with so *full* a mind – bad, good, & indifferent, I grant you, but full & overflowing.

Miss Hays I have seen. . . .

Of Miss Hay's intellect I do not think so highly, as you, or rather, to speak sincerely, I think, not *contemptuously*, but certainly very *despectively* thereof. – Yet I think you likely in this case to have judged better than I – for to hear a Thing, ugly & petticoated, ex-syllogize a God with cold-blooded Precision, & attempt to run Religion thro' the body with an Icicle – an Icicle from a Scotch Hog-trough –! *I* do not endure it! – my Eye beholds phantoms – & "nothing is, but what is not." –

Have you seen Mrs Robinson lately? How is she? – Remember me in the kindest & most respectful phrases to her. – I wish, I knew the particulars of her complaint. For Davy has discovered a perfectly new Acid, by which he has restored the use of limbs to persons who had lost them for many years, (one woman 9 years) in cases of supposed Rheumatism. At all events, Davy says, it can do no harm, in Mrs Robinson's case – & if she will try it, he will make up a little parcel & write her a letter of *instructions* &c. – Tell her, & it is the truth, that Davy is exceedingly delighted with the two Poems in the Anthology. – N.B. Did you get my Attempt at a Tragedy from Mrs Robinson? –

To Mrs Smith I am about to write a letter, with a book – be so kind as to inform me of her direction.

Mrs Inchbald I do not like at all – every time, I recollect her, I like her less. That segment of a *look* at the corner of her eye – O God in heaven! it is so cold & cunning – ! thro' worlds of wildernesses I would run away from that look, that heart-*picking* look. 'Tis marvel-lous to me, that you can like that Woman. –

– In all other respects I could not be better off – except perhaps the two passengers – one a gross worldly minded fellow, not deficient in sense or judgment, but inert to every thing except Gain & eating / – the other, a woman once housekeeper in Gen. Fox's Family, a crea-ture with a horrible Superfluity of Envelope, a Monopolist & paten-

tee of flabby Flesh: or rather *Fish*. Indeed she is at once Fish, Flesh, &
Foul: tho' no chicken. And so unutterably feeble in her mind &
Thought, tho' she has been in all parts of the World, & seen all sorts
of people. O Christ! for a sea sick woman [man?] to see the man eat,
& this Mrs Carnosity talk about it. She eats every thing by a choice /
"I must have that little potatoe" / – (baked in grease under the meat)
"it looks so smilingly at one." – "Do cut me if you please ["] (for she
is so fat, she cannot help herself) "that small bit – just there, Sir! – a
leettle tiny bit *below*, if you please." – "Well! I have brought plenty of
pickles, I *always* think &c" / "I have always three or four jars of
brandy cherries with me; for with boil'd rice now &c for I always
think &c" – and true enough, if it can be called thinking, she does
always think upon some little damned article of eating that belongs
to the Housekeeper's Cupboards & Locker. And then her plaintive
Yawns / such a mixture of moan & petted Child's dry *Cry*, or *Try* at
a Cry, in them / And she said to me this morning, "how unhappy,
I always think, one always is, when there is nothing & nobody, as
one may say, about *one* to amuse *one*. It makes me so *nervou[s."]* She
eats, drinks, snores – & simply the being stupid & silly & vacant the
learned Body calls nervous. – Shame on me for talking about her /

There are two Passengers besides me / the one a half pay Lieutenant,
turned small Merchant, who with a bright eye over a yellow-purple
face that betrays to me that half his Liver is gone or going, has said
4 or 5 times aloud, that good wine never did any man any harm / &
an unconscientiously fat Woman, who would have wanted Elbow
Room on Salisbury Plain / a body that might have been in a less
spendthrift mood of Nature sliced into a company, & a reasonable
Slice allotted to her as Corporal! I think, I never saw so large a
woman, such a monopolist, patentee, abstract, of superfluous Flesh!
– *Enough of her* – in a double sense of the Phrase. –

Beautiful, feminine, attractive, without affectation – add to this amus-
ing and (female foibles out of the question which we scarcely wish
away) of excellent Good Sense – yet with all this not permanently
lovely <or loveable.> How can this be? They are loveless – if any trait
of the Lover appear, it is to each other. To each other I have noticed
a soft, soothing, and caressing character. But to men, however intimate, they uniformly bear the semblance of persons to be attended

to / ~~not~~ they will *do* indeed every thing that can be wished – but they will *look* nothing, *say* <attune> nothing. In vain, shall the Husband or Lover or Brother or Friend expect from either the flush, the overflow, the rapture, after long absence – in vain, the triumph & that best, dearest part of Success to a pure & susceptible Being, tha~te~ (more than mere) Sympathy of Joy ~in~ with the person beloved, the anticipation of which had been no weak motive to his effort, and one of the sweetest rewards of <his> Success. – O that suppressed Gladness & attempted Calmness, when the Smile passed off from the Lips moves to the Eyes or perhaps to the Nose, with which the fond Lover tells his success – & the broad sweet tumult of Joy with wc͞h the Beloved hears him!

A few ideal women exist – not only Sara Hutchinson, described later as an ideal marriage partner, but also the sister of Dr Crompton of Eaton, encountered on his Watchman *tour of 1796 and remembered here in a letter of 1812.*[43]

Mary & Charlotte will smile at my extravagance; but I have never ceased from my first acquaintance (nearly 17 years) to love and venerate in her the heavenliest Vision possible on Earth; viz. the Ideal of Womanhood. O how they both would love her! Tho' her elder children are now men & women, I seem to see no change in her. The Bodily holds in *her* the same relation to the Spiritual, as appropriate *Words* to pure and sweet conceptions – the Mortal is swallowed up in the Immortal, not destroyed but interfused and glorified. She explains to my feelings that most venial, because most beautiful, of all forms of Idolatry, the adoration of maiden Motherhood visualized & realized in the Virgin & Child. But it is more than this. – I must add the commanding Submissiveness, the dignified & elevating Humility of the Matron; the seriousness, the equability, the *for-ever*-ness of the conjugal affection still blended with, never disparted from, the delicacy & wakefulness of First-love! I must add too sincerity & constancy with the truest & justest Subordination in her attachments, from the Acquaintance who is received with courtesy to the Friend who is welcomed with an Interest that transcends while it accompanies gladness. In short, you cannot be with her without becoming *better*, & THEREFORE wise: & besides this, her very questions improve *my* understanding oftentimes more than the answers of even wise men. – Now as I have written this as if with the blood of my inmost Heart, so let me without suspicion of insincerity conclude by affirming, that few indeed are the women, in my sphere of acquaintance, to whom I could write thus, as confident as I now am, that as far as they credited my description, they would be delighted with it. –

Most, however, live only in the pages of Shakespeare.[44]

The opinion once prevailed, but, happily, is now abandoned, that Fletcher alone write for women; – the truth is, that with very few, and those partial, exceptions, the female characters in the plays of Beaumont and Fletcher are, when of the light kind, not decent; when heroic, complete viragos. But in Shakespeare all the elements of womanhood are holy, and there is the sweet,yet dignified feeling of all that *continuates* society, as sense of ancestry and of sex, with a purity unassailable by sophistry, because it rests not in the analytic processes, but in that sane equipoise of the faculties, during which the feelings are representative of all past experience, – not of the individual only, but of all those by whom she has been educated, and their predecessors even up to the first mother that lived. Shakespeare saw that the want of prominence, which Pope notices for sarcasm, was the blessed beauty of the woman's character, and knew that it arose not from any deficiency, but from the more exquisite harmony of all the parts of the moral being constituting one living total of head and heart. He has drawn it, indeed, in all its distinctive energies of faith, patience, constancy, fortitude, – shown in all of them as following the heart, which gives its results by a nice tact and happy intuition, without the intervention of the discursive faculty, – sees all things in and by the light of the affections, and errs, if it ever err, in the exaggerations of love alone. In all the Shakspearian women there is essentially the same foundation and principle; the distinct individuality and variety are merely the result of the modification of circumstances, whether in Miranda the maiden, in Imogen the wife, or in Katharine the queen.

Coleridge describes the differences of men from women (some of which might have been developed in his proposed novel on the subject): their reactions to infidelity provide one example.[45]

Würde, Worthiness, Virtue consist in the mastery over the sensuous & sensual Impulses – but Love requires Innocence / Let the Lover

ask his Heart whether he can endure that his Mistress should have
struggled with a sensual impulse for another man, tho' she overcame
it from a sense of Duty to him? – Women are LESS offended with Men,
from the vicious habits of men in part, & in part from the Difference
of bodily constitutions – yet still to a pure and truly loving woman
it must be a painful thought / That he should struggle with &
overcome Ambition, Desire of Fortune, superior Beauty, &c <or with
objectless Desire> is ~~not~~ pleasing; but *not* that he has struggled with
positive appropriated Desire / i.e. Desire *with* an object. –

*Their concern about handwriting (as he declares to Mrs J. J. Morgan) provides
another.*[46]

You write a good hand, & you express yourself naturally & like an
unaffected Gentlewoman – but in the name of Love & Friendship,
have you known me so long as to fear that my Regard for you, or my
respect for your Understanding, could be increased or diminished
by your Style or your Hand-writing? – If that were at all possible, it
could only happen from your Style being too blue-stocking fine &
correct, & your Handwriting *too* exquisite. So help me Conscience! I
should always anticipate a more natural Letter, more really wise, &
more unaffectedly affecting, the more ill-spelt Words there were in
it; & the fewer Stops & divided Sentences. – You yourselves *cannot*
write half as sweetly & heart-touchingly, as with *your* thoughts &
feelings you would have done, if you had never heard of Grammar,
Spelling, &c. – O curse them – at least as far as Women are concerned. The longer I live, the more do I loathe in stomach, & deprec-
ate in Judgement, all, *all* Bluestockingism. The least possible of it
implies at least two *Nits*, in one egg a male, in t'other a female – & if
not killed, O the sense of the Lady will be *Lice*nce! Crathmo-crawlo!

*Others include a tendency to dwell on doleful subjects, a quickness in judging the
human (but not the divine or devilish) in a man, a lack of education in the means of
retaining a man's affection, and the ability to control spaces tidily as opposed to
delighting in particular forms.*[47]

It is a remark that I have made many times & many times shall
repeat, I guess – that Women are infinitely fonder of clinging to &
beating about, hanging upon & keeping up & reluctantly letting fall,

any doleful or painful or unpleasant subject, than men of the same class & rank. . . .

. . . Is it want of generalizing power & even instinct? I was thinking of Uncles (Petrus), Batchelors, Reason acting without Love, & therefore attracting Rages / for it must have some Leidenschaft –

Women have a quick sense of the Human, bad & good, but none of the divine, or perhaps of the devilish, in a man – They can easily catch his intentions, difficultly his square contents – and are better judges of his *Coloridng*, than of his Design & Composition –

Of the one main mightly Defect of Female Education – every thing is taught but Reason & the Means of retaining Affection – This, this, O! it is worth all the rest told 10,000 times – how to quit a Husband, how to receive him on his Return, how never to recriminate – in short, the power of pleasurable Thoughts & Feelings – & the *Mischief* of giving pain, or (as often happens, when a Husband comes home from a Party of old Friends, Joyous & full of Heart) the love killing Effect of cold, dry, uninterested looks & Manners –

What I have written in the 3rd page of this Book, let me here take another Chance of bringing back in my Recollection as one possible mean of Compensating for my many heavy crimes of Omission – namely, that of enforcing as a part of Female Education, nay, habitual, from earliest Childhood, the virtuous blessed Art of blessing in marriage Life – in all its minutiæ – with the reasons & conscience-motives for each of which, brought *next* to their Creed as human Beings, & *as* their Creed, as Women.

Now a well-attuned and sensitive female mind must have the whole of the given Space *in keeping* – it requires the callus of an extreme Stimulation to be able to endure the rags, brushes & broken gallipots of an Allston, or the scattered Books, fluttering Pamphlets, & dusty Paper-wilderness of a Wordsworth. – I know but two individuals, who combine both, viz – ~~the fem~~ Lady-like *Wholeness* with creative delight in *particular* forms – & these are Mr Robert Southey, Poet Laureat &c &c &c, and Mr Sam. Tayl. Coleridge, whose whole Being has been unfortunately little more than a far-stretched Series of Et Ceteras. Calne, Wiltshire – 20 May, 1815. –

Observations on the affections of women, particularly as compared with those of men.[48]

<Hints and Fragments of "Men and Women, a Novel" – Mem. To write out the *Story*: that if I die, my friend M. may make use of it – & incorporate the various remarks in my different Pocket books. –> I have observed – indeed, it is the experience of my Life – that none are so eager, so restlessly eager, to *repay* an obligation as Women: and from the same cause Women in general have no *gratitude*. They feel the *Load* of the *Obligation* instead of *Sympathizing* with the Love and Kindness that constituted its whole value. A in deep distress is relieved by B with a sum of 200£, the Whole that B. possessed in the World – and with it B. gave his whole Time, and Anxiety – did 20 things, he could not have found courage to do for himself – & never dreamt of any return but Love for Love. – Well (exclaims C & D.) I shall never be happy till we can repay the obligation, my dear! – the very first money, we can possibly spare – &c – The money is re-turned – Thank God! now we *have got rid of that obligation*. – This originates in same source, as the universal habit among Women, that seems indeed almost instinct, of *recrimination*. – Their nature is extroitive, while in men we find introition – It is a *pun*, but in this sense Women may be paradoxically asserted to be *reflecting* Sub-stances – even as a Mirror that absorbs no ray but *reflects* all.

Yet where the Sexual Instinct with all its moral adjuncts takes its natural Course, the Affection for the Lover, then for the Husband, and finally for the Husband & Child corrects these qualities, and often turns them into truly feminine excellences. But if the Affections of <a> Woman are concentered to a woman, under the *name* of friendship or any other; but with the exclusiveness of Love; then these qualities are sure to corrupt into pride, vindictiveness, dis-quieting curiosity – ah me! what not? – <Here ends the Passage for the Novel.>

That which I have to strive for now in the discipline of my own mind is independence of [female] *Society* – Month after month the conviction strengthens in me, that it is my penance and my Duty to devote my future Life to *Work*, exclusive of all other views but the compensation <to my Children & Friends> for the indolence and ravage of intellect, which the dire self-punishing Vice of Opium has effected! – O merciful Redeemer! Grant me, grant me but Faith as a mustard grain that I may be able to remove this mountain into the briny Sea of true and effective Repentance! –

December, 1815. *Calne.*

Women have their heads in their hearts. Man seems to have been destined for a superior being: as things are, I think women generally better creatures than men. They have weaker appetites and weaker intellects, but much stronger affections. A man with a bad heart has been sometimes saved by a strong head: but a corrupt woman is lost for ever. Boys are usually prettier infants than girls.

Wordsworth said he could make nothing of Love except that it was Friendship accidentally combined with Desire. Whence I conclude that Wordsworth was never in love. For what shall we say of the feeling which a man of sensibility has towards his wife with her baby at her breast? How pure from sensual Desire – yet how different from Friendship!

Sympathy constitutes Friendship – but in Love there is a sort of Antipathy or opposing Passion. Each strives to be the other, and both together make up a one whole.

"Most women have no character at all" said Pope, and meant it for satire. Shakespeare, who knew man and woman better, saw that in fact it was the perfection of woman to be *characterless*. Every man wishes for Desdemonas, Ophelias and creatures who, though they may not always *understand* you, do always *feel* you and *feel* with you.

Men are not more generous than women. Men desire the happiness of women apart from themselves, chiefly, if not only, *when and where* it would be an imputation upon a woman's affections for her [?not] to be happy: and women on their part, seldom cordially carry their wish for their husband's happiness and enjoyment beyond the threshold. Whether it is that women have a passion for nursing, or from whatever cause, they invariably discourage all attempts to seek for health itself, beyond their own abode. When balloons, or these new roads upon which they say it will be possible to travel fifteen miles an hour, for a day together, shall become the common mode of travelling, women will become more locomotive: – the health of all classes will be materially benefitted. Women will then spend less time in attiring themselves – will invent some more simple head gear, or dispense with it altogether.

Thousands of women, attached to their husbands by the most endearing ties, and who would deplore their death for months, would oppose a separation for a few weeks in search of health, or assent so reluctantly, and with so much dissatisfaction, as to deprive the remedy of all value – rather make it an evil. I speak of affectionate natures and of the various, but always selfish, guises of self will.

Caresses and endearment on this side of sickening *fondness*, and affectionate interest in all that concerns himself, from a wife freely chosen are what every man loves, whether he be communicative or reserved, staid or sanguine. But affection, where it exists, will always prompt or discover its own most appropriate manifestation. All men, even the most surly, are influenced by affection, even when little fitted to excite it. I could have been happy with a servant girl had she only in sincerity of heart responded to my affection.

3

The Difficulty of Sustaining Humanity

(a) LAPSES FROM HUMAN INDEPENDENCE

To be human, in Coleridge's sense, is not a natural state but one that must constantly be reaffirmed by choices. In a notebook of 1827 he summarised this painful responsibility: 'for man what is not won by himself, by himself will be lost'. Unlike the animals, who remain as they are born, man is born naked, mute, ignorant. 'Even these must be Products of his own Act, he must win them by his Will.'[1] In view of this responsibility to choose a distinctly human life for oneself and to prevent lapses into a behaviour that was always potentially bestial – to prevent oneself from becoming 'loveless as the fish, merciless as the snake that kills by poison & cruel as the tiger that indulges its lust of destruction ere yet he appeases his thirst & hunger' – it was not surprising that the will sometimes failed, that human beings ceased to be entirely human. Balancing the multiple elements of the person was equally difficult; individual human beings sometimes failed to sustain their own coherence.

Efforts towards consciousness, wholeness, free agency and humane effectiveness were burdensome. Many forces conspired to subvert the coherence and identity of individuals: economic forces made them dependent; psychological weakness and addictions deprived them of will and/or volition; mob action submerged them under the *volonté generale*, easily manipulated by rabble rousers.

One of Coleridge's most frequently acknowledged contributions to modern thought is his focus on failures of will and volition through unconscious forces and inexplicable fractures in the personality. Investigation of his own failures in this regard led him to reject simple theories such as Socrates' doctrine that if we knew the good we would do it,[3] or that once truth was made evident people would follow it.[4] Many forces within the self and outside it undermined naïve notions of an easy congruence between the desire to do good and the capacity to act on it. Coleridge went on to examine various kinds of dependency, whether of women and poor people, whose free agency was necessarily compromised by financial want, or of those who were carried along to inhuman acts by the force of mobs that obliterated individuality, or of those addicted to drugs or alcohol.

Coleridge's ardent belief in human will was tempered by realistic analysis of the many ways in which this free will collapses. Contemporary students of addiction, for example, are often impressed by Coleridge's advanced analysis of his 'divided being' in a letter to J. J. Morgan about his own addiction.[5] This and other self-examinations disclosed the many divisions within the person, the many cross-roads at which decisive action could be waylaid. Finer and finer distinctions among the moments of self-control and self-loss showed how easily the human being lapses from human behaviour, becomes bestial or thing-like, can no longer will or do the good. Coleridge's self-examination revealed intricate psychological labyrinths which entangled his capacity for ethical action. 'Will-wantonness' was a term he invented for the phenomenon.[6] Eruption of psychological trouble was not to be identified with clinical madness: he saw friends and associates struggling with numerous inner schisms, while Mary Lamb, repeatedly admitted to the madhouse, stood firm and cheerful. At the worst times of his own addiction, on the other hand, he wished to be confined himself. His investigation drew on the philosophers of the 'age of reason', for it is often forgotten how perceptively David Hartley and John Locke acknowledged the forces of disintegration in the human mind (even if not with the exhaustiveness of Robert Burton's earlier *Anatomy of Melancholy*), noting with close attention the anxieties, addictions, oblivions and manias that debased or disconnected the centre of human nature; an interest which not only contributed to the study of insanity in that period but may have thrown light more permanently on its forms.[7] In his observations in notebooks and letters Coleridge carried on this task still more subtly.

The need to extend the conventional categories of madness to include, for example, maladies of the Will.[8]

Medicine hitherto has been too much confined to *passive* works – as if fevers &c – were the only human calamities. A Gymnastic Medicine is wanting, not a mere recommendation but a system of forcing the Will & *motive faculties* into action. There are a multitude of cases wčh should be treated as Madness – i.e. the genus Madness should be extended & more classes & species made, in practise, tho' of course, not in name.

A disease of the active imagination.[9]

. . . there is a state of mind, wholly unnoticed, as far as I know, by any Physical or Metaphysical Writer hitherto, & which yet is necessary to the explanation of some of the most important phænomena of Sleep & Disease / it is a transmutation of the *succession* of *Time* into the *juxtaposition* of *Space*, by which the smallest Impulses if quickly & regularly recurrent, *aggregate* themselves – & attain a kind of visual magnitude with a correspondent Intensity of general Feeling. – The simplest Illustration would be the *circle* of Fire made by whirling round a live Coal – only here the mind is passive. Suppose the same effect produced ab intra – & you have a clue to the whole mystery of frightful Dreams, & Hypochondriacal Delusions. – I merely *hint* this; but I could detail the whole process, complex as it is. – Instead of "an imaginary aggravation &c" it would be better to say – "an *aggregation* of slight Feelings by the force of a diseasedly retentive Imagination." –

Ghastly dreams in sea-sickness.[10]

Yet I can scarcely imagine a less desirable mode of Death than to be drowned at Sea in a Cabin, sea-sick, with that sick flatulence at the Stomach which would make a sadder Sleep of every act of composure, and resignation, & their natural bodily aids & accompaniments, the resting the Head & the closing of the Eyelids – & of these Sleeps, these Horrors, these frightful Dreams of Despair when the sense of individual Existence is full & lively only <for one> to feel oneself powerless, crushed *in* by every power – a stifled boding, one abject miserable Wretch / yet hopeless, yet struggling, removed from all touch of Life, deprived of all notion of Death / strange mixture of Fear and Despair – & that passio purissima, that mere Passiveness with Pain (the essence of which is perhaps Passivity – & which our word – mere Suffering – well comprizes –) in which the Devils are the Antithesis of Deity, who is Actus Purissimus, and eternal Life, as they are an ever-living Death. / – and all this vanishes on the casting off a puff of ill-tasted Gas from the Stomach / But O mercy! what a Dream to *expect* Death with what a pillow-mate for a Death-bed!

Self-disgust at his own failure.[11]

Oct. 21st 1804 – Monday night – Syracuse. – O my God! or if I dare not continue in that awful feeling! yet oh whatever is good in me, even tho' not in the *Depth*, tho' not in that which is the Universal & Perfect in us yet oh! by ~~the~~ all the ministering Imperfections of my nature that were capable of subserving the Good – O why have I shunned & fled like a cowed Dog from the Thought that yesterday was my Birth Day, & that I was 32 – So help me Heaven! as I looked back, & till I looked back I had imagined I was only *31* – so completely has a

whole year passed, with scarcely the fruits of a *month*. – O Sorrow &
Shame! I am not worthy to live – Two & thirty years. – & this last
year above all others! – I have done nothing! No I have not even
layed up any material, any inward stores, – of after action! – O no!
still worse! still worse! body & mind, habit of bedrugging the feelings, & bodily movements, & habit of dreaming without distinct or
rememberable [. . . . .]

Mid-life crisis.[12]

Wednesday Night, 18th May, 1808. – Important remark of Stuart,
with whom I never converse but to receive some distinct and
rememberable Improvement – (at least and if it be not remembered,
it is the fault defect of my memory, which, alas! grows weaker daily,
or the a fault of from my Indolence in not noting it down, as I do this)
that there is a period in a man's Life, varying in various men, from
35 to 45 – & operating most strongly in Batchelors, Widowers, or
those worst & MISERABLEST OF WIDOWERS, UNHAPPY HUSBANDS, in which
a man finds himself at the *Top of the Hill* – & having attained perhaps
what he wishes begins to ask himself – What is all this for? – begins
to feel the *vanity* of his pursuits – becomes half-melancholy, gives in
to wild dissipation, or self-regardless Drinking – and some not content with these – not *slow* – poisons, destroy themselves – & leave
their ingenious female, or female-minded friends, to fish out some
motive for an act which proceeded from a motive-making Impulse,
which would have acted even without a motive – even as <the>
Terror <in Nightmairs> a bodily sensation, tho' it most often creates
calls up† consonant Images, yet – as I know by experience, can affect
equally without any – or if not so, yet like gunpowder in a Smithy,
tho' it will not go off without a spark, is *sure* to receive one – if not
this hour, yet the next. – I had *felt* this Truth; but never saw it before

† O Heaven! 'twas frightful! now run down, and star'd at
  By shapes more ugly, than can be remember'd –
  Now seeing nothing and imagining nothing
  But only being afraid – stifled with fear
  And every goodly, each familiar Form
  Had a strange somewhat that breath'd Terror on me –
  　　　　　　　　From my Mss Tragedy –

so clearly; it came upon me at Malta, under the melancholy dreadful feeling of finding myself to be *Man*, by a distinct division from Boyhood, Youth, and *"Young Man"* – Dreadful was the feeling – before that Life had flown on so that I had always been *a Boy*, as it were – and this sensation had blended in all my conduct, my willing acknowledgement of superiority, & *in truth*, my meeting every person, as a superior, at the first moment – O Hope! O Hopelessness!

Yet if men survive this period, they commonly become chearful again – that is a comfort – for mankind – not for me!

The procrastination of despair.[13]

When your Ladyship's Letter arrived, I do not recollect, and as I write from Ambleside, I cannot enquire – but it arrived with two others at a time, when I was labouring under a depression of spirits, little less than absolute Despondency. It is so difficult to convey to another a state of feeling and it's accompaniments, which one believes and hopes that other has never experienced – I can only say, that one of the symptoms of this morbid state of the moral Being is an excessive sensibility and strange cowardice with regard to every thing that is likely to affect the Heart, or recall the consciousness to one's own self and particular circumstances. Especially, in Letters –. A mere letter of Business or from an indifferent person is received and opened at once; but from any one loved or esteemed seems formidable in proportion to that very regard and affection. The sick and self-deserting Soul, incapable of renouncing it's activity, merges it in subjects the most abstruse and remote from it's immediate Duties and Bearings, and so obtains a *forgetfulness*, a sort of counterfeit of that true substantial tranquillity, which a satisfied Conscience alone can procure for us: – "I will do it after I have read this Chapter –" – "or tomorrow morning" – & so on – till warned by experience the mind is ashamed any longer to *lie* to it's own self by any positive promise, and procrastinates indefinitely.–

Why are people more ready to call themselves fools than villains?[14]

O that my Readers would look round the World, as it now is, and make to themselves a faithful Catalogue of its many Miseries! From what do these proceed, and on what do they depend for their continuance? Assuredly for the greater part on the actions of Men, and those again on the want of a vital Principle of virtuous action. We live by Faith. The essence of Virtue subsists in the Principle. And the Reality of this, as well as its Importance, is believed by all Men in Fact, few as there may be who, bring the Truth forward into the light of distinct Consciousness. Yet all Men feel, and at times acknowledge to themselves, the true cause of their misery. There is no man so base, but that at some time or other, and in some way or other, he admits that he is not what he ought to be, though by a curious art of self-delusion, by an effort to keep at peace with himself as long and as much as possible, he will throw off the blame from the amenable part of his nature, his moral principle, to that which is independent of his will, namely, the degree of his intellectual faculties. Hence, for once that a man exclaims, how dishonest I am, on what base and unworthy motives I act, we may hear a hundred times, what a Fool I am! curse on my Folly? and the like.

Yet even this implies an obscure sentiment, that with clearer conceptions in the understanding, the Principle of Action would become purer in the Will. Thanks to the image of our Maker not wholly obliterated from any human Soul, we dare not purchase an exemption from guilt by an excuse, which would place our amelioration out of our own power. Thus the very man, who will abuse himself for a fool but not for a Villain, would rather, spite of the usual professions to the contrary, be condemned as a Rogue by other men, than be acquitted as a Blockhead.

(i) Dependency on Drugs and Alcohol

In Malta Coleridge watches the addictions that he cannot control, protesting meanwhile that his opium-taking has always been indulged in for defensible reasons.[15]

I in despair drank three glasses running of whisky & water / the violent medicine answered – I ~~was~~ have been feeble in body ~~here this~~ during the next day, & active in mind – & how strange that with so shaken a nervous System I never have the Head ache! – I verily am a stout-headed, weak-bowelled, and O! most pitiably weak-*hearted* Animal! But I leave it, <as I wrote it> – & likewise have refused to destroy the stupid drunken Letter to Southey, which I wrote in the sprawling characters of Drunkenness/~~&~~ If I should perish without having the power of destroying these & my other pocket books, the history of my own mind for my own improvement. O friend! Truth! Truth! but yet Charity! Charity! I have never loved Evil for its own sake; & <no! nor> n̄ ever sought pleasure for its own sake, but only as the means of escaping from pains that coiled round my mental powers, as a serpent around the body & wings of an Eagle! <My sole sensuality was *not* to be in pain! ->

The divided being that has resulted.[16]

Who that thus lives with a continually divided Being can remain healthy! <And who can long remain body-crazed, & not at times use unworthy means of making his Body the fit instrument of his mind? Pain is easily subdued compared with continual uncomfortableness – and the sense of stifled Power! – O this is that which made poor Henderson, Collins, Boyce, &c &c &c – *Sots!* – awful Thought – O it is horrid! – Die, my Soul, die! – Suicide – rather than this, the worst state of Degradation! It is less a suicide! S.T.C.> – I work hard, I do the duties of common Life from morn to night / but verily – I raise my limbs, "like lifeless *Tools*" – The organs of motion & outward action perform their functions at the stimulus of a galvanic fluid applied by the *Will*, not by the Spirit of Life that makes Soul and Body one. Thought and Reality two distinct corresponding Sounds, of which no man can say positively which is the ~~Sound~~ Voice and which the Echo.

In the autumn of 1808 he believes himself cured.[17]

I am hard at work – and feel a pleasure and eagerness in it, which I had not known for years – a consequence and reward of my courage in at length [having] overcome the fear of dying suddenly in my Sleep, which and, heaven knows! which alone had seduced me into the fatal habit of taking enormous quantities of Laudanum, and latterly, of spirits too – the latter merely to keep the former on my revolting Stomach. – I am still far enough from well – my lungs are slightly affected, as by asthma, and my bowels dreadfully irritable; but I am far better than I could have dared expect. I left it off *all at once*; & drink nothing but Toast and Water, or Lemonade made with Creme of Tartar. If I entirely recover, I shall deem it a sacred Duty to publish my Case, tho' without my name – for the practice of taking Opium is dreadfully spread. – Throughout Lancashire & Yorkshire it is the common Dram of the lower orders of People – in the small Town of Thorpe the Druggist informed me, that he commonly sold on market days two or three Pound of Opium, & a Gallon of Laudanum – all among the labouring Classes. Surely, this demands legislative Interference –

He falls back on limited dosing a few months later but finds himself in better spirits.[18]

For years I had with the utterest pangs of Self-disapprobation struggled in secret against the habit of taking narcotics. My Conscience indeed fully acquitted me of taking them from the weakness of Self-indulgence, or for the sake of my pleasurable sensation, or exhilaration of Spirits – in truth, the effects were the very contrary. From the disuse my spirits and pleasurable feelings used gradually to increase to the very Hour, when my circulation became suddenly distur[bed,] a painful and intolerable Yawning commenced, soon followed by a vio[lent] Bowel-complaint – and the evacuations – being chiefly dark blood in the form of . . . Gra[vel –] gave proof that the Liver had ceased to perform it's proper functions – in short, I had the strongest convictions that if I persisted, I should die. Still however, I had no other ground for this conviction than my own feelings – and therefore was never sure, that I was not acting guiltily. – At length, I made a fair Trial under the eye of a Physician, determining whatever might be the result, henceforward never to conceal anything of any kind from those who loved me and lived with me. The result was, that it could not be abandoned without Loss of Life – at least, not at once – but such has been the blessed Effect upon my Spirits of having no Secret to brood over, that I have been enabled to reduce the Dose to one *sixth* part of what I formerly took – and my Appetite, general Health, and mental Activity are greater than I have known them for years past. – O had you conjectured the inward Anguish that was consuming me (for it is a goodness of Providence to me that I cannot do wrong without severe Self-punishment) both in your Heart and in that of dear Mrs Estlin's, Pity would have suspended all condemnation for my real or apparent neglects of the Duties, which I owed to my friends, my family and my own Soul. –

In truth, I have been for years almost a paralytic in mind from self-dissatisfaction – brooding in secret anguish over what from so many baffled agonies of Effort I had thought and felt to be inevitable, but which yet from moral cowardice and a strange tyrannous Reluctance to make any painful Concern of my own the subject of Discourse – a reluctance strong in exact proportion to my esteem and affection for the persons, with whom I am communing – I had never authorized my conscience to pronounce inevitable by submitting my case carefully & faithfully to some Physician. I have however done it at last – and tho' the result after a severe Trial proved what I had anticipated, yet such is the Blessedness of walking altogether in Light, that my Health & Spirits are better [than] I have known them for years. But of all this hereafter.

By April 1814, however, his condition has become desperate.[19]

O dear Friend! – I have too much to be forgiven to feel any difficulty in forgiving the cruellest enemy that ever trampled on me: & *you* I have only to *thank*. – You have no conception of the dreadful Hell of my mind & conscience & body. You bid me, pray. O I do pray inwardly to be able to *pray*; but indeed to pray, to pray with the faith to which Blessing is promised, this is the reward of Faith, this is the Gift of God to the Elect. O if to feel how infinitely worthless I am, how poor a wretch, with just free will enough to be deserving of wrath, & of my own contempt, & of none to merit a moment's peace, can make a part of a Christian's creed: so far I am a Christian –

S. T. C.

The first outward and sensible Result of Prayer is a penitent Resolution, joined with a consciousness of weakness in effecting it (yea, even a dread too well grounded, lest by breaking & falsifying it the soul should add guilt to guilt by the very means, it has taken to escape from Guilt – so pitiable is the state of unregenerated man!). Now I have resolved to place myself in any situation, in which I can remain for a month or two as *a Child*, wholly in the Power of others – But alas! I have no money –

Letters of the following month describe a renewed struggle to free himself from the effects of 'this free-agency-annihilating poison'.[20]

My dear Morgan

If it could be said with as little *appearance* of profaneness, as there is feeling or intention in my mind, I might affirm; that I had been crucified, dead, and buried, descended into *Hell*, and am now, I humbly trust, rising again, tho' slowly and gradually. I thank you from my heart for your far too kind Letter to Mr Hood – so much of it is true that such as you described I always wished to be. I know, it will be vain to attempt to persuade Mrs Morgan or Charlotte, that a man, whose moral feelings, reason, understanding, and senses are perfectly sane and vigorous, may yet have been *mad* – And yet nothing is more true. By the long long Habit of the accursed Poison my Volition (by which I mean the faculty *instrumental* to the Will, and by which alone the Will can realize itself – it's Hands, Legs, & Feet, as it were) was compleatly deranged, at times frenzied, dissevered itself from the Will, & became an independent faculty: so that I was perpetually in the state, in which you may have seen paralytic Persons, who attempting to push a step forward in one direction are violently forced round to the opposite. I was sure that no ease, much less pleasure, would ensue: nay, was certain of an accumulation of pain. But tho' there was no prospect, no gleam of Light before, an indefinite indescribable Terror as with a scourge of ever restless, ever coiling and uncoiling Serpents, drove me on from behind. – The worst was, that in *exact proportion* to the *importance* and *urgency* of any Duty was it, as of a fatal necessity, sure to be neglected: because it added to the Terror above described. In exact proportion, as I *loved* any person or persons more than others, & would have sacrificed my Life for them, were *they* sure to be the most barbarously mistreated by silence, absence, or breach of promise. – I used to think St James's Text, "He who offendeth in one point of the Law, offendeth in all", very harsh; but my own sad experience has taught me it's aweful, dreadful Truth. – What crime is there scarcely which has not been included in or followed from the one guilt of taking opium? Not to speak of ingratitude to my maker for the wasted Talents; of ingratitude to so many friends who have loved me I know not why; of barbarous neglect of my family; excess of cruelty to Mary & Charlotte, when at Box, and both ill – (a vision of Hell to me when I think of it!) I have in this one dirty business of Laudanum an hundred times deceived, tricked, nay, actually & consciously LIED. – And yet *all* these vices are so opposite to my nature, that but for this *free-agency-annihilating* Poison, I verily believe that I should have suffered myself to have been cut to pieces rather than have committed any one of them.

At length, it became too bad. I used to take [from] 4 to 5 ounces a day of Laudanum, once . . . [ou]nces, i.e. near a Pint – besides great quantities [of liquo]r. From the Sole of my foot to the Crown of [my h]ead there was not an Inch in which I was not [contin]ually in torture: for more than a fortnight no [sleep] ever visited my Eye lids – but the agonies of [remor]se were far worse than all! – Letters past between Cottle, Hood, & myself – & our kind Friend, Hood, sent Mr Daniel to me. At his second Call I told him plainly (for I had sculked out the night before & got Laudanum) that while I was in my own power, all would be in vain – I should inevitably cheat & trick *him*, just as I had done Dr Tuthill – that I must either be removed to a place of confinement, or at all events have a Keeper. – Daniel saw the truth of my observations, & my most faithful excellent friend, Wade, procured a strong-bodied, but decent, meek, elderly man, to super-intend me, under the name of my Valet – All in the House were forbidden to fetch any thing out by the Doctor's order. – Daniel generally spends two or three hours a day with me – and already from 4 & 5 ounces has brought me down to four tea-spoonfuls in the 24 Hours – The terror & the indefinite craving are gone – & he expects to drop it altogether by the middle of next week – Till a day or two after that I would rather not see you.

My dear Morgan

To continue from my last – Such was the direful state of my mind, that (I tell it you with horror) the razors, penknife, & every possible instrument of Suicide it was found necessary to remove from my room! My faithful, my *inexhaustibly patient* Friend, WADE, has caused a person to sleep by my bed side, on a bed on the floor: so that I might never be altogether alone – O Good God! why do such good men love me! At times, it would be more delightful to me to lie in the Kennel, & (as Southey said) "unfit to be pulled out by any honest man except with a pair of Tongs." – What *he* then said (perhaps) rather unkindly of me, was prophetically true! Often have I wished to have been thus trodden & spit upon, if by any means it might be an atonement for the direful guilt, that (like all others) first *smiled* on me, like Innocence! then crept closer, & yet closer, till it had thrown it's serpent folds round & round me, and I was no longer in my own power! – *Something* even the most wretched of Beings (*human* Beings at least) owes to himself – & this I *will* say & *dare* with truth say – that never was I led to this wicked direful practice of taking Opium or Laudanum by any desire or expectation of exciting *pleasurable* sensations; but purely by *terror*, by cowardice of pain, first of mental pain, & afterwards as my System became weakened, even of bodily Pain.

My Prayers have been fervent, in agony of Spirit, and for hours together, incessant! still ending, O! only for the merits, for the agonies, for the cross of my blessed Redeemer! For I am nothing, but evil – I can do nothing, but evil! Help, Help! – I believe! help thou my unbelief! –

Mr Daniel has been the wisest of physicians to me. I cannot say, how much I am indebted both to his Skill and Kindness. But he is one of the few rare men, who can make even their Kindness Skill, & the best and most unaffected Virtues of their Hearts *professionally* useful.

In June he entreats that a full account of his condition be given after his death.[21]

For I am unworthy to call any good man friend – much less you, whose hospitality and love I have abused; accept, however, my intreaties for your forgiveness, and for your prayers.

Conceive a poor miserable wretch, who for many years has been attempting to beat off pain, by a constant recurrence to the vice that reproduces it. Conceive a spirit in hell, employed in tracing out for others the road to that heaven, from which his crimes exclude him! In short, conceive whatever is most wretched, helpless, and hopeless, and you will form as tolerable a notion of my state, as it is possible for a good man to have.

I used to think the text in St. James that "he who offended in one point, offends in all," very harsh; but I now feel the awful, the tremendous truth of it. In the one crime of OPIUM, what crime have I not made myself guilty of! – Ingratitude to my Maker! and to my benefactors – injustice! *and unnatural cruelty to my poor children*! – self-contempt for my repeated promise – breach, nay, too often, actual falsehood!

After my death, I earnestly entreat, that a full and unqualified narration of my wretchedness, and of its guilty cause, may be made public, that at least some little good may be effected by the direful example!

Knowing his own propensity for addiction, Coleridge observes its incidence among working men and women, among the Irish, and in sots among his friends.[22]

The short Debate on the Petition introduced by Mr Grattan from the Irish Brewers, praying that the Duty on Spirits might be restored to its former rate (*i.e.* from 2*s*. 6*d*. to 5*s*. 8*d*. per gallon) has excited more thought in our minds, and awakened a deeper interest, than many discussions which have filled all our columns. We must be blind indeed, not to perceive the more than ordinary and only not supreme importance of the Revenue at the present moment. A collision of vital interests must needs be a subject of grief and anxiety to every lover of his country; and sincerely do we hope that in the present case some means may be found to reconcile them. But where the health and the morals of a whole Island, and with them both its industry and public tranquillity are at stake, the Revenue cannot be said so much to make sacrifices, as to refrain from borrowing for the present craving, sums which must be repaid, by subtraction, at a most usurious interest, in a time, perhaps, of still greater necessity. It is well known how nearly allied to frenzy are the effects of spirituous liquors on men who have strong feelings and few ideas. The quantity of stimulus, which taken by a man of education, surely as it will hasten the decay of all his powers, would yet, for the time, only call them into full energy –

> And only, till unmechaniz'd by Death,
> Make the Pipe vocal to the Player's breath.

The same quantity renders an uneducated man, of undisciplined habits, a frantic wild beast. Nor do these effects cease with the temporary intoxication; but engender habits of restlessness, a proneness to turbulent feelings, even when the man is sober, in short, a general inflammability of temperament. Nor can it be denied, whatever may be its causes, that there exists a certain nationality of constitution, which occasions the poison of spirituous drinks to act with greater malignity in some countries than in others.

Apply these facts to the lower classes of the Irish, whom such indefatigable pains are taken to intoxicate with another poison, a malignant hatred to Great Britain, and a persuasion, that to the oppression and tyranny of the British Government they are indebted for all the miseries they either feel or imagine; and that the hesitation to concede the eligibility to 33 great offices of State to the wealthy

Catholics by some marvellous circuit of operation, strips the cottager, or rather *hoveller*, of every comfort, and keeps him half-fed, half-cloathed, and half-human! Apply these facts to those districts in our Sister Island, where a large majority of the inhabitants with the third or fourth glass of whisky *"pruriunt in pugnam,"* itch for a riot; and if there is no quarrel higher at hand between the Caravats or —, we forget the name – the Anti-caravats begin to enquire after a rebellion! Reflect in short on the passion and appetite of the lower Irish for spirits, the effects of these spirits on them, and the mournfully large proportion which their numbers bear to those of the middle and higher classes – and then deduce the consequences of the poison being rendered so cheap, that a man may be mad-drunk for *three-pence*! Much injury has arisen, as well as many errors, from the indiscriminate application of the maxim, "Things find their level." – *Things* may find their level; but the *minds* and bodies of men do not. Drunkenness will not wheel round again to sobriety; nor sloth to industry; nor will disorderly habits and turbulent inquietude sink down again into peaceableness and obedience to the law.

It is an undoubted Fact of human nature, that the sense of impossibility quenches all will. Sense of utter inaptitude does the same. The man shuns the beautiful Flame, which is eagerly grasped at by the Infant. The sense of a disproportion of certain after harm to present gratification, produces effects almost equally uniform: though almost perishing with thirst, we should dash to the earth a goblet of Wine in which we had seen a Poison infused, though the Poison were without taste or odour, or even added to the pleasures of both. Are not all our Vices equally inapt to the universal end of human actions, the Satisfaction of the agent? Are not their pleasures equally disproportionate to the after harm? Yet many a Maiden, who will not grasp at the fire, will yet purchase a wreathe of Diamonds at the price of her health, her honor, nay (and she herself knows it at the moment of her choice), at the sacrifice of her Peace and Happiness. The Sot would reject the poisoned Cup, yet the trembling hand with which he raises his daily or hourly draught to his lips, has not left him ignorant that this too is altogether a Poison. I know, it will be objected, that the consequences foreseen are less immediate; that they are diffused over a larger space of time; and that the slave of Vice hopes well, where no hope is. This, however, only removes the question one step further: for why should the distance or diffusion of known consequences produce so great a difference? Why are men the dupes of the present moment? Evidently because the conceptions are indistinct in the one case, and vivid in the other; because all confused conceptions render us restless; and because Restlessness can drive us to Vices that promise no enjoyment, no not even the cessation of that Restlessness. This is indeed the dread Punishment attached by Nature to habitual Vice, that its Impulses wax as its Motives wane. No object, not even the light of a solitary Taper in the far distance, tempts the benighted Mind from before; but its own restlessness dogs it from behind, as with the iron goad of Destiny.

In October 1820 Coleridge writes a letter for his son Hartley to send to the Provost and Fellows of Oriel College, pleading with them to exonerate him from charges of 'sottishness' and reverse the consequent dismissal from his probationary fellowship. (The dependency denied in this letter was to become increasingly evident in the next few years.)[23]

. . . disclaiming all ref[er]ence to any expressions used or communications made, by individuals in their individual character, by letter or in conversation, I here, secondly, protest against the charge of *frequent* acts of Intoxication, if by the word frequent more than two or at the utmost three single instances be meant; and declare that I am permitted by my conscience to admit the truth even of so many, only as far as by intoxication a culpable degree of Intemperance be understood, and not if by intoxication a temporary deprivation of my mental & bodily faculties, such as we commonly mean to express when we say that a man is thoroughly *drunk*, i.e. either does not know what he is doing or saying, or will be incapable of recollecting it on the return of sobriety, or (recollecting the same, or having had it brought to his recollection & knowledge) disclaims what he had said or done, as said or done in the suspension of his judgement & moral will; or finally, has lost or greatly impaired his powers of communicating his meaning, and effectuating his purposes, ex. gr. staggering, or stammering, or using one set of words when he meant another.

I solemnly declare that but for the recollection of *one* incident, viz. that on my returning from a wine party given on the occasion of a degree passing, the Servant desired me to take care of my Candle, from which I inferred both at the time & again on the next morning (for the words were my first thought on awaking) that I must have had the appearance & marks of Intoxication, and felt (not without self-reproach & sincere grief) that I must have drunk too much, & beyond what any occasion could justify, above all in a man whose duty, moral and prudential, it was with peculiar solicitude to eschew all scandal, and every approach to an evil example – but for the recollection of this one incident & the rightful inference from the same, I solemnly declare that I could not without offending against my own conscience have pleaded guilty to more than the negative (though still, and with unfeigned penitence, I admit, the serious) offence of not having been sufficiently anxious & careful in the performance of the positive duty, that of making myself an example of the opposite virtue – of behaviour decorous and circumspect and of Temperance beyond suspicion.

Writing to J. H. Green in 1833, Coleridge advocates temperance societies, sanatoriums and the drinking of beer instead of spirits.[24]

It is seldom, my dearest Friend! that I find myself differing from you in judgements of any sort. It is more than seldom, that I am left in doubt and query on any judgement of your's of a *practical* nature – for on the good ground of some 16 or more years' experience I feel a take-for-granted faith in the dips and pointings of the needle, in every decision of your *total* mind. – But in the instance, you spoke of this afternoon, viz. your persistent rebuttal of the Temperance-Society Man's Request, tho' I do not feel *sure* that you are not in the Right, yet I do feel as if I should have been more delighted, and more satisfied, if you had intimated your compliance with it. I feel, that in this case I should have had *no* doubt; but that my mind would have leapt forwards with content, like a key to a loadstone.

Assuredly, you might – at least, you would have a very promising chance of effecting considerable *Good* – and you might have commenced your address with your own remark of the superfluity of any Light of Information afforded to an habitual Dram Drinker respecting the unutterable evil and misery of his thraldom. As wisely give a physiological Lecture to convince a man of the pain of Burns, while he is lying with his head on the bars of the Fire-grate, instead of snatching him off. But in stating this you might most effectingly & preventively for others describe the misery of that condition in which the impulse waxes as the motive wanes. Mem. There is a striking passage in my FRIEND on this subject – & a no less striking one in a School boy theme of mine, now in Gillman's Possession, & in my own hand, written when I was fourteen, with the simile of the treacherous Current & the Maelstrom – But this might give occasion for the suggestion of one new charitable Institution, under Authority of a Legislative Act – namely, a Maison de Santé (what do the French call it?) for Lunacy & Ideocy of the *Will* – in which with the full consent of, or at the direct instance of the Patient himself, and with the concurrence of his Friends, such a person under the certificate of a Physician might be placed under medical & moral coercion. I am convinced, that London would furnish a hundred Volunteers in as many days from the Gin-shops – who would swallow their glass of poison in order to get courage to present themselves to the Hospital in question – And a similar Institution might exist for a higher class of Will-Maniacs or Impotents. – Had such a House of Health been in existence, I know who would have entered himself as a Patient some five & 20 years ago. –

2 Class – To the persons still capable of self-cure – and lastly, to the young who have only begun – & not yet begun – and the urgency of connecting the Temperance Society with the *Christian* Churches, of all denominations – the *classes* known to each other – & deriving strength from *religion*. This is a beautiful part or might have been made so of the Wesleian Church –

These are but raw Hints. But unless the Mercy of God should remove me from my sufferings earlier than I dare hope or pray for, we will talk the subject over, again: as well as of the reasons *why* Spirits in any form, as such, are so much more dangerous morally & in relation to the forming [of a] Habit than Beer or Wine – Item – If a Government were truly paternal, a healthsome and sound Beer would be made universal – aye, and for the lower Half of the middle classes Wine might be imported, good and generous, from 6d to 8d per quart –

In a late notebook he ponders whether a Christian society could follow Islam in prohibiting alcohol.[25]

Meditating on the wide waste of Humanity effected by intemperance, the lust of intenser Life from nervous excitement by physical stimulants, a Sceptic, who had studied Gibbon, Voltaire, &c, with too much predilection, declared it a great ground of preference, of Mohamedanism as compared with Christianity, that Mahomet had absolutely forbidden Wine. . . . Mahomet forbade wine. His faithful Followers take Opium, & smoke Bang. Is that better? . . . had Christ forbidden Wine, Christians might have drunk Gin, punch, &c. . . . Would you have it commanded – Man shall not take into the body, by any organ, any substance that shall excite the sensations, that shall act on the nervous system? The Prohibition would include every fresh Breeze, every morsel of food that the hungry man takes – No! Religion forbids drunkenness, forbids intemperance, forbids any enjoyment of the outward creature which is not for the well-being of the Enjoyer – forbids any use that is against the true use – and this places the commandment in the only sphere, in which it can effectuate itself, in the Court of Conscience. Mahomet placed it in the Court of Excise, in which the *letter* of the Law alone can be enforced.

(ii) Dependency on the Will of the Group

Coleridge's hostility to mob action is expressed strongly in 1795.[26]

The Example of France is indeed a "Warning to Britain". A nation wading to their Rights through Blood, and marking the track of Freedom by Devastation! Yet let us not embattle our Feelings against our Reason. Let us not indulge our malignant Passions under the mask of Humanity. Instead of railing with infuriate declamation against these excesses, we shall be more profitably employed in developing the sources of them. French Freedom is the Beacon, that while it guides us to Equality should shew us the Dangers, that throng the road.

The annals of the French Revolution have recorded in Letters of Blood, that the Knowledge of the Few cannot counteract the Ignorance of the Many; that the Light of Philosophy, when it is confined to a small Minority, points out the Possessors as the Victims, rather than the Illuminators, of the Multitude. The Patriots of France either hastened into the dangerous and gigantic Error of making certain Evil the means of contingent Good, or were sacrificed by the Mob, with whose prejudices and ferocity their unbending Virtue forbade them to assimilate. Like Sampson, the People were strong – like Sampson, the People were blind.

Wilder features characterize the second class. Sufficiently possessed of natural sense to despise the Priest, and of natural feeling to hate the Oppressor, they listen only to the inflammatory harangues of some mad-headed Enthusiast, and imbibe from them Poison, not Food; Rage, not Liberty. Unillumined by Philosophy, and stimulated to a lust of revenge by aggravated wrongs, they would make the Altar of Freedom stream with blood, while the grass grew in the desolated halls of Justice. These men are the rude materials from which a detestable Minister manufactures conspiracies. Among these men he sends a brood of sly political monsters, in the character of sanguinary Demagogues, and like Satan of old, "the Tempter ere the Accuser," ensnares a few into Treason, that he may alarm the whole into Slavery. He, who has dark purposes to serve, must use dark means – light would discover, reason would expose him: he must endeavour to shut out both – or if this prove impracticable, make them appear frightful by giving them frightful names. . . .

. . . Yet they possess a kind of wild Justice well calculated to spread them among the grossly ignorant. To unenlightened minds, there are terrible charms in the idea of Retribution, however savagely it be inculcated. The Groans of the Oppressors make fearful yet pleasant music to the ear of him, whose mind is darkness, and into whose soul the iron has entered.

His misgivings increase between 1806 and 1817 as he observes the power of dema-gogues such as William Cobbett and fears that mob action may lead to a 'Fool-and-Knave-ocracy'.[27]

Of the profanation of the Sacred word, *the People* – [every/any] brutal Burdett-Mob, assembled on some drunken St Monday of Faction, is *the People* forsooth – & ~~now~~ each leprous ragamuffin, like a Circle in Geometry, is at once one, and all – & calls his own brutal Self, "us, the People!" – and who are the Friends of the People? Not those who would wish to elevate each of them, or at least, the Child who is to take his place in the flux of Life & Death, into something worthy of Esteem & capable of Freedom, but those who flutter & infuriate them, as they *are*. – A contradiction in the very thought! For if really, they are good & wise, virtuous and well-informed, how weak must be the motives of discontent to a truly moral Being – but if the contrary, and the motives for discontent proportionally strong, how without guilt and absurdity appeal to them, as Judges & arbiters? He alone is entitled to a share in the government of all, who has learnt to govern himself – there is but one possible ground of a Right to Freedom, viz. to understand & revere its Duties.

That the Cobbetts & Hunts address you (= the lower Ranks) as Beasts who have no future Selves – as if by a natural necessity you must *all* for ever remain poor & slaving. But what is the *fact*? How many scores might each of you point out in your own neighborhood of men raised to wealth or comfort from your own ranks? –

It is for this reason, that I entertain toward the Jeffrieses, Cobbetts, Hunts, and all these creatures – and to the Foxites, who have fostered the vipers – a feeling more like Hatred than I ever bore to other Flesh and Blood. So clearly do I see and always have seen, that it must end in the suspension of Freedom of all kind. Hateful under all names these wretches are most hateful to me as Liberticides. – The work attributed to Bonaparte says – Liberty is for a Few, Equality for all – Alas! dear Sir! what is Mankind but *the Few* in all ages? Take them away, and how long, think you, would the rest differ from the Negroes or New Zealanders – Strip Waithman for instance of every thing that he does and talks, as a Barrel organ, without really *understanding* one word of what he says, one ultimate end of what he does – leave him, for instance, on a South sea Island, & with no other words to talk in but what the savages can supply him with – and think, in what one respect would Waithman differ from one of these Savages in his inward soul and in any reality of Being – but for the worse? – O that *Conscience* permitted me to dare tell the whole Truth! I would, methinks, venture to brave the fury of the great and little Vulgar, as the Advocate of an insufferable Aristocracy. But either by an Aristocracy, or a Fool-and-Knave-ocracy man must be governed. –

(iii) Economic Dependency

In the 1809 Friend, *Coleridge describes the effects on children and women of dependency, depriving them of their free agency as individuals.*[28]

Children are excluded from all political Power – are they not human beings in whom the faculty of Reason resides? Yes? but in them the faculty is not yet adequately developed. But are not gross Ignorance, inveterate Superstition, and the habitual Tyranny of Passion and Sensuality, equal Preventives of the development, equal impediments to the rightful exercise of the Reason, as Childhood and early Youth? Who would not rely on the judgement of a well-educated English Lad, bred in a virtuous and enlightened Family, in preference to that of a brutal Russian, who believes that he can scourge his wooden Idol into good humour, or attributes to himself the merit of perpetual Prayer, when he has fastened the Petitions, which his Priest has written for him, on the wings of a Windmill? Again: Women are likewise excluded – a full half, and that assuredly the most innocent the most amiable half, of the whole human Race, is excluded, and this too by a Constitution which boasts to have no other foundations but those of universal Reason! Is Reason then an affair of Sex? No! But Women are commonly in a state of *dependence*, and are not likely to exercise their Reason with freedom. Well! and does not this ground of exclusion apply with equal or greater force to the Poor, to the Infirm, to Men in embarrassed Circumstances, to all in short whose maintenance, be it scanty or be it ample, depends on the Will of others? How far are we to go? Where must we stop? What Classes should we admit? Whom must we disfranchise? The objects, concerning whom we are to determine these Questions, are all Human Beings and differenced from each other by *degrees* only, and these degrees too oftentimes changing. Yet the Principle on which the whole System rests is, that Reason is not susceptible of degree.

The twin human yearnings for Freedom and Dependence are seen as engendering a kind of madness that yet presupposes the possibility of their being reconciled in true love.[29]

We all love to be a little mad, when we are certain that there is no Witness or Noticer of our madness. Two Master-feelings are gratified – *Freedom & Dependence*. – Who can be himself, who does not at times prove to himself that he is *free*? Who ~~that~~ does not the same moment yearn to feel himself dependent? What is that third which makes a synthesis of this Thesis and its Antithesis? Love! – All things in Heaven & on Earth & beneath the Earth are but ~~as~~ one Triplicity revealing itself in an endless series of Triplicities, of which the common Formula is A + (– A) = B.

(b) MISTAKING PERSONS FOR THINGS

Indignation towards slave-owners, industrialists, legislators and government leaders for their mistreatment of human beings was a recurring element in Coleridge's prose writings from 1795 to 1833. While directing his
outrage against specific abuses, he was at pains to show how those abuses
arose from false principles – pre-eminently the mistaking of human beings
for things – along with the middle-class obsession with objects, identified by
him as 'fetishism'.

Coleridge feared that the treatment of persons as things by industrialists
or social engineers was the result of utilitarian theories like those of Adam
Smith which permitted the dehumanisation of men and women labourers in
the process of enumerating and separating them as useful mechanisms for
production. Such processes were supplemented by philosophical and psychological theories, most potently enunciated by David Hume in his
'bundle' theory of personality, that the existence of a coherent centre of
personality was an illusion. Philosophical scepticism could in this way sap
belief in personal integrity and in other people's freedom to act.

Coleridge often repeated Kant's insistence that, whereas things were means
to an end, persons were ends in themselves. Coleridge also recognised,
nevertheless, that personal identity could become fragmented and discontinuous, and that some persons might indeed encourage others to treat them
as things. He invented the word 'be-thing'd' to cover some of these debase-
ments.

While his reasons for anger at specific abuses are evident enough, his
analysis of modern 'fetishism' belonged to a longer line of thought about
human relationships. In his 'Opus Maximum' he argued that upper-class
children were being stimulated by accumulations of objects rather than by
beloved family members; instead of seeing themselves mirrored in other
persons, as they might in an old-fashioned or poor farming family, they
came to associate themselves with these objects, and valued themselves
accordingly. They were then liable to sacrifice their independent judgements as persons to powerful figures who offered them objects for gain;
because they did not see themselves as persons, they did not recognise the
personhood of others and so became brutalised, in a cycle that could progressively worsen.[30] Many professions, he maintained – even that of medicine – had ceased to value persons above things and joined the 'fetishism' of
the time.[31]

Lecturing in 1795 Coleridge attacks the dehumanising forces of poverty and starva-
tion in his own country.[32]

Wherein am I made worse by my ennobled neighbour? do the childish titles of aristocracy detract from my domestic comforts, or prevent my intellectual acquisitions? but those institutions of society
which should condemn me to the necessity of twelve hours daily

toil, would make my *soul* a slave, and sink *the rational* being in the mere animal. It is a mockery of our fellow creatures' wrongs to call them equal in rights, when by the bitter compulsion of their wants we make them inferior to us in all that can soften the heart, or dignify the understanding. Let us not say that this is the work of time – that it is impracticable at present, unless we each in our individual capacities do strenuously and perseveringly endeavour to diffuse among our domestics those comforts and that illumination which far beyond all political ordinances are the true equalizers of men.

They too, who live *from Hand to Mouth*, will most frequently become improvident. Possessing no *stock* of happiness they eagerly seize the gratifications of the moment, and snatch the froth from the wave as it passes by them. Nor is the desolate state of their families a restraining motive, unsoftened as they are by education, and benumbed into selfishness by the torpedo touch of extreme Want. Domestic affections depend on association. We love an object if, as often as we see or recollect it, an agreeable sensation arises in our minds. But alas! how should *he* glow with the charities of Father and Husband, who gaining scarcely more, than his own necessities demand, must have been accustomed to regard his wife and children, not as the Soothers of finished labour, but as Rivals for the insufficient meal!

To unenlightened minds, there are terrible charms in the idea of Retribution, however savagely it be inculcated. The Groans of the Oppressors make fearful yet pleasant music to the ear of him, whose mind is darkness, and into whose soul the iron has entered.
    This class, at present, is comparatively small – Yet soon to form an overwhelming majority, unless great and immediate efforts are used to lessen the intolerable grievances of our poorer brethren, and infuse into their sorely wounded hearts the healing qualities of knowledge. For can we wonder that men should want humanity, who want all the circumstances of life that humanize? Can we wonder that with the ignorance of Brutes they should unite their ferocity? peace and comfort be with these! But let us shudder to hear from Men of dissimilar opportunities sentiments of similar revengefulness. The purifying alchemy of Education may transmute the fierceness of an ignorant man into virtuous energy – but what remedy shall we apply to him, whom Plenty has not softened, whom Know-

ledge has not taught Benevolence? This is one among the many fatal effects which result from the want of fixed principles.

. . . the Ancients fatted their Victims for the Altar, we prepare ours for sacrifice by leanness. War ruins our Manufactures; the ruin of our Manufactures throws Thousands out of employ; men cannot starve: they must either pick their countrymen's Pockets – or cut the throats of their fellow-creatures, because they are Jacobins. If they chuse the latter, the chances are that their own lives are sacrificed: if the former, they are hung or transported to Botany Bay. And here we cannot but admire the deep and comprehensive Views of Ministers, who having starved the wretch into Vice send him to the barren shores of new Holland to be starved back again into Virtue. It must surely charm the eye of humanity to behold Men reclaimed from stealing by being banished to a Coast, where there is nothing to steal, and helpless Women, who had been

Bold from despair and prostitute for Bread,

find motives to Reformation in the sources of their Depravity, refined by Ignorance, and famine-bitten into Chastity. Yet even these poor unfortunates, these disinherited ones of Happiness, appear to me more eligibly situated than the wretched Soldier – because more innocently! Father of Mercies! if we pluck a wing from the back of a Fly, not all the Ministers and Monarchs in Europe can restore it – yet they dare to send forth their mandates for the Death of Thousands, and if they succeed call the Massacre Victory.
. . . What remains? Hunger. Over a recruiting place in this city I have seen pieces of Beef hung up to attract the half-famished Mechanic. It has been said, that GOVERNMENT, though not the best preceptor of Virtue, procures us security from the attack of the lower Orders. – Alas! why should the lower Orders attack us, but because they are brutalized by Ignorance and rendered desperate by Want? And does Government remove this Ignorance by Education? And does not GOVERNMENT increase their want by Taxes? – Taxes rendered necessary by those national assassinations called Wars, and by that worst Corruption and Perjury, which a reverend Moralist has justified under the soft title of "secret Influence!" The poor Infant born in an English or Irish Hovel breathes indeed the air and partakes of the light of Heaven: but of its other Bounties he is disinherited. The

powers of Intellect are given him in vain: to make him work like a brute Beast he is kept as ignorant as a brute Beast. It is not possible that this despised and oppressed Man should behold the rich and idle without malignant envy. And if in the bitter cravings of Hunger the dark Tide of Passions should swell, and the poor Wretch rush from despair into guilt, then the GOVERNMENT indeed assumes the right of Punishment though it had neglected the duty of Instruction, and hangs the victim for crimes, to which its own wide-wasting follies and its own most sinful omissions had supplied the cause and the temptation. And yet how often have the fierce Bigots of Despotism told me, that the Poor are not to be pitied, however great their necessities: for if they be out of employ, the KING wants men! – They may be shipped off to the Slaughter-house abroad, if they wish to escape a Prison at home! – Fools! to commit ROBBERIES, and get hung, when they might MURDER with impunity – yea, and have Sixpence a day into the bargain!

(i) Slavery

He cites evidence concerning the effects of slavery that draws on eye-witness accounts.[33]

Perhaps from the beginning of the world the evils arising from the formation of imaginary wants have been in no instance so dreadfully exemplified as in the Slave Trade & the West India Commerce! We receive from the West Indias Sugars, Rum, Cotton, log-wood, cocoa, coffee, pimento, ginger, indigo, mahogany, and conserves – not one of these are necessary – indeed with the exception of cotton and mahogany we cannot with truth call them even useful, and not one is at present attainable by the poor and labouring part of Society. In return for them we export a vast quantity of necessary Tools, Raiment, and defensive Weapons – with great stores of provision – so that in this Trade as in most others, the poor with unceasing toil first raise and then are deprived of the comforts which they absolutely want in order to procure Luxuries which they must never hope to enjoy – If the Trade had never existed, no one human being would have been less comfortably cloathed, housed, or nourished – Such is its value – to estimate the price, we pay for it, it will be well to give a brief History of a slave-vessel and its contents – and first the manning – The wages, which able seamen receive in this Trade, are

very considerably greater than in any other – and there is no exception made to the most profligate character. That must be dreadful
indeed, to which unprincipled Avarice finds it necessary to hold out
such extraordinary Temptations – These however have little weight
with seamen so long as ships of any other description are fitting out
– the great Bulk of the Cargo are procured (according to Clarkson)
by the most infamous allurements. There are certain Landlords, who
allured by the high Wages given them in this trade, the advance
money of two months, and the promises of the merchant, open
houses for their reception. These, having a general knowledge of the
Ships and Seamen in the Port and being always on the look out
entice such as are more unwary or in greater distress than the rest
into their houses. They entertain them with Music and Dancing, and
keep them in an intoxicated state for some Time. In the interim the
Slave-merchant comes and makes his application – the unfortunate
men are singled out – their Bill is immediately brought them – they
are *said* to be more in debt than even two months' advance money
will discharge. They have therefore the alternative made them of a
Slave-vessel or a Gaol. While the crew are in this manner collecting,
the articles of agreement are prepared – some of which are too
iniquitous to be omitted. I extract them from Clarkson's Essay – The
first Clause is, that the Crew shall conform and demean themselves
in every respect according to the late act of Parliament for the better
regulation of Seamen in his *Majesty's* service. The fourth clause is,
That if they shall commence any action either at Common Law or at
a Court of Admiralty, either on account of any thing in these presents
contained, or on account of any other matter whatsoever that may
happen during the Voyage, without first referring it to the arbitra-
tion of the officers or owners within twenty Days after their arrival
at the port of discharge, they shall forfeit 50 pounds. In the first
Clause by the artful Substitution of the word Majesty's instead of
Merchant's service, and by the penalty contained in this last clause,
the officers think themselves authorised in inflicting the most savage
Punishments – so far Clarkson – Whether or not these Iniquities
have been discontinued since the late Regulations we do not know –
that before they took place, the Sailors were treated with hideous
cruelty there are unanswerable proofs. Nor indeed can any Regulations make it even probable that the men belonging to Slave-ships
can be treated <with> humanity – for the officers, employed as the
immediate Instrument of buying, selling and torturing human Flesh,
must from the moral necessity of circumstances become dead to

every feeling of confession. From the brutality of their Captain and the unwholesomeness of the Climate through which they pass, it has been calculated that every Slave Vessel from the Port of Bristol loses on an average almost a fourth of the whole Crew – and so far is this Trade from being a nursery for Seamen, that the Survivors are rather shadows in their appearance than men and frequently perish in Hospitals after the completion of the Voyage – many die in consequence of the excesses, with which [they indulge] themselves on Shore as compensations for the intolerable severities they undergo. In Jamaica many rather than re-embark for the<ir> native Country beg from door to door, and many are seen in the streets dying daily in an ulcerated state – and they who return home, are generally incapacitated for future service by a complication of Disorder[s] contracted from the very nature of the Voyage – so that these different accounts being added together, it was calculated that by the prosecution of the Slave Trade in the year 1786, not less than 1950 seamen were lost to the service of this Country. Thus were the objects of the Trade perfectly innocent, yet the means by which it is carried on are so destructive and iniquitous as to brand with ignominy every nation that tolerates it. But what is the Object! and how procured? The purchase of Man!

. . . Such is the infamous and detestable policy of the Europeans[:] they inoculate the petty tyrants of Africa with their own vices – they teach them new wants, to gratify which they bribe them to murder, that they themselves may inflict the most grievous ills of slavery upon the survivors – the wretched slaves taken on the field of battle, or snatched from the burning ruins of their villages are led down to the ships – they are examined stark naked male and female, and after being marked on the breast with a red hot iron, with the arms and names of the company or owner, who are the purchasers; they are thrust promiscuously into the ship – when on board they are always fettered with leg-shack[l]es & handcuffs, two and two – right and left – they lie in a crowded and cramped state, having neither their length nor breadth, we may form some idea of the hot & pestilent vapours arising from their confinement between the decks by the fact that the very timbers of the vessel are rotted by them, so that a slave ship is considered as lasting only half the time of another – so dreadful is this confinement between the decks, that slaves who have been thrust down at night in health have been brought up dead in the morning. These indeed are happy and the miserable survivors use every effort to obtain the same dreadful remedy – the negroes have been known to choak themselves by throwing back their tongues so <as> effectually to prevent respiration – others continue sullenly to refuse all food – for this resolution they are flogged, both their hands handcuffed, both their feet shackled – a collar with a chain fastened round the neck, and often that infernal engine of torture the thumb screw is applied – an engine so exquisitely cruel as to be used by the Spanish Inquisition – their allowance of water for the day is little more than a pint – in the afternoon they are made to dance, and flogged if they refuse – they have been heard to sing too in their captivity, and this has been mentioned as a proof that they cared little for slavery – but a witness who knew their language heard them sing, & their songs were songs of lamentation.

When the vessel arrives at its destined port, they are again exposed to sale & examined with an unfeeling indecency that may not be described – picked out at the pleasure of the purchaser – the wife is separated from her husband – the mother from her child and if they linger with each other at this moment of separation the lash is again applied. . . .

It would lacerate the feelings too much to detail the dreadful cruelties exercised upon the negro slaves. one law decrees that "after proclamation is issued against slaves that run away, it is lawful for any person whatever to kill and destroy such slaves by such ways and means as he shall think fit" – the author who records this adds One Gentleman, whilst I was abroad, *thought fit* to roast his slave alive.

The law of Barbadoes decrees "That if any negro under punishment by his master or his order, for running away, or any other misdemeanour, *shall suffer in life or member, no person whatever shall be liable to any fine* therefore. But if any man of *wantonness or bloody-mindedness or cruel intention, wilfully kill a negro* of his own, he shall pay into the public treasury, fifteen pounds sterling! and not be liable to any other punishment and forfeiture for the same.["]

It is calculated that one hundred and fifty thousand negroes are annually imported into the European colonies – add to these at least one fifth of the number who die during passage, and the long list of those murdered in the wars which the traffic occasions it is a catalogue of crimes and miseries that will leave an indelible spot upon human nature.

The diminution of the human species by this infernal trade mocks calculation –

. . . Mere men may shudder at heart-withering Wretchedness of their fellow-men – but Princes, Dukes, & Earls soar above these vulgar feelings, and I suppose are happy in the opportunity of proving that they have nothing in common with us, and that they are distinguished not by their Titles only, but by their superiority to all the weak feelings of Pity and Justice. The jealous spirit of Liberty placed the Elector of Hanover on the Throne of Britain and the Duke of Clarence one of his illustrious descendants, made his maiden speech in favour of the Slave Trade! – Enormities at which a Caligula might have turned pale, are authorised by our Legislature, and jocosely defended by our Princes – and yet (O Shame! where is thy Blush!) we have the impudence to call the French a Nation of *Atheists*! They who believe God, believe him to be the loving Parent of all men – and is it possible that they who really believe and fear the Father should fearlessly authorise the oppression of his children! the Slavery and tortures, and dreadful murders of tens of thousands of his Children.

. . . Had all the people who petitioned for the abolition of this execrable Commerce instead of bustling about and shewing off with all the vanity of pretended Sensibility, simply left off the use of Sugar and Rum, it is demonstrable that the Slave-merchants and Planters must either have applied to Parliament for the abolition of the Slave Trade or have suffered the West India Trade altogether to perish – a consummation most devoutly to be wished –

The Abbé Raynal computes that at the time of his writing 9000 nine millions of Slaves have been consumed by the Europeans. Add one million since for it is more than 20 years since he wrote his book – And recollect that for one slave procured ten at least are slaughtered that a fifth die in the passage and a third in seasoning and the unexaggerated computation will turn out that one hundred and eighty million of our fellow creatures have been murdered. Murdered! – That were friendly – Recollect that all these were torn from the bleeding breast of domestic affection, that each one had Wives, Brethren, Sons and Daughters – that each one of these suffered all the Horrors of Toil and Torture and that his greatest Transport was at the moment when his fellow Slaves danced around him a congratulatory Dance of Death. Culminate the sum total of Misery – and ye, who have caused it ask of yourselves this fearful Question – if the God of Justice inflicts on us that mass only of anguish which we have wantonly heaped on our Brethren what will Hell be? and who are they that have caused this misery? who are they that have joined in this Tartarean confederacy? where are these detested Kidnappers, Tyrants, Assassins who have done all this wrong – who have (as far as in them lay) first racked and then killed 180,000,000 men? In all reasonings neglecting the intermediate Lines ~~which~~ we must attributed the final effect to the first Cause and what is the first and constantly acting cause of the Slave Trade – that cause by which it exists and without which it would immediately die? Is it not self-evidently ~~a~~ the consumption of its Products! and does not then the Guilt rest on the Consumers? and is it not an allowed axiom in Morality That Wickedness may be multiplied but cannot be divided and that the Guilt of all attaches to each one who is knowingly an accomplice? For that each accomplice does not do more ill is owing to his want of opportunity – he does all he can – and what he does *not* do, is the Goodness of Providence, ~~is~~ not his own! There are two Classes of Men I wish that they were always one – Those who profess themselves Christians and those who (Christians or Infidels) profess themselves the zealous Advocates of Freedom! I address myself first of all to those who independent of political distinction profess themselves Christian[.] As you hope you live with Christ hereafter you are commanded to do unto others as ye would that others should do unto you! Would you choose that Slave Merchants should incite an intoxicated Chieftain to make War on your Tribe to murder your Wife and Children before your face and drag them with yourself to the Market – Would you choose to be sold, to have the hot iron hiss upon your breast, to be thrown down into the hold of a ship ironed with so many fellow victims so closely crammed together that the heat and stench arising from your diseased bodies should rot the very planks of the Ship? Would you choose to work sixteen hours a day to procure foolish Luxuries for others and be repaid for it with a red herring? Would you choose that *others* should do this unto you? and if you shudder with selfish Horror at the very thought do you yet dare to be the occasion of it to others! If one tenth part only of you [who] profess yourselves Christians, were to leave off not all the West India Commodities but only Sugar and Rum – the one useless and the latter pernicious all this Misery might be avoided – Gracious Heaven! at your meals you rise up and pressing your hands to your bosom ye lift up your eyes to God and say O Lord bless the Food which thou hast given us! A part of that Food among most of you is sweetened with the Blood of the Murdered. Bless the Food which thou hast given us! O Blasphemy! Did God give Food mingled with Brothers blood! Will the Father of all men bless the Food of Cannibals – the food which is polluted with the blood of his own innocent Children? Surely if the inspired Philanthropist of Galilee were to revisit earth and be among the feasters as at Cana he would not change Water into Wine but haply convert the produce into the things producing, the occasioned into the things occasioning! Then with our fleshly eye should we behold what even now truth-painting Imagination should exhibit to us – instead of sweetmeats Tears and Blood, and Anguish – and instead of Music groaning and the loud Peals of the Lash –

– Pause

And there are zealous Friends of Freedom who have heard these arguments even to Satiety, yet feel them not, or affecting to feel do not obey their dictates!

•   •   •

. . . True Benevolence is the only possible Basis of Patriotism, and I am afraid, that what with sensuality and Vanity, and yet more disgusting Pride – true Benevolence is a rare Quality among us. Sensibility indeed we have to spare – what novel-reading Lady does not over flow with it to the great annoyance of her Friends and Family – Her own sorrows like the Princes of Hell in Milton's Pandemonium sit enthroned bulky and vast – while the miseries of our fellow creatures dwindle ~~with~~ into pigmy forms, and are crowded, an unnumbered multitude, into some dark corner of the Heart where the eye of sensibility gleams faintly on them at long Intervals – But a keen feeling of trifling misfortunes is selfish cowardice not virtue.

But I have heard another argument in favor of the Slave Trade, namely, that the Slaves are as well off as the Peasantry in England! Now this argument I have [seen] in publications on the Subject – and were I the attorney General, I should *certainly* have prosecuted the author for sedition & treasonable Writings. For I appeal to common sense whether to affirm that the Slaves are as well off as our Peasantry, be not the same as to assert that our Peasantry are as bad off as Negro Slaves – and whether if the Peasantry believed it there is a man amongst them who [would] not rebel? and be justified in Rebellion?

Outrage at the trade in human beings continues to be expressed at intervals through his life.

On the freeing of his slaves in George Washington's will.[34]

Of a mixed nature, partly belonging to the patriot, and partly to the master of a family, is the humane, earnest, and solemn wish concerning the emancipation of the slaves on his estate. It explains, with infinite delicacy and manly sensibility, the true causes of his not having emancipated them in his life time; and should operate as a caution against those petty libellers, who interpret the whole of a character by a part, instead of interpreting a part by the whole. We feel ourselves at a loss which most to admire in this interesting paragraph, the deep and weighty feeling of the general principle of universal liberty; or the wise veneration of those fixed laws in society, without which that universal liberty must for ever remain impossible, and which, therefore, must be obeyed even in those cases, where they *suspend* the action of that general principle; or, lastly, the affectionate attention to the particular feelings of the slaves themselves, with the ample provision for the aged and infirm. Washington was no "architect of ruin!"

On treating slaves as things.[35]

In Trade, from its most innocent form to the abomination of the African commerce nominally abolished after a hard-fought battle of twenty years, no distinction is or can be acknowledged between Things and Persons. If the latter are part of the concern, they come under the denomination of the former. Two objects only can be proposed in the management of an Estate, considered as a *Stock* in Trade – first, that the Returns should be the largest, quickest, and securest possible; and secondly, with the least out-goings in the providing, over-looking, and collecting the same – whether it be expenditure of money paid for other men's time and attention, or of the tradesman's own, which are to him *money's worth*, makes no difference in the argument. Am I disposing of a bale of goods? The man whom I most love and esteem must yield to the stranger that outbids him; or if it be sold on credit, the highest price, with equal security, must have the preference. I may fill up the deficiency of my friend's offer by a private gift, or loan; but as a tradesman, I am bound to regard honesty and established character themselves, as *things*, as *securities*, for which the known unprincipled dealer may offer an unexceptionable substitute. Add to this, that the security being equal, I shall prefer, even at a considerable abatement of price, the man who will take a thousand chests or bales at once, to twenty who can pledge themselves only for fifty each. For I do not seek trouble for its own sake; but among other advantages I seek wealth for the sake of freeing myself more and more from the necessity of taking trouble in order to attain it. The personal worth of those, whom I benefit in the course of the Process, or whether the persons are really benefited or no, is no concern of mine. The Market and the Shop are open to all.

Do the vices of slaves constitute an excuse for slavery?[36]

THE VICES OF SLAVES NO EXCUSE FOR SLAVERY

It often happens, that the slave himself has neither the power nor the wish to be free. He is then *brutified*; but this apathy is the dire effect of slavery, and so far from being a justifying cause, that it contains the grounds of its bitterest condemnation. The Carolingian race bred up the Merovingi as beasts; and then assigned their unworthiness as the satisfactory reason for their dethronement. Alas! the human being is more easily weaned from the habit of commanding than from that of abject obedience. The slave loses his soul when he loses his master: even as the dog that has lost himself in the street, howls and whines till he has found the house again, where he had been kicked and cudgelled, and half-starved to boot. As we however or our ancestors must have inoculated our fellow-creatures with this wasting disease of the soul, it becomes our duty to cure him; and though we cannot immediately make him free, yet we can, and ought to, put him in the way of becoming so at some future time, if not in his own person yet in that of his children. The French are not capable of freedom. Grant this! but does this fact justify the ungrateful traitor, whose every measure has been to make them still more incapable of it?

A comment on the mingling of advertisements for runaway horses and runaway slaves in a Jamaica newspaper.[37]

What a History! Horses and Negroes! Negroes and Horses! It makes me tremble at my own Nature! – Surely, every religious and conscientious Briton is equally a debtor in gratitude to Thomas Clarkson, and his fellow labourers, with every African: for on the soul of every individual among us did a portion of guilt rest, as long as the slave trade remained legal.

(ii) Terror and Militarism

In 1795 the American patriots are defended for having resisted the dehumanising cruelty of British policy in the War of Independence.[38]

The principles industriously propagated by the friends of our Government are opposite to the American Constitution – and indeed to Liberty every where; and in order to form a just estimate of our excesses, let us recollect that prominent feature of the late War – *Scalping*!
. . . The Fiend, whose crime was Ambition, leapt over into this Paradise – Hell-hounds laid it waste. *English* Generals invited the Indians "to banquet on blood:" the savage Indians headed by an Englishman attacked it. Universal massacre ensued. The Houses were destroyed: the Corn Fields burnt: and where under the broad Maple trees innocent Children used to play at noontide, there the Drinkers of human Blood, and the Feasters on human Flesh were seen in horrid circles, counting their scalps and anticipating their gains. The English Court bought Scalps at a fixed price! SCALPING this *pious* Court deemed a fit punishment for the crimes of those, whose only crime was, that being Men, and the descendants of Britons, they had refused to be Slaves. Unconditional Submission was the only Terms offered to the Americans – and Death the immediate Menace. Our Brethren, (if indeed we may presume to call so exalted a race *our* Brethren,) indignantly rejected the terms, and resolved to hazard the execution of the menace. For this the Horrors of European Warfare afforded not a sufficient Punishment. Inventive in cruelty and undistinguishing in massacre, Savages must be hired against them: human Tygers must be called from their woods, their attacks regulated by Discipline, and their Ferocity increased by Intoxication. But did not this employment of merciless Scalpers rouse the indignation of Britons?

Contemplating fears of invasion in April 1798, Coleridge surveys the inhumanities perpetrated by his fellow-Englishmen.[39]

We have offended, Oh! my countrymen!
We have offended very grievously,
And been most tyrannous. From east to west
A groan of accusation pierces Heaven!
The wretched plead against us; multitudes
Countless and vehement, the sons of God,
Our brethren! Like a cloud that travels on,
Steamed up from Cairo's swamps of pestilence,
Even so, my countrymen! have we gone forth
And borne to distant tribes slavery and pangs,
And, deadlier far, our vices, whose deep taint
With slow perdition murders the whole man,
His body and his soul! Meanwhile, at home,
All individual dignity and power
Engulfed in Courts, Committees, Institutions,
Associations and Societies,
A vain, speech-mouthing, speech-reporting Guild,
One Benefit-Club for mutual flattery,
We have drunk up, demure as at a grace,
Pollutions from the brimming cup of wealth;
Contemptuous of all honourable rule,
Yet bartering freedom and the poor man's life
For gold, as at a market!

•   •   •

Alas! for ages ignorant of all
Its ghastlier workings, (famine or blue plague,
Battle, or siege, or flight through wintry snows,)
We, this whole people, have been clamorous
For war and bloodshed; animating sports,
The which we pay for as a thing to talk of,
Spectators and not combatants! No guess
Anticipative of a wrong unfelt,
No speculation on contingency,
However dim and vague, too vague and dim
To yield a justifying cause; and forth,
(Stuffed out with big preamble, holy names,
And adjurations of the God in Heaven.)

We send our mandates for the certain death
Of thousands and ten thousands! Boys and girls,
And women, that would groan to see a child
Pull off an insect's leg, all read of war,
The best amusement for our morning meal!
The poor wretch, who has learnt his only prayers
From curses, who knows scarcely words enough
To ask a blessing from his Heavenly Father,
Becomes a fluent phraseman, absolute
And technical in victories and defeats,
And all our dainty terms for fratricide;
Terms which we trundle smoothly o'er our tongues
Like mere abstractions, empty sounds to which
We join no feeling and attach no form!
As if the soldier died without a wound;
As if the fibres of this godlike frame
Were gored without a pang; as if the wretch,
Who fell in battle, doing bloody deeds,
Passed off to Heaven, translated and not killed:
As though he had no wife to pine for him,
No God to judge him!

Writing in The Courier *in 1816, he condemns German treatment of the Jews.*[40]

If it be true that the Senate of Lubeck have ordered the Jews settled
there to leave that city, we can only remark that Lubeck deserves to
be deprived of her title and privileges as a free and independent city.
In the first place, it is a direct violation of the 16th Article of the
German Confederation, by which it is declared that the Jews should
continue in the full enjoyment of all their present rights and privileges, and await a further decision. In the second place, it is a shocking outrage upon the principles of humanity and hospitality. It is not
pretended that this expulsion is for any crimes committed. But even
that charge could not apply to a whole community – to the aged, the
infirm, the female, and the infant. We have ever thought that the
treatment which the Jews have received has been a disgrace to all
countries and to all nations. The fate of never having a home – of
being a people without a people's country – of being dispersed over
every part of the world, is hard enough – But to have superadded the
fact of being treated as criminals and outcasts – of having the pun-

ishment of guilt without the commission of guilt – of having their very names pass into a synonym for all that is bad and tricking, and false and foul – to be the mock and scorn of the rabble – to have the "very dogs bark at them" as they pass, is a degree of suffering to which no race were ever exposed from the creation of the world – And this has been their lot for ages. If they have been hard and griping in their dealings, may it not have been occasioned by the treatment they have received? To treat men as if they were incapable of virtue is to make them so. If it be said that the Almighty has decreed them to be wanderers and outcasts, we reply that that Divine Being has no where told us to persecute them. If we wish to make them Christians, is persecution the best method? Is the severe treatment they have received from Christians the most likely way to dispose them in favour of the Christian Religion? We trust that a better and a kinder system will be adopted, and that if the age we live in, be in deeds, and not only in words, the enlightened age it is said to be, it will be shewn in a juster treatment of the Jews.

(iii) Industry and Trade

In 1806 Coleridge resolves to take up the cause of oppressed women workers.[41]

Let me try – that I may have at least one good thought to alleviate the pang of dying away – to pursue steadily the plan of opening the eyes of the public to the real situation of Needle-workers, and of women in general. Mary Lamb has promised me Facts in abundance.

Child labour becomes one of Coleridge's most passionate causes, perhaps also under the influence of Mary Lamb.

An inquiry in 1816 into the hours of work for children.[42]

Among the useful labours of the Select Committees of the House of Commons during last Session, one of the most useful perhaps was the inquiry into the *state of the children employed in manufactories*. It did, we must confess, excite other feelings besides those of surprise to find children employed in manufactories 13 hours a-day. Which, we ask, ought most to excite our surprise, that any parents can consign, or any manufactories receive children to be so employed?

We were quite pleased with the answer of Dr. Baillie, who, upon being asked, "At what age may children, without endangering their health, be admitted into factories, to be regularly employed 13 hours a-day, allowing them one hour and a half to go and return from meals, and one hour for instruction?" replied, "I should say, that there was no age, no time of life whatever, where that kind of labour could be compatible, in most constitutions, with the full mainten-ance of health." Certainly not: But for children to be employed so long! What time can they have for proper instruction – what for that which is necessary to health at that tender age, running about or playing in the open air? The confinement to one spot, to one posi-tion, cannot we should think but be injurious to faculties both [of] body and mind. But it is attempted in the examination before the Committee, to shew that such employment is not injurious. In one manufactory it is said, of 875 persons there were not more than from two to five deaths: and in another of 289 persons, two only died in 1815. Be it so, and allowing the full weight to these facts, we then say, that the injury to health might not be then visible, that no disease might then have broken out. But we ask, whether the very privation at that early age of that exercise in the open air, of those plays which are not more necessary to the amusement of children than to their health, may not, and does not lay the foundation of disorders, which may and must break out at a more advanced period of life?

Dr. Baillie thinks "that seven years old is the earliest age at which children ought to be employed in factories, and then only four or five hours a day; at eight and nine years of age, six and seven hours; afterwards they might be employed ten hours, and beyond that there ought to be no increase of labour."

His work on behalf of children in the cotton factories.[43]

Ill Health; two Lectures a week; humble, but as hireless as ardent, Efforts to support by my pen the hopeless cause of our poor little White-Slaves, the children in our cotton Factories, against the un-pitying cruel spirit of Trade, and the shallow heart-petrifying Self-conceit of our Political Economists, and the *Philosophy* of best name in this vast Temple of Mammon; – these and other Businesses of less Size but no less the imperious Creditors of my *time*, must be my excuse for not having called on you.

The case laid out in Swiftian terms in 1818.[44]

Sir,

As I understand it to be the intention of Mr. Phillips, and other distinguished and disinterested Members of the House of Commons, to oppose, *totis viribus*, a most pernicious and arbitrary Act, which is to be read a third time after the recess, and which is impudently declared to be a Bill for the Relief of the Children employed in Cotton Factories, permit me to second, as far as I am able, their pious endeavours, by pointing out the necessary comfort, health, and happiness, inherent in the present system of management in the many factories, which, like oaks, have attained their perfection by slow advances; but which, in proportion as their sources of nourishment are cut off, must inevitably languish and decay. Nor is this the only danger consequent to this measure, which I shall have the satisfaction of pointing out to the notice of your readers; for I trust I shall be able to inspire all reasonable men with horror, at a measure, which, by a fatal precedent, will open the door to legislative interference in other cases of free labour, and thus unhinge and overset the natural relations and competitions which maintain the due subordination, and social order of the State.

First then, I trust, your readers will readily admit, that the inconvenience of a *part* ought in every case to yield to the advantage of the *whole*; and if *so*, why this mischievous outcry about these helpless children, as they are called? Are they not employed for the general advantage? Besides, are they not kept from a state of idleness – the worst misfortune that can befall the age of infancy, by a healthful and innocent employment? Are they not living in warm comfortable rooms, at a temperature of 80 to 90 degrees, into which no drafts of air, so fatal in the production and increase of pulmonary complaints, are admitted? Here they are, not seated at their work, like clerks in a counting-house, but, in the gaiety of their hearts, suffered to run about during the day. What parent, let me ask, whose breast was animated with the tenderest affection, would, for an instant, hesitate, if he had it in his power, to let his children participate in what is not, in fact, labour, but ought rather to be called healthful exercise and recreation? But it is difficult to satisfy the over-scrupulousness of some minds. The advocates of this measure have asserted, that this recreation of fourteen or fifteen hours a day, is, forsooth, excessive! That the children frequently grow rickety, are afflicted with various fatal disorders, and die. But surely is not such unnecessary philanthropy sickening, and repulsive to the cultivated, and unprejudiced mind?

. . . Our population is already excessive. Even in this highly refined condition of society, have we sufficient bread for the multitude of poor unfortunate wretches, with which our streets and prisons are swarming, without depriving ourselves and families of this staff of our existence? Should we wish to increase the evil, when, even at this moment, with the rapid counteraction that our cotton factories afford, the poors' rates are felt as an intolerable load by all classes of the community? Besides, let me add, as a philosopher and a physiologist, that in infancy the feelings and sensations are by no means so acute, and that if they must suffer, and endure – and it is acknowledged by all hands to be the lot of the majority of mankind to suffer and endure – better let it be, when the misery is *least* acutely felt, and the frame will *most readily* sink exhausted beneath the burden. But this is the age of sensibilities, and the disease is epidemic. It has spread, like a pestilence, from the West Indies to our own shores; and now we hear of nothing, but charitable institutions for relieving the poor and impotent, instead of salutary laws for preventing their multiplication; our prisons, and madhouses, have been searched with indecent curiosity, as if no means whatever should be used for relieving the superabundant population; and now, as if to give a death-blow to our commerce, our cotton factories, in which so much capital is sunk, are to be stopped for two or three hours in each day, in order that children may be restored to that health, of which, if they were but sent young enough, as they could not know, so neither would they be able to estimate the loss.

But it has been urged that when these children are sinking under the fatigue of the employment, and are exhausted by the heat of the rooms, that the stick and the strap are applied by the overlookers to keep them to their duty. And where, let me ask, is the hardship or cruelty of this indispensable course of proceeding? Is not a state of discipline necessary to the well-being of every institution? At school, where, under other circumstances, they would probably be, is not the lash freely and frequently applied? Is it not the same on board our ships, and in our Bridewells? And are not warm rooms to be preferred to the cold and damp of a prison, which would assuredly be their fate were they not thus humanely rescued from destruction? But, should any legislative measure be enacted to restrict their labour to twelve hours a-day, I maintain that it will be an act of the basest ingratitude. What! when a body of spirited individuals come forward, in the most handsome manner, to lighten the burdens of the community by the employment of thousands, and to increase the wealth of the kingdom by supplying an article of the most extensive demand in our external commerce; and is this to be the return? Are they to be deprived, in a great measure, of the very means by which these national advantages are obtained? The money sunk in machinery is, for some hours in each day, to be unprolific, in order that children, from a mistaken humanity, may pass their time in *ennui*, and idleness. Here then, for a moment, let us pause, that the enlightened and unsophisticated reader may ponder upon the impolicy as well as the injustice of this measure, before I enter upon the last, but not least interesting portion of my letter.

It is of singular importance in this seat of liberty, that voluntary labour should be left free, and unshackled. Between the master and the servant there should be no restrictions whatever either on one side, or on the other. Competition is the life of trade, and trade, the sinews, bones, and muscles of the State. Now, nobody will deny that these children are free agents, capable of judging, whether their labour be commensurate with their strength, and whether or no the term of their employment be prejudicial to their health and comfort. Undoubtedly they are free agents; and as they have neither individually, nor collectively, petitioned Parliament to step forward for their protection, we have a right fairly to conclude, that they are well satisfied with their present condition, and that this is an act to which they have not given their sanction or concurrence. But this is not the first instance of legislative want of wisdom. There is another Act, either passing or passed the House, for the restriction of free labour. Climbing boys, as they are called, must, without any application from themselves, in these tearful times, be restricted in the exercise of their honest calling; and because of some few instances of unfortunate severity, which have been wantonly obtruded before the public eye, the trade is to suffer, and we are to be inconvenienced by the substitution of machines. It is in vain to dream of national prosperity, if such fetters are to be put upon free labour. If we once begin to legislate upon mere trifles, and matters of little importance, where shall we stop? Surely not until we have limited, from a tender regard for his health, the number of dishes on my Lord Mayor's table, and prescribe to him the hour at which he is to retire to bed.

But this legislation in cases of mere humanity is pregnant with fatal dangers to our most glorious Constitution. A renovated spirit of Luddism will infect these very children, whose present love and veneration for the machines, by which they are enabled to support their aged parents, can only be exceeded by the love and respect they bear towards their indulgent masters. But how fearfully will the scene be changed! Give them but the notion that they are under the protection of the laws, and instead of quietly piecing the yarn, and of cleaning the machinery during dinner, their little hearts will be beating high for radical reform, annual Parliaments, and universal suffrage.

Thus have I attempted, and I hope with some success, to open the public eye to its real interest. If this measure is to pass, our commerce will be materially injured; the interest of capital sunk in machinery will be comparatively unproductive; Luddism will enter, with blazing torch, the happy and peaceful retreats of our factories; and we shall have to choose between the suspension either of the Habeas Corpus, or of the Master Spinners of the town of Manchester. Let us then hear no more useless defences of Sir Robert Peel's Bill. I am willing, as you see, in the first instance, to try the effect of sound and serious argument; but should this fail, and the public be again stormed by a letter from Atticus, I shall be constrained to try the effect of ridicule, to laugh men out of their prejudices, and thus dissipate all this silly alarm about the health, comfort, and moral condition of little children.

PLATO

(c) HUMAN EVIL

Although Coleridge explored the daily failures of human beings to sustain their humanness, arguing that false values inculcated by eighteenth-century materialism led many to mistreat others, his mind circled incessantly around the question of human evil. The question is inherent in the poem that first propelled him into fame, 'The Rime of the Ancient Mariner', which begins with the commission of a wanton evil deed prompted apparently by an unthinking impulse on the part of the mariner. In the allegorical narrative that follows, the harmony of man and nature is broken and an unending sequence of punishment and suffering initiated. The question of human evil continued to haunt the ambiguities of the subtly devised 'Christabel'. Both poems may be seen as explorations of the origins of evil in an individual's lack of insight and of the complicity of good but weak people in the evil actions of others. As the extracts in this section indicate, Coleridge believed in original sin, in the depravity of man, and in the necessity of some myth of the fall to account not only for active evil but also for everyday viciousness.

Only for a brief time had he hoped that environment alone might explain these 'lapses'.

Coleridge's fascination with 'great bad men' (to use Stephen Bygrave's phrase[45]) led him to examine the evil principle at work in actions both historical and fictional. When he analysed the psychology of Shakespeare's villains Iago and Edmund, or of Milton's Satan, he used the same penetration into the labyrinths of human depravity as in his examinations of Robespierre, Napoleon and other tyrants. While his description of Iago's behaviour as 'the motive-hunting of motiveless Malignity'[46] is well-known, his analysis of Edmund in *King Lear* also demonstrated a striking understanding of the complex springs of evil: goaded by his father's 'degrading and licentious Levity' about his illegitimate birth, Edmund suffered 'the ever-trickling flow of Wormwood and gall into the wounds of Pride – the corrosive Virus which inoculates Pride with a venom not its own, with Envy, Hatred, a lust of that Power which in its blaze or radiance would hide the dark spots on his disk – pangs of shame, personally undeserved, and therefore felt as wrongs – and a blind ferment of vindictive workings toward the occasions and causes'.[47] Similar penetration into secret viciousness characterises Coleridge's analyses of contemporary living villains whose nature he had perceived from their public words and deeds. He was prophetic of modern students of human wickedness such as Mary Midgley in seeing evil as the result of projecting one's own evil on to another by self-duplicity and self-deception, or, in Simone Weil's formulation, as the 'gloomy, monotonous, barren, boring' result of 'emptiness at the core of the individual'.[48]

Coleridge's belief in original sin grew during his lifetime, drawing both on Jacob Boehme, who saw evil as 'the centrifugal falling-away from God, the centre, when one becomes the many', and on Schelling's *Of Human Freedom* (1805), which pictured the human will as 'anchored in the irrational creative ground, the power of darkness'.[49] Lockridge summarises the inevitability of evil that arises, in Coleridge's view, in the exercise of free will: 'since human freedom means in its essence the freedom to separate oneself from the will of God, the free and active personality is by definition presumptuous'.[50] Coleridge's clearest statement of 'satanic pride and rebellious self-idolatry'[51] appeared in the *Lay Sermons*. In his late theology, as enunciated in *Aids to Reflection*, acknowledgement of human depravity was set firmly at the heart of the need for religious faith.

Despite his adherence to a doctrine of original sin, however, he was shocked at the image of a God who would punish the children for the deeds of their first parents; to have to take the blame for such sin as 'original' seemed clearly unjust.[52] This problem he attempted to solve by reading 'Adam' as the genus Man and finding within all people the rebellious will as part of their inherent nature. 'Original sin' originates in the will of everyone in turn; it is 'original' in the sense that it is a fresh beginning, rather than the continuation of a previous chain of guilt. Each individual originates evil when he or she acts according to the Will in disregard of Reason. In originating acts that are evil or otherwise, moreover, human beings affirm their distinction from nature, which originates nothing, but continues in a chain of mechanism of cause and effect. (See extracts from *Aids to Reflection*.) Persons can forfeit their free will by choosing to sink into the chain of circumstances, becoming beasts or things, but (unless one is a maniac) doing so is itself one choice among many.

As Coleridge looked at the political scene, he saw evil operating through false sentimentality, cynicism, distrust and terror. He noted the inhuman coldness of William Pitt, but also saw his power facilitated by 'the short-sightedness of the careful; the carelessness of the far-sighted'.[53] The errant will exhibited itself not only in crimes against others and the self, but also in quotidian failures of sympathy and resolve, sometimes disguised in the false morality of prudence, a calculating self-interest that alienates one from one's fellow-beings and narrows one's vision. The word 'prudent', which continued to mean wise, sapient, judicious, using forethought and careful deliberation, gathered its negative connotations only during this period: the earliest such example in the *Oxford English Dictionary*, indeed, is from Coleridge himself in 1833; yet he had already been using it for decades (as did Jane Austen in *Pride and Prejudice*) to characterise those who follow the most politic and profitable course, are skilful in adapting means to ends, or, more generally, calculate their self-advancement with a shrewd coldness lacking spontaneous generosity of heart. He did not need to look far from home to find such prudence. His friends Southey and Wordsworth, in particular, demonstrated the hard-heartedness that could come from prosperity or ambition for it. Of Wordsworth's happy marriage Coleridge wrote, 'A blessed Marriage is the intensest sort of Prosperity, & all Prosperity, I find, hardens the Heart – and happy people become so *very prudent* & far-sighted.'[54] In Southey he early noted 'callousness in personal feelings', 'blunt-ness of conscience', 'self-centering Resolve'. The materialism of the age contributed to this 'bluntness of conscience': Too continuous an attention to objects 'ossified' or 'paralysed' 'the imaginative powers'; so also the 'habitual slavery to the eye', relying on the outward rather than the inward sense, led to a 'hardness and heart-hardening spirit of contempt', and 'debased [the] moral being'.[55]

In a lecture of 1795 Coleridge inveighs against the many forms of evil involved in prosecuting the war against France, including the selfishness and indifference of ordinary people not immediately touched by the war.[56]

Thus from the influence of the understanding they continued to do what the heart sickened at; but a course of action, which the heart disapproves, will vitiate the heart and make it callous: and when the heart is vitiated, the understanding will not long remain pure. But TERROR intoxicates more than strong wine; with the which, who forcibly drenches another man, is the real cause and sole responsible agent of all the excesses, which in the hour of drunkenness he shall have committed. It was a truth easily discovered, a truth on which our Minister has proceeded, that valour and victory would not be the determiners of this War. *They* would prove finally successful whose resources enabled them to hold out the longest. The commerce of France was annihilated; her money'd-men were slow and cold from that selfishness, with which Mammon fails not to incrust the heart of his votaries. Immense armies were to be supported – immense to the confusion of the faith of posterity. Alas! Freedom weeps . . .

. . . finally, of us will justice require a dreadful account of whatever guilt France has perpetrated, of whatever miseries France has endured. Are we men? Freemen? rational men? And shall we carry on this wild and priestly War against reason, against freedom, against human nature? If there be one among you, who departs from me without feeling it his immediate duty to petition or remonstrate against the continuance of it, I envy that man neither his head or his heart!

There is observable among the Many a false and bastard sensibility that prompts them to remove those evils and those evils alone, which by hideous spectacle or clamorous outcry are present to their senses, and disturb their selfish enjoyments. Other miseries, though equally certain and far more horrible, they not only do not endeavour to remedy – they support, they fatten on them. Provided the dunghill be not before their parlour window, they are well content to know that it exists, and that it is the hot-bed of their pestilent luxuries. – To this grievious failing we must attribute the frequency of wars, and the continuance of the Slave-trade. The merchant finds no argument against it in his ledger: the citizen at the crouded feast is not nauseated by the stench and filth of the slave-vessel – the fine lady's nerves are not shattered by the shrieks! She sips a beverage sweetened with human blood, even while she is weeping over the refined sorrows of Werter or of Clementina. Sensibility is not Benevolence. Nay, by making us tremblingly alive to trifling misfortunes, it frequently prevents it, and induces effeminate and cowardly selfishness. Our own sorrows, like the Princes of Hell in Milton's Pandemonium, sit enthroned "bulky and vast:" while the miseries of our fellow-creatures dwindle into pigmy forms, and are crouded, an innumerable multitude, into some dark corner of the heart.

Writing in The Courier *in 1811, he notes the prostration of the soul before power.*[57]

The error, which of all others most besets the public mind, and which yet of all others is the most degrading in its nature, the most tremendous in its consequences, is an inward prostration of the soul before enormous power, and a readiness to palliate and forget all iniquities to which prosperity has wedded itself; as if man was only a puppet without reason and free-will, and without the conscience which is the offspring of their union, a puppet played off by some unknown power! as if success were the broad seal of Divine approbation, and tyranny itself the Almighty's inauguration of a Tyrant!

In several notebook entries between 1803 and 1815 (the second of which recalls The Ancient Mariner) *he grapples with the subtle nature of evil.*[58]

I will at least make the attempt to explain to myself the Origin of moral Evil from the *streamy* Nature of Association, which Thinking = Reason, curbs & rudders / how this comes to be so difficult / Do not the bad Passions in Dreams throw light & shew of proof upon this Hypothesis? – Explain those bad Passions: & I shall gain Light, I am sure – A Clue! A Clue! – an Hecatomb à la Pythagoras, if it unlabyrinths me. – Dec. 28, 1803 – Beautiful luminous Shadow of my pencil point following it from the Candle – rather going before it & illuminating the word, I am writing. 11 o'clock / – But take in the blessedness of Innocent Children, the blessedness of sweet Sleep, &c &c &c: are these or are they not contradictions to the evil from *streamy* association? – I hope not: all is to be thought *over* and *into* – but what is the height, & ideal of mere association? – Delirium. – But how far is this state produced by Pain & Denaturalization? And what are these? – In short, as far as I can see any thing in this Total Mist, Vice is imperfect yet existing Volition, giving diseased Currents of association, because it yields on all sides & *yet* is – So think of Madness: – O if I live! Grasmere, Dec. 29. 1803.

Hawk with ruffled Feathers resting on the Bowsprit – Now shot at & yet did not move – how fatigued – a third time it made a gyre, a short circuit, & returned again / 5 times it was thus shot at / left the Vessel / flew to another / & I heard firing, now here, now there / & nobody shot it / but probably it perished from fatigue, & the attempt to rest upon the wave! – Poor Hawk! O Strange Lust of Murder in Man! – It is not cruelty / it is mere ~~un~~ non-feeling from non-thinking.

Friday, Nov. 23, 1804.
One of the heart-depraving Habits & Temptations of men in power, as Governors, &c &c is to make *instruments* of their fellow-creatures – & the moment, they find a man of Honor & Talents, instead of loving & esteeming him, they wish to *use him* / hence that self-betraying side & down look of cunning &c – and they justify & inveterate the habit by believing that every individual who approaches has selfish designs upon them.

Neither must we divide *men* too much – even the poor & most sinful Sinner is still a *man* – and tho' he needs the terror of menace, & selfish motives, he is yet capable of being operated on additionally by the higher impulse of Conscience & Love – in order, without *some* impulse of this kind he never would *believe* a hereafter sufficiently to be acted on by the former –. Never therefore strip any man of his *humanity* – Whatever is in man, he has, however imperfectly developed, however filmed or obstructed –

Those who think lowliest of themselves, perhaps with a *feeling* stronger than rational comparison would justify, are apt to feel & express undue asperity for the Faults or Defects of those whom they habitually have looked up to as their Superiors – For placing themselves very low, perhaps too low, whenever a series of experiences, struggled against for a while, have at length convinced the mind, that in such & such a moral habit the long idolized Superior is far below even itself, the grief & anger will be in proportion – "If even I could never done this, O anguish! that HE, so much my Superior, should do it – if even I with all my infirmities have not this defect, this selfishness, that HE should have it –" –

    This is the course of thought – Men are bad enough; & yet they often think themselves worse than they are; among other causes, by a reaction from their own uncharitable Thoughts of others – The poisoned Chalice is brought back to our own Lips – May 23, 1808.

An idea has just occurred to me – it seems important. Is not *Sin*, or Guilt, the first thing that makes the idea of *a* God necessary, instead of το θειον [the divine] – therefore is not the incarnation a beautiful consequence & revelation of the το θειον [the divine] first revealing itself as ὁ Θεος [God]? The idea escapes from me as I write it; purify the mind by humility & self consciousness wholly *retrospective*, & again try to retrace it. To see the Gospel in a new light again – & again read Spinoza – to think vices mere necessitated movements, relative only as stench or roughness, we *know* to be false – but take it in the Kantean idea, as the Anti-type of a the moral Law – suppose it like Cohesion – as that simply causing coherence, so this essentially demanding *morality* – & what becomes of Sinners? I feel the Clouds – yet sure there is something here. –

O me! there are Secrets of so painful a nature, that like hatched Insects <they> would fain eat their way out of the Heart; but meeting with a strong kind of Fear & Pity and Delicacy & ignorance in what way to relieve the anguish, ~~of~~ which the disclosure would inflict on a noble soul already too unhappy, turn round and seem to eat their way in & to the depth of the Heart! – Good cannot come from evil – and the Eye is a Window not only from which the Soul sees, but thro' which it may be seen! Closed Shutters & locked Doors are but Transparencies, I find, to an Observer, whose penetration has been perfected by much experience!

In a letter to his brother George in 1798 he avows his belief in original sin and in a human 'darkening' from the womb.[59]

Of Guilt I say nothing; but I believe most steadfastly in original Sin; that from our mothers' wombs our understandings are darkened; and even where our understandings are in the Light, that our organization is depraved, & our volitions imperfect; and we sometimes see the good without *wishing* to attain it, and oftener *wish* it without the energy that wills & performs – And for this inherent depravity, I believe, that the *Spirit* of the Gospel is the sole cure.

The belief is restated more emphatically in his 1810 'Confession of Faith' and analysed again in Aids to Reflection.[60]

4.   I believe, and hold it as the fundamental article of Christianity, that I am a fallen creature; that I am of myself capable of moral evil, but not of myself capable of moral good, and that Guilt is justly imputable to ~~be~~ me prior to any given act, or assignable moment of time, in my Consciousness. I am born a child of Wrath. This fearful Mystery I pretend not to understand – I cannot even conceive the possibility of it – but I know, that it is so! My Conscience, the sole fountain of certainty, commands me to believe it, and would itself be a contradiction, were it not so – and what is real, must be possible.

. . . I profess a deep conviction that Man was and is a *fallen* Creature, not by accidents of bodily constitution, or any other cause, which *human* Wisdom in a course of ages might be supposed capable of removing; but diseased in his *Will*, in that Will which is the true and only strict synonime of the word, I, or the intelligent Self.

Writing to Joseph Cottle in 1815, he distinguishes between crime and vice, and links the latter with addiction.[61]

If you should have time to look over Dr Williams' larger work, in addition to what I have remarked in the slips of Paper, you will not fail to observe a sophism grounded on the admitted fact of the incapability to act aright in minds habitually vicious. This, we all know, constitutes the difference between a crime and a vice: and makes the latter, even tho' comparatively trifling in each individual act, more hopeless and therefore of deeper Evil than any single Crime, however great: if only it be not such as involves as the condition of it's possibility, a prior vicious Habit. This, I long ago observed, is the dire Curse of all habitual Immorality, that the impulses wax as the motives wane – like animals caught in the current of a Sea-vortex, (such as the Norwegian Maelstrohm) at first they rejoice in the pleasurable ease with which they are carried onward, with their consent yet without any effort of their will – as they swim, the servant gradually becomes the Tyrant, and finally they are sucked onward against their will: the more they see their danger, with the greater and more inevitable rapidity are they hurried toward and into it –. Now from this fact Dr Williams deduces, that the inability to will good is no excuse for not doing so – in genere, and without reference to the *origin* of the inability – forgetting that our conscience never condemns us for what we cannot help unless this *"cannot in praesenti"* is the result of a *"would not a preterito"* – all moral Evil is either *cum* voluntate or *de* voluntate –. N.B. a voluntas causata is a contradiction, unless as causa sui. – Take Dr Williams's own instances – suppose the man stated as utterly incapable of loving God to have been created with this incapability, and you no more blame him than you blame a rattle snake for his Poison. – All Law human and divine acknowledges this distinction – as in the criminality of murder committed in drunkenness, and the impunibility of the same act committed in madness –.

In a philosophical lecture he argues against the Socratic doctrine that to know the good is to do it.[62]

The great point which Socrates laid down was this, that ignorance was the ground of all vice and therein of all misery, and that knowledge on the contrary was the source of all virtue and therein of all happiness. To this object he constantly tended, but it was evident to a thinking man that either it was an argument in a circle, or it led to the destruction of the very essence of virtue. For if he meant, which he could not, that no man does a crime knowing it to be a crime and knowing that its effect will be a disproportionate one to the misery, to his future being, compared to the gratification he immediately receives from it, it is notoriously false. Every drunkard that lifts with trembling hands his glass to his lips and even sheds tears over it, knowing the anguish it will occasion, is a proof against it. No, it is impossible as the whole experience of the world shews. It is not an ignorance of the effects that will arise from it, but to get rid of the pain arising from the want of it, and that just in proportion as the pleasure declines, so the temptation, as it is called, or the motive, becomes equal; then does the good, become most tremendous. Not a single ray of pleasure beforehand, but the daily round of habit from behind, *that* presses on the human mind. It could not be taken, therefore, in this sense. For we all know, we are so well persuaded in our own mind, that what we call criminals are aware at the time they commit the crime both of its criminality and of its consequences to themselves, that wherever we can make out a fair case of compleat ignorance, we acquit the being of guilt and place him either as an idiot, or a madman, or as by law we do, as a child. So little is it possible that in this sense vice can originate, properly speaking, in ignorance. But if on the other hand Socrates meant that vice was not possible, was not compatible with the clear perfect insight into the very nature of the action of the soul, and such a commanding idea to the mind as comprises a perfect science, how is this to be given? For his great doctrine was that it could be taught. The only answer to be made was: it must be given to a mind predisposed to it. And hence he uses the word *apatheia*, not *ignoria*, for ignorance. This is merely a concession of the point in dispute, for then there is something attached to knowledge and the condition of it, not knowledge itself, which is necessary to make this knowledge efficacious or influential. So that in truth we see that knowledge without this is without avail. And therefore the foundation of virtue must be laid in something to which knowledge indeed is highly natural, which in its general effects must lead to knowledge, but which in itself is a higher principle than knowledge; <*it must be*> placed, namely, in the will, if I may venture to use such a phrase, and in that religion which is innate in man only because it is felt by the very necessity of it.

A meditation in the 1809 Friend *on power, absence of principle and 'villainy entrenched and barricadoed by villainy'.*[63]

Often have I reflected with awe on the great and disproportionate power, which an individual of no extraordinary talents or attainments may exert, by merely throwing off all restraint of Conscience. What then must not be the power, where an Individual, of consummate wickedness, can organize into the unity and rapidity of an individual will, all the natural and artificial forces of a populous and wicked nation? And could we bring within the field of imagination, the devastation effected in the moral world, by the violent removal of old customs, familiar sympathies, willing reverences, and habits of subordination almost naturalized into instinct, the mild influences of reputation, and the other ordinary props and aidances of our infirm Virtue, or at least, if Virtue be too high a name, of our well-doing; and above all, if we could give form and body to all the effects produced on the Principles and Dispositions of Nations by the infectious feelings of Insecurity, and the soul-sickening sense of Unsteadiness in the whole Edifice of civil Society; the horrors of Battle, though the miseries of a whole War were brought together before our eyes in one disastrous Field, would present but a tame Tragedy in comparison.*

If then the power with which Wickedness can invest the human being be thus tremendous, greatly does it behove us to enquire into its Source and Causes. So doing we shall quickly discover that it is not Vice, as Vice, which is thus mighty; but *systematic* Vice! Vice self-consistent and entire; Crime corresponding to Crime; Villainy entrenched and barricadoed by Villainy; this is the condition and main cons[ti]tuent of its power. The abandonment of all *Principle* of Right enables the Soul to chuse and act upon a *Principle* of Wrong, and to subordinate to this one Principle all the various Vices of Human nature. For it is a mournful Truth, that as Devastation is incomparably an easier Work than Production, so all its means and instruments may be more easily arranged into a scheme and System. Even as in a Siege every Building and Garden which the faithful Governor must destroy as impeding the defensive means of the Garrison, or furnishing means of Offence to the Besieger, occasions a Wound in feelings which Virtue herself has fostered: and Virtue, because it is Virtue, loses perforce part of her energy in the reluctance, with which she proceeds to a business so repugnant to her wishes, as a choice of Evils. But He who has once said with his whole heart, Evil be thou my Good! has removed a world of Obstacles by the very decision, that he will have no Obstacles but those of force and brute matter. . . . Happily for Mankind, however, the obstacles which a consistent evil mind no longer finds in itself, it finds in its own unsuitableness to Human nature. A limit is fixed to its power: but within that limit, both as to the extent and duration of its influence, there is little hope of checking its career, if giant and united Vices are opposed only by mixed and scattered Virtues, and those too, probably, from the want of some combining Principle, which assigns to each its due Place and Rank, at civil War with themselves, or at best

---

* Nay, it would even present a sight of comfort and of elevation, if this Field of Carnage were the sign and result of a national Resolve, of a general Will so to die, that neither Deluge nor Fire should take away the name of Country from their Graves, rather than to tread the same clods of Earth, no longer a Country, and themselves alive in nature but dead in infamy. What is Greece at this present moment? It is the Country of the Heroes from Codrus to Philopæmen; and so it would be, though all the Sands of Africa should cover its Corn Fields and Olive Gardens, and not a Flower left on Hybla for a Bee to murmur in.

perplexing and counteracting each other. Thus even in the present Hour of Peril we may hear even good Men painting the horrors and crimes of War, and softening or staggering the minds of their Brethren by details of individual wretchedness; thus under pretence of avoiding Blood, withdrawing the will from the defence of the very source of those blessings without which the blood would flow idly in our veins! thus lest a few should fall on the Bulwarks in glory, preparing us to give up the whole State to baseness, and the children of free Ancestors to become Slaves, and the Fathers of Slaves.

The story of Maria, raped in a churchyard near her father's grave, demonstrates a 'madness of the heart'.[64]

I have sate for some minutes with my pen resting: I can scarce summon the courage to tell, what I scarce know, whether I ought to tell. Were I composing a Tale of Fiction, the Reader might justly suspect the purity of my own heart, and most certainly would have abundant right to resent such an incident, as an outrage wantonly offered to his imagination. As I think of the circumstance, it seems more and more like a distempered dream: but alas! what is guilt so detestable other than a dream of madness, that worst madness, the madness of the heart? I cannot but believe, that the dark and restless passions must first have drawn the mind in upon themselves, and as with the confusion of imperfect sleep, have in some strange manner taken away the sense of reality, in order to render it possible for a human being to perpetrate what it is too certain that human beings have perpetrated.

The assertion that sin cannot arise by force of circumstance, rather that 'original sin' is forever originating in the human powers of each individual, provides a central argument in Aids to Reflection.[65]

The *Christian* likewise grounds *his* philosophy on assertions [which] are in immediate reference to three ultimate *Facts*; namely, the Reality of the LAW OF CONSCIENCE; the existence of a RESPONSIBLE WILL, as the subject of that law; and lastly, the existence of EVIL – of Evil essentially such, not by accident of outward circumstances, not derived from its physical consequences, nor from any cause, out of itself. The first is a Fact of Consciousness; the second a Fact of Reason necessarily concluded from the first; and the third a Fact of History interpreted by both.

A Sin is an Evil which has its ground or origin in the Agent, and not in the compulsion of Circumstances. Circumstances are compulsory from the absence of a power to resist or control them: and if this absence likewise be the effect of Circumstance (*i.e.* if it have been neither directly or indirectly caused by the Agent himself) the Evil *derives* from the Circumstances; and therefore (in the Apostle's sense of the word, Sin, when he speaks of the exceeding sinfulness of Sin) such *evil* is not *sin*; and the person who suffers it, or who is the compelled instrument of its infliction on others, may feel *regret*, but cannot feel *remorse*. So likewise of the word origin, original, or originant. The reader cannot too early be warned that it is not applicable, and, without abuse of language, can never be applied, to a mere *link* in a chain of effects, where each, indeed, stands in the relation of a *cause* to those that follow, but is at the same time the *effect* of all that precede. For in these cases a cause amounts to little more than an antecedent. At the utmost it means only a *conductor* of the causative influence: and the old axiom, Causa causæ causa causati, applies, with a never-ending regress to each several link, up the whole chain of nature. But this (as I have elsewhere shown at large) *is* Nature: and no *Natural* thing or act can be called originant, or be truly said to have an *origin* in any other. The moment we assume an Origin in Nature, a true *Beginning*, an actual First – that moment we rise *above* Nature, and are compelled to assume a *supernatural* Power. (Gen. i. 1.)

For if it be Sin, it must be *original*: and a State or Act, that has not its origin in the will, may be calamity, deformity, disease, or mischief; but a *Sin* it cannot be. It is not enough that the Act appears voluntary, or that it is intentional; or that it has the most hateful passions or debasing appetite for its proximate cause and accompaniment. All these may be found in a Mad-house, where neither Law nor Humanity permit us to condemn the Actor of Sin. The Reason of Law declares the Maniac not a Free-Agent; and the Verdict follows of course – Not guilty. Now Mania, as distinguished from Idiocy, Frenzy, Delirium, Hypochondria, and Derangement (the last term used specifically to express a suspension or disordered state of the Understanding or Adaptive Power) is the Occultation or Eclipse of Reason, as the Power of ultimate ends. The Maniac, it is well known, is often found clever and inventive in the selection and adaptation of means to *his* ends; but his *ends* are madness. He has lost his Reason. For though Reason, in finite Beings, is not the Will – or how could the Will be opposed to the Reason? – yet is the *condition*, the *sine qua non* of a *Free*-will.

Sin is Evil having an *Origin*. But inasmuch as it is *evil*, in God it cannot originate: and yet in some *Spirit* (*i.e.* in some *supernatural* power) it *must*. For in *Nature* there is no origin. Sin therefore is spiritual Evil: but the spiritual in Man is the Will. Now when we do not refer to any particular Sins, but to that state and constitution of the Will, which is the ground, condition, and common Cause of all Sins; and when we would further express the truth, that this corrupt *Nature* of the Will must in some sense or other be considered as its own act, that the corruption must have been self-originated; – in this case and for this purpose we may, with no less propriety than force, entitle this dire spiritual evil and source of all evil, that is absolutely such, Original Sin. (I have said, "the corrupt *Nature* of the Will." I might add, that the admission of a *Nature* into a spiritual essence by its own act *is* a corruption.)

Satanic pride and remorseless despotism as characterised in historic figures.[66]

But neither can reason or religion exist or co-exist as reason and religion, except as far as they are actuated by the WILL (the platonic Θυμός,) which is the sustaining, coercive and ministerial power, the functions of which in the individual correspond to the officers of war and police in the ideal Republic of Plato. In its state of immanence (or indwelling) in reason and religion, the WILL appears indifferently, as wisdom or as love: two names of the same power, the former more intelligential, the latter more spiritual, the former more frequent in the Old, the latter in the New Testament. But in its utmost abstraction and consequent state of reprobation, the Will becomes satanic pride and rebellious self-idolatry in the relations of the spirit to itself, and remorseless despotism relatively to others; the more hopeless as the more obdurate by its subjugation of sensual impulses, by its superiority to toil and pain and pleasure; in short, by the fearful resolve to find in itself alone the one absolute motive of action, under which all other motives from within and from without must be either subordinated or crushed.

This is the character which Milton has so philosophically as well as sublimely embodied in the Satan of his Paradise Lost. Alas! too often has it been embodied in *real* life! Too often has it given a dark and savage grandeur to the historic page! And wherever it has appeared, under whatever circumstances of time and country, the same ingredients have gone to its composition; and it has been identified by the same attributes. Hope in which there is no Chearfulness; Stedfastness within and immovable Resolve, with outward Restlessness and whirling Activity; Violence with Guile; Temerity with Cunning; and, as the result of all, Interminableness of Object with perfect Indifference of Means; these are the qualities that have constituted the COMMANDING GENIUS! these are the Marks, that have characterized the Masters of Mischief, the Liberticides, and mighty Hunters of Mankind, from NIMROD to NAPOLEON. And from inattention to the possibility of such a character as well as from ignorance of its elements, even men of honest intentions too frequently become fascinated.

In several notebook entries Coleridge analyses the selfish prudence and expedience encouraged by the teachings of writers such as William Paley and visible in the conduct even of Wordsworth.[67]

Among the countless arguments against the Paleyans state this too – Can a wise Moral Legislator have made *Prudence* the true principle, ground, and guide of moral conduct, when in almost all cases in which there is any temptation to act wrong, the first appearances of Prudence are in favor of immorality – and to ground the contrary on a principle of Prudence, it is necessary to refine, to calculate, to look far onward into an uncertain future – Is this a guide, a primary guide, that forever requires a guide against itself? – Is it not a strange system which sets prudence against prudence? – Compare this with the *Law* of *Conscience* – is it not its specific character, to be immediate, positive, unalterable? – In short a priori state the requisites of a moral guide – apply them 1st to Prudence – & then to the Law of pure Reason or Conscience – & we need [not] fear the result, if the Judge is pure from all bribes, & prejudice.

Shew likewise that this preference of prudence, or distant to immediate prudence, of magnitude imagined & judged of by faintness, to a lesser understood but greater apparent magnitude with vividness & immediate action on the senses & passions, is impossible for men in general without a moral principle – that these cases of calculation in honest men are really nothing but Conscience acting in an unworthy disguise –

Draw the difference between the greater, if we arrive at – and the greater, for the present & which really is – detract from the distant magnitude an equivalent for its uncertainty, (this to the Judgment) and another for its faintness – (this to the feelings) – and what is to decide our choice? – O assuredly, before we set about making the comparison, we knew and felt, ~~before~~ that the one was *right* and the other *wrong* – and this it is that enables us to prefer the former, nay, it is this which enables us even to pause long enough to meet the calculation – an uneasiness, a sad misgiving at the inmost heart throws *a damp* over the vivid flame of the present advantage, ~~and~~ or the wall of *flame* would shut out all distance as effectually as a Wall of *Stone* . . .

Prudence – what are its real dictates as drawn from every man's experience in late manhood, and sobered from the intoxication of youth, hope & love – how cold, how dead'ning; what a dire vacuum they would leave in the soul – if the high and supreme sense of Duty did not form a root, out of which other Prospects budded – *Ex. gr.* – a fair review of what I hoped, believed, seemed to *know* & *possess*, of my friendship & attachment to & with Asra Hutchinson and the "Grasmerians" – !! !! – "Dorothy" !! – and above all the deadly disappointment in Mary. Yet such must be the result of all full reliance on human Love, or human fidelity! – What <then> is the clear dictate of *Prudence*? Assuredly, to *like* only, – & never to be so attached as to be stript naked by the Loss – A Friend may be a great Coat – a Beloved a Couch – but never, never, our necessary cloathing, our only means of quiet Heart-repose! – And yet with this the mind of a generous Man would be so miserable, that Prudence itself would fight against Prudence – & advise to drink off the draft of Hope spite of the horrid & bitter dregs of Disappointment, <with> which ~~assuredly will end~~ the draught will assuredly finish!

A most important truth, that the Law of Justice, that is, of unconditional Obedience to the Conscience knits us to earth, to the flesh and
blood of our human nature with all its food and fuel of Affections,
local attachments, predilections of Language & Country, while it at
once prophecies & proves another & spiritual State of Being. On the
contrary, the doctrine of Expedience inevitably unloosens the Soul
from its centripetal Instincts, makes man a thing of generalities and
ideal abstractions, Shadows in which no life is, no power – and yet
destroys the faith in a supersensual world by undermining its very
grounds – at best to substitute the mock props, props unpropped, of
historical Evidence thus like a spherical Balloon we ~~lose Earth &~~
float between earth & heaven without belonging to either.

The effects of prudence on the wholeness and vitality of human feeling.[68]

The widest maxims of Prudence are like Arms without Hearts,
disjoined from those Feelings which flow forth from Principle as
from a fountain: and so little are even the genuine maxims of expedience likely to be perceived or acted upon by those who have been
habituated to admit nothing higher than Expedience, that I dare
hazard the assertion, that in the whole Chapter of Contents of European Ruin, every Article might be unanswerably deduced from the
neglect of some maxim that had been repeatedly laid down, demonstrated, and enforced with a host of illustrations in some one or other
of the Works of Machiavelli, Bacon, or Harrington.

4

Transmitting Humanity

(a) MARRIAGE

Of all the institutions that formalise human relations to others in the world, marriage was the one that most divided Coleridge, leaving him tormented between theory and reality. He believed profoundly in marriage as an institution that gave stability to society and fostered the growth of the individual. While acknowledging his error in having rushed at a very early age into his union with Sara Fricker, he believed marriage to be indissoluble, offering at its best the highest form of earthly love, the most complete friendship: it was the centre of an irradiating series of attachments and widening affections which made possible more distant benevolences. Throughout his career he continued to express his belief that 'Reciprocal & Exclusive Love [was] the undoubted Source of Marriage, domestic Charities, thence of Society, of all that secures, softens, ornaments, elevates, disanimalizes, coelestializes the human Being – and the human Being must surely be deemed the principal tho' not sole end of this planet.' 'Marriage', he continued, was 'as essential to the growth & preservation & progressive perfection of the *Man*, as Coition to the propagation of the *Animal*'.[1]

For all his praise of marriage, he knew how painfully it could fail, counting himself among the very large proportion of 'good, great, and learned Men [who] have been made miserable (many even heart broken) by ill-tempered Wives'.[2] Men of genius were susceptible because they 'form an ideal in their own minds, and then . . . christen it by the name of . . . an existing Woman' and because they had a more intense conscience than men of the world, were more sensitive, felt more deeply. As a susceptible, quick, even passionate genius, Coleridge was particularly attracted by intelligent women such as Mary 'Perdita' Robinson. He also believed that if he had been free to marry Wordsworth's sister-in-law Sara Hutchinson he would have found just the ideal of domestic affection he was seeking. Yet his belief in the indissolubility of marriage only made this possibility more corrosive. As he put it in an arresting metaphor, 'The Torch of Love may be blown out wholly; but not that of Hymen. Whom the flame, and its cheering Light and genial Warmth no longer bless, him the Smoke stifles – for the Spark is inextinguishable save by Death.'[3]

In correspondence with this schism between theory and reality, the extracts in this section are divided between Coleridge's general observations and advice on marriage (some given long after his separation from his wife), and his experience of marriage as revealed in letters to or about his wife, dwelling on their incompatibility and mutual destructiveness.

Writing in barely subdued anguish to Southey in December 1794, he declares his willingness to accept the loss of his first love, Mary Evans, and to follow the path of duty and marriage to Sara Fricker.[4]

Southey! my ideal Standard of female Excellence rises not above that Woman. But all Things work together for Good. Had I been united to her, the Excess of my Affection would have effeminated my Intellect. I should have fed on her Looks as she entered into the Room – I should have gazed on her Footsteps when she went out from me.

To lose her! – I can rise above that selfish Pang. But to marry another – O Southey! bear with my weakness. Love makes all things pure and heavenly like itself: – but to marry a woman whom I do *not* love – to degrade her, whom I call my Wife, by making her the Instrument of low Desire – and on the removal of a desultory Appetite, to be perhaps not displeased with her Absence! – Enough! – These Refinements are the wildering Fires, that lead me into Vice.

Mark you, Southey! – *I will do my Duty.*

Local customs surprise the traveller in Germany, as he reveals in 1799 to Thomas Poole.[5]

I am pestered every ball night to dance, which very *modestly* I refuse – They dance a most infamous dance called the Waltzen – There are perhaps 20 couple – the Man & his Partner embrace each other, arms round waists, & knees almost touching, & then whirl round & round, the whole 20 couple, 40 times round at least, to lascivious music. This they dance at least three times every ball night – There is no Country on the Earth where the married Women are chaste like the English – here the married Men intrigue or whore – and the Wives have their Cicisbeos. I entreat you, suspect *me* not of any Cicisbeo affair – I am no Puritan; but yet it is not customs or manners that can extinguish in me the Sacredness of a married Woman, or quench the disgust I feel towards an Adultress – It is here as in France – the single Women are chaste, but Marriage seems to legitimate Intrigue – This is the chief moral objection I have to Infidels – In Individuals it may not operate – but when it is general, it always taints the domestic Happiness of a People – .

His views in 1801 on the indissolubility of marriage.[6]

Carefully have I *thought thro'* the subject of marriage & deeply am I
convinced of it's indissolubleness. – If I separate, I do it in the earnest
desire to provide for her & [the]m; that while I live, she may enjoy
the comforts of life; & that when I die, something may have been
accumulated that may secure her from degrading Dependence. When
I least love her, then m[ost] do I feel anxiety for her peace, comfort,
& welfare. Is s[he] not the mother of my children? And am I the man
not to know & feel this? –

The pains of domestic unhappiness, as described in his 1802 verse letter to Sara
Hutchinson.[7]

> I speak not now of those habitual Ills
> That wear out Life, when two unequal Minds
> Meet in one House, & two discordant Wills –
>   This leaves me, where it finds,
> Past cure, & past Complaint – a fate austere
> Too fix'd & hopeless to partake of Fear!
>
> But thou, dear Sara! (dear indeed thou art,
> My Comforter! A Heart within my Heart!)
> Thou, & the Few, we love, tho' few ye be,
> Make up a world of Hopes & Fears for me.
> And if Affliction, or distemp'ring Pain,
> Or wayward Chance befall you, I complain
> Not that I mourn – O Friends, most dear! most true!
>   Methinks to weep with you
> Were better far than to rejoice alone –
> But that my coarse domestic Life has known
> No Habits of heart-nursing Sympathy,
> No Griefs, but such as dull and deaden me,
> No mutual mild Enjoyments of it's own,
> No Hopes of it's own Vintage, None, O! none –
> Whence when I mourn'd for you, my Heart might borrow
> Fair forms & living Motions for it's Sorrow.

In two subsequent letters of July and October he relates that attempts to mend the
marriage seem to be succeeding.[8]

I rejoice for you as well as for myself, that I am able to inform you, that now for a long time there has been more Love & Concord in my House, than I have known for years before. I had made up my mind to a very aweful Step – tho' the struggles of my mind were so violent, that my sleep became the valley of the shadows of Death / & my health was in a state truly alarming. It did alarm Mrs Coleridge – the thought of separation wounded her Pride – she was fully persuaded, that deprived of the Society of my children & living abroad without any friends, I should pine away – & the fears of widowhood came upon her – And tho' these feelings were wholly selfish, yet they made her *serious* – and that was a great point gained – for Mrs Coleridge's mind has very little that is *bad* in it – it is an innocent mind –; but it is light, and *unimpressible*, warm in anger, cold in sympathy – and in all disputes uniformly *projects* itself *forth* to recriminate, instead of turning itself inward with a silent Self-questioning. Our virtues & our vices are exact antitheses – I so attentively watch my own Nature, that my worst Self delusion is, a compleat Self-knowledge, so mixed with intellectual complacency, that my q[uick]ness to see & readiness to acknowledge my faults is too often frustrated by the small pain, which the sight of them give[s] me, & the consequent slowness to amend them. Mrs C. is so stung by the very first thought of being in the wrong that she never amends because she never endures to look at her own mind at all, in it's faulty parts – but shelters herself from painful Self-enquiry by angry Recrimination. Never, I suppose, did the stern Match-maker bring together two minds so utterly contrariant in their primary and organical constitution. Alas! I have suffered more, I think, from the amiable propensities of my nature than from my worst faults & most erroneous Habits – and I have suffered much from both – But as I said – Mrs Coleridge was made *serious* – and for the first time since our marriage she felt and acted, as beseemed a Wife & a Mother to a Husband, & the Father of her children – She promised to set about an alteration in her external manners & looks & language, & to fight against her inveterate habits of puny Thwarting & unintermitting Dyspathy – this immediately – and to do her best endeavors to cherish other *feelings*. I on my part promised to be more attentive to all her feelings of Pride, &c &c and to try to correct my habits of impetuous & bitter censure –. We have both kept our Promises – & she has found herself so much more happy, than she had been for years before, that I have the most confident Hopes, that this happy Revolution in our domestic affairs will be permanent, & that this external Conformity will gradually generate a greater inward Likeness of thoughts, & attachments, than has hitherto existed between us. Believe me, if you were here, it would give you a deep delight to observe the difference of our *minutely* conduct towards each other, from that which, I fear, could not but have disturbed your comforts, when you were here last. Enough. But I am sure, you have not felt it tedious –

After my return to Keswick I was, if possible, more miserable than before. Scarce a day passed without such a scene of discord between me & Mrs Coleridge, as quite incapacitated me for any worthy exertion of my faculties by degrading me in my own estimation. I found my temper injured, & daily more so; the good & pleasurable Thoughts, which had been the support of my moral character, departed from my solitude – I determined to go abroad – but alas! the less I loved my wife, the more dear & necessary did my children seem to me. I found no comfort except in the driest speculations – in the ode to dejection, which you were pleased with, these Lines in the original followed the line – My shaping Spirit of Imagination.

> For not to think of what I needs must feel,
> But to be still and patient, all I can,
> And haply by abstruse Research to steal
> From my own Nature all the natural Man –
> This was my sole resource, my only plan,
> And that which suits a part infects the whole
> And now is almost grown the Temper of my Soul. –

I give you these Lines for the Truth & not for the Poetry –. – However about two months ago after a violent quarrel I was taken suddenly ill with spasms in my stomach – I expected to die – Mrs C. was, of course, shocked & frightened beyond measure – & two days after, I being still very weak & pale as death, she threw herself upon me, & made a solemn promise of amendment – & she has kept her promise beyond any hope, I could have flattered myself with: and I have reason to believe, that two months of tranquillity, & the sight of my now not colourless & cheerful countenance, have really made her feel as a Wife ought to feel. If any woman wanted an exact & copious Recipe, "How to make a Husband compleatly miserable", I could furnish her with one – with a Probatum est, tacked to it. – Ill tempered Speeches sent after me when I went out of the House, ill-tempered Speeches on my return, my friends received with freezing looks, the least opposition or contradiction occasioning screams of passion, & the sentiments, which I held most base, ostentatiously avowed – all this added to the utter negation of all, which a Husband expects from a Wife – especially, living in retirement – & the consciousness, that I was myself growing a worse man / O dear Sir! no one can tell what I have suffered. I can say with strict truth, that the happiest half-hours, I have had, were when all of a sudden, as I have been sitting alone in my Study, I have burst into Tears. – But better days have arrived, & are still to come.

In letters to his wife during that winter he tries to distinguish between their characters and gives her his version of the reasons for their unhappiness.[9]

I love warm Rooms, comfortable fires, & food, books, natural scenery, music &c; but I do not care what *binding* the Books have, whether they are dusty or clean – & I *dislike* fine furniture, handsome cloathes, & all the ordinary symbols & appendages of artificial superiority – or what is called, *Gentility*. In the same Spirit, I dislike, at least I seldom like, Gentlemen, gentlemanly manners, &c. I have no Pride, as far as Pride means a desire to be *thought* highly of by others – if I have any sort of Pride, it consists in an indolent . . .

So much for myself – & now I will endeavor to give a short sketch of what appears to be the nature of your character. – As I seem to exist, as it were, almost wholly within myself, in *thoughts* rather than in *things*, in a particular warmth felt all over me, but chiefly felt about my heart & breast; & am connected with *things without* me by the pleasurable sense of their immediate Beauty or Loveliness, and not at all by my knowledge of their average value in the minds of people in general; & with *persons without* me by no ambition of their esteem, or of having rank & consequence in their minds, but with people in general by general kindliness of feeling, & with my especial friends, by an intense delight in fellow-feeling, by an intense perception of the Necessity of Like to Like; so you on the contrary exist almost wholly in the world *without* you / the Eye & the Ear are your great organs, and you depend upon the eyes & ears of others for a great part of your pleasures.

Indeed, my dear Love! I did not write to you that Letter from the Passage without much pain, & many Struggles of mind, Resolves, & Counter-resolves. Had there been nothing but your Feelings concerning Penrith I should have passed it over – as merely a little tiny Fretfulness – but there was one whole sentence of a very, very different cast. It immediately disordered my Heart, and Bowels. If it had not, I should not have written you; but it is necessary, absolutely necessary for you to know, how such things do affect me. My bodily Feelings are linked in so peculiar a way with my Ideas, that you cannot *enter into* a state of Health so utterly different from your own natural Constitution – you can only see & know, that so it is. Now, what we know only by the outward fact & not by sympathy & inward experience of the same, we are ALL of us too apt to forget; & incur the necessity of being *reminded* of it by others. And this is one among the many causes, which render the marriage of unequal & unlike Understandings & Dispositions so exceedingly miserable. Heaven bear me witness, [I often say inly – in the words of Christ – Father forgive her! she knows not what she does] – Be assured, my dear Love! that I shall never write otherwise than *most* kindly to you, except after great *Aggressions* on your part: & not then, unless my reason convinces me, that some good end will be answered by my Reprehensions. – My dear Love! let me in the spirit of love say two things / 1. I owe duties, & solemn ones, to you, as my wife; but I owe equally solemn ones to Myself, to my Children, to my Friends, and to Society. Where Duties are at variance, dreadful as the case may be, there must be a Choice. I can neither retain my Happiness nor my Faculties, unless I move, live, & love, in perfect Freedom, limited only by my own purity & self-respect, & by my incapability of loving any person, man or woman, unless I at the same time honor & esteem them. My Love is made up $\frac{9}{10}$ths of fervent wishes for the permanent *Peace* of mind of those, whom I love, be it man or woman; & for their Progression in purity, goodness, & true Knowledge. Such being the nature of my Love, no human Being can have a right to be jealous. My nature is quick to love, & retentive. Of those, who are within the immediate sphere of my daily agency, & bound to me by bonds of Nature or Neighbourhood, I shall love each, as they appear to me to deserve my Love, & to be capable of returning it. More is not in my power. If I would do it, I could not. That we can love but one person, is a miserable mistake, & the cause of abundant unhappiness. I can & do love many people, dearly – so dearly, that I really scarcely know, which I love the best. Is it not so with every good

mother who has a large number of Children – & with many, many
Brothers & Sisters in large & affectionate Families? – Why should it
be otherwise with Friends? Would any good & wise man, any warm
& wide hearted man marry at all, if it were part of the Contract –
Henceforth this Woman is your only friend, your sole beloved! all
the rest of mankind, however amiable & akin to you, must be only
your acquaintance! – ? It were well, if every woman wrote down
before her marriage all, she thought, she had a *right* to, from her
Husband – & to examine each in this form – By what *Law* of God, of
Man, or of general reason, do I claim *this* Right? – I suspect, that this
Process would make a ludicrous Quantity of Blots and Erasures in
most of the first rude Draughts of these Rights of Wives – infinitely
however to their own Advantage, & to the security of their true &
genuine Rights. 2. – Permit me, my dear Sara! without offence to
you, as Heaven knows! it is without any feeling of Pride in myself, to
say – that in sex, acquirements, and in the quantity and quality of
natural endowments whether of Feeling, or of Intellect, you are the
Inferior. Therefore it would be preposterous to expect that I should
see with your eyes, & dismiss my Friends from *my* heart, only
because you have not chosen to give them any Share of *your* Heart;
but it is not preposterous, in me, on the contrary I have a *right* to
expect & demand, that you should to a certain degree love, & act
kindly to, those whom I deem worthy of my Love. – If you read this
Letter with half the Tenderness, with which it is written, it will do
you & both of us, GOOD; [& contribute it's share to the turning of a
mere Cat-hole into a Dove's nest!] You know, Sally Pally! I must
have a Joke – or it would not be me! –

. . . And heaven knows! I build up my best hopes on my attempts to
conciliate your Love, & to call it forth into hourly exercise, & gentle
compliances, by setting you the example of respectful & attentive
manners. We cannot get rid of our faulty Habits all at once; but I am
fully sensible, that I have been faulty in many things; tho' justice to
myself compels me to add, not without provocation. But I wish to
confine my whole attention to my own faults – & it is my hourly &
serious Resolve to endeavor to correct all little overflows of Temper,
& offensive vehemence of manner, look, & language – & above all
things never, never either to blame you, or banter you in the presence of a third person. On the other hand, you must make your mind
to receive with love & a ready & docile mind any thing that I say

seriously & lovingly to you, when we are alone: because, my dear
Love! I must needs grow desperate, if I should find, that it is not only
the *manner* of being found fault with that i[rritated you, but I canno]t
& will not endure to . . .

. . . encourage every Thought & Feeling that may tend to make me
love you more – & make a merit to myself of bearing with your little
corrosions, & apparent unimpressibilities. You are a good woman
with a pleasing person, & a healthy understanding – superior certainly to nine women in ten, of our own rank, or the rank above us
– & I will be not only contented but grateful, if you will let me be
quite tranquil – & above all, my dear Sara! have confidence in my
honor & virtue – & suffer me to love & to be beloved without
jealousy or pain. Depend on it, my dear Wife! that the more you
sympathize with me in my kind manners & kind feelings to those of
Grasmere, the more I shall be likely to sympathize with you in your
opinions respecting their faults & imperfections. I am no Idolater at
present; & I solemnly assure you, that if I prefer many parts of *their*
characters, opinions, feelings, & habits to the same parts of your's, I
do likewise prefer much, very much of your character to their's – Of
course, I speak *chiefly* of Dorothy & William – because Mrs
Wordsworth & her Sister are far less remote from you than they – &
unless I am grievously deceived, will in some things become less so
still. – God send us Peace & Love – My dear Love! what a new year's
Blessing it would be – O & surely it shall be. My heart is full of Hope
& full of Love! – . . .

. . . In one thing, my dear Love! I do prefer you to any woman, I
ever knew – I have the most unbounded Confidence in your Discre-
tion, & know it to be well grounded.

By 1806 he writes to the Wordsworths that the situation has become irreparable.[10]

Every attack that could be made on human weakness has been
made; but, fortunately for so weak a moral being as I am, there was
an indelicacy and artifice in these which tho' they did not percept-
ibly lessen my anguish, yet made my shame continually on the
watch, made me see always, and without the possibility of a doubt,
that mere selfish desire to have a *rank* in life and not to be believed
to be that which she really was, without the slightest wish that what
was should be otherwise, was at the bottom of all. Her temper, and

selfishness, her manifest dislike of me (as far as her nature is capable of a *positive* feeling) and her self-encouraged admiration of Southey as a vindictive feeling in which she delights herself as satirizing me &c. &c. . . .

We have *determined* to part absolutely and finally; Hartley and Derwent to be with me but to visit their Mother as they would do if at a publick school.

It is also described to his brother George (whose displeasure was to be lasting).[11]

. . . it is absolutely necessary that I should put you in possession of the true state of my domestic Affairs – the agony, which I feel on the very thought of the subject and the very attempt to write concerning it, has been a principal cause not only of the infrequency & omission of my correspondence with you, but of the distraction of all settled pursuits hitherto –

In short, with many excellent qualities, of strict modesty, attention to her children, and economy, Mrs Coleridge has a temper & general tone of feeling, which after a long – & for six years at least – a patient Trial I have found wholly incompatible with even an endurable Life, & such as to preclude all chance of my ever developing the talents, which my Maker has entrusted to me – or of applying the acquirements, which I have been making one after the other, because I could not be doing nothing, & was too sick at heart to exert myself in drawing from the sources of my own mind to any perseverance in any regular plan. The few friends, who have been Witnesses of my domestic Life, have long advised separation, as the necessary condition of every thing desirable for me – nor does Mrs Coleridge herself state or pretend to any objection on the score of attachment to me.

He tells the Morgans in 1808 that his wife has alienated him from his children.[12]

Are they then not *my* children too? I have indeed no other proof, and can have none, than their Faces & their Hearts; but I have to maintain them, to brood over them, to hope and fear and pray & weep for them. Whether or no they be my Children, I am quite certain, that I am *their* Father. Did this Woman bring me a Fortune? or give me rank? or procure me introductions & interest? or am I now maintained in Idleness by her money? – O that I had the Heart to do what

Justice & Wisdom would dictate – & bring her to her Senses! – Henceforward, I will trouble you no more with this hateful Subject. But only think just enough of it, not to remain too much surprized that my Spirit was so weighed down by her unfeelingness, her seeming pleasure at the anticipation of my being speedily got quit of – me, who in the worst of times had ever felt & expressed as much Joy in her Health, as my Wife, and mother of my Children, as if I had been married to you, or Charlotte, or Mrs Wordsworth or Sara Hutchinson – I say, wonder not that I was overs[et – that I se]emed to look round a Wilderness, to hear in the distance the yel[l & ro]ar of fierce animals. . . .

●   ●   ●

. . . O Friend! *you* cannot comprehend how the poison works – to know, that an ungrateful woman has infused dislike of me into the mind of my own child, the first-born & darling of my Hopes. –

A few days later he writes to Daniel Stuart that, by contrast to his wife, Sara Hutchinson represents his ideal woman.[13]

If Sense, Sensibility, sweetness of Temper, perfect Simplicity and an unpretending nature, joined to shrewdness & entertainingness, make a valuable Woman, Sara H. is so – for the combination of natural Shrewdness and disposition to innocent humor joined with perfect Simplicity & Tenderness is what distinguishes her from her Sister, whose character is of a more solemn Cast. Had Captn Wordsworth lived, I had hopes of seeing her blessedly married, as well as prosperously – but it is one of the necessary Results of a Woman's having or acquiring feelings more delicate than those of women in general, not to say of the same Rank in Society, that it exceedingly narrows the always narrow circle of their Prospects, and makes it a stroke of Providence when they are suitably married. O! to a man of sensibility, especially if he have not the necessity of turmoiling in life, & can really concenter his mind to quiet enjoyment, there is no medium in marriage between great happiness and thorough Misery – but that Happiness is so great, that all outward considerations become ridiculous to a man who has enjoyed it, if in opposition to the possession of a Woman, who is capable of being at once a Wife, a Companion, and a Friend.

I have within the last fortnight received such a tremendous Proof of what a man must suffer who has been induced to unite himself to a Woman, who can be neither of the three in any effective sense, that (as what sinks deepest most easily comes uppermost) it has led me into a digression very remote from the subject of my Letter.

Living without his wife, Coleridge begins to speculate freely in letters and notebooks of 1808 to 1810 on the theory of marriage.[14]

Exclusive of Health, Virtue, and respectable Connections, there seem to me to be just four points, on which a wise man ought to make calm and most deliberate questions – and unless he can answer *all* four queries in the affirmative, he has no chance to be happy – and if he be a man of feeling, no possibility even of being comfortable. 1. Is A a woman of plain good sense, as manifested by sound judgment as to common occurrences of Life, and common persons, and either possessing information enough, or with an understanding susceptible of acquiring it, enough, I say, to be and to become a companion? In few words, has she good sense with average quickness of understanding? 2. Is she of a sympathizing disposition, in *general* – does she possess the sensibility, that a good man expects in an amiable Woman? – 3. Has she that steadiness of moral feeling, that simplicity undebauched by lust of admiration, that sense of duty joined with a constancy of nature, which enables her to concentrate her affections to their proper Objects in their proper proportions and relations – to her Sisters, Brothers, Parents, *as* Sisters, Brothers, Parents, to her children as her Children, to her Husband as her Husband? – N.B. The second & third Query by no means supersede each other. I know a woman of great sensibility, quick & eager to sympathize, yet ever carried away by the present object – a wholly uncentering Being. This Woman is a pleasant companion, a lively Housemate, but O! she would *starve* the Heart, and wound the pride as well as affections, of a Husband – she cannot be a *Wife*. – Again, Mrs Southey is a woman answering tolerably well in affirmative to the third query – She loves her Husband almost too exclusively, & has a great constancy of affection, such as it is. But she sympathizes with nothing, she enters into none of his peculiar pursuits – she only loves *him*; – she is therefore a respectable Wife, but not a Companion. Dreary, dreary, would be the Hours, passed with her – amusement, and all the detail of whatever cheers or supports the spirits, must be sought elsewhere. Southey finds them in unceasing Authorship, never interrupted from morning to night but by sleep & eating. –

4 and lastly. Are all these 3 classes of necessary qualities combined with such manners & such a person, as is striking to you – as suits your feelings, & coalesces with your old associations, as a man, as both a *bodily* and *intellectual* man? –

I feel a deep conviction, that any man looking soberly & watching patiently, might obtain a full solution to all these queries, with scarce the possibility of being deluded. He will see too, whether she is highly esteemed & deeply beloved by her Sister, Brother, oldest Friends, &c –. If there be an atmosphere of true affection & domestic feelings in her family, he cannot help himself breathing it, & perceiving that he breathes it. But alas! alas! is it because it is the most important step of human Life, that therefore it so often happens, that it is the only one, in which even wise men have acted foolishly – from haste, or passion, or inquietude from singleness, or mistaken notions of Honor leading them to walk into the Gulph with their eyes open! God preserve my friend from this worst of miseries! God guide my friend to that best of earthly goods, which makes us better by making us happier, & again happier by making us better! –

Never marry but for Love; but see that thou lovest what is lovely. W. Penn's Reflections & Maxims. –

Prefer Person before Money, good Temper with good sense before Person – and let all, wealth, easy temper, strong Understanding, and Beauty be as nothing to thee unless accompanied by Virtue in Principle & in Habit. –

Suppose competence, health, & female Honesty – then a happy Marriage depends on four Things – 1. an understanding proportionate to thine = a recipiency at least of thine – 2. Natural sensibility & lively Sympathy in general – 3. Steadiness in attaching & retaining sensibility to its proper Objects in its proper proportions. . . . 4. Mutual Liking – including Person, & all the thousand obscure sympathies that determine conjugal Liking, including Love & Desire, to A rather than to B. –

This seems very obvious & almost trivial – and yet all unhappy marriages arise from the not honestly putting & sincerely answering each of these 4 Questions – either negatived, marriage is imperfect, & in hazard of discontent –

It is assuredly a noticeable fact, that so large a proportion of good, great, and learned Men have been made miserable (many even heart broken) by ill-tempered Wives. – That *Pride* of the English Church, & honor of Protestantism in general, *Hooker*, how affecting his domestic History! – Milton, & who was that Painter, who literally died heart-broken, & in the anguish of his Spleen having to paint the Gate of Hell painted exact Portraits of himself & his Wife at the Altar, in the ceremony of Marriage? – In our Days, Parr, Priestley, Cooper of Manchester / Sometimes, I can count up a prodigious number / but I am particularly struck with Elias Benoit, a French Prot: Min: who records that by every caprice of bad Temper, & low avarice, & utter deadness to all worthy Things or Persons, loving no one but especially hating her Husband's Friends, she had been the Scourge of her wretched Mate 47 years, & he ascribes his not having had his Heart broken to the pleasure & calmness with which in consequence of his most often miserable and always Joyless Home he had habitually looked forward to Death, and the resignation, with which he met all other calamities / his home misery having disarmed all other Evils. – The causes are / 1 incaution from quick sensibility of mind and body –. 2. Disposition of men of genius in early Life & till chastised by bitter experiences to form an ideal in their own minds, and then to christen it by the name of, & to conceit it as incarnated in the person, of some an existing Woman. 3. Quick sense of honor, dread of their own conscience, which makes them often persevere if once they have payed marked attentions, or payed direct addresses, even after their eyes have been opened – in cases where Men of the World would feel no scruple and anticipate no Blot on their characters. 4. In learned and pious Recluses Ignorance of the World, Newness to Women of any Elegance of Dress or Manner, and the accumulation of suppressed Instincts. 5. After marriage men of Genius, in Arts or Letters are more at home than men in general /

6 They have more opportunity of observing defects, more in the way of suffering fits of bad Temper – 7. They have more sensibility than the generality of even well-educated men, & therefore, what they have more opportunity to see, they feel more deeply – as when they are happy, when a Mary Wordsworth blesses them, they are happy in a sense undreamt of by the World – so likewise do *they* most pine under the want of sympathy & [?loveliness/liveliness] and to them to be miserable in this is to be miserable in all. 8. A woman unfit for them becomes worse, than should perhaps an

otherwise have been ~~having~~ from meeting with no sympathy, vice versa, in ~~the~~ *her* favorite amusements of large Parties, Card-playing, talking Scandal &c.

Reciprocal & Exclusive Love the undoubted Source of Marriage, domestic Charities, thence of Society, of all that secures, softens, ornaments, elevates, disanimalizes, cœlestializes the human Being – and the human Being must surely be deemed the principal tho' not sole end of this planet, for it is manifest that he is destined to be its sole Inhabitant, by a right of *property* – Is it then to be believed, is there any one analogy to render it credible, that the wisdom of God would leave so paramount, so wide-grasping an end to mere prudence, as its source – which prudence can in truth be found or expected only when the domestic Charities have pre-existed – to mere calculations of the bad consequences of polygamy, or promiscuous Lust –. If Marriage be as essential to the growth & preservation & progressive perfection of the *Man*, as Coition to the propagation of the *Animal* – if for the latter Nature has provided a security in *Lust*, is it to be imagined that she has provided no aid, no predisposing & peculiar cause & efficient of the former in our being – Impossible! – Love is as much an element as Lust – tho' it may require, as Reason does, a more genial Climate of Circumstances to make it *manifest* as Love – Yet even in the wildest it exists till it be destroyed – and why is it more wonderful that by some vices we should destroy Love in our Nature than that by others we destroy Lust – as by extreme Intemperance? –

The Torch of Love may be blown out wholly; but not that of Hymen. Whom the flame, and its cheering Light and genial Warmth no longer bless, him the the Smoke stifles – for the Spark is inextinguishable save by Death –

I was meditating on the fact & musing what the final cause might be, that Providence had ordained in the great majority of men that the sexual disquietudes should commence several years before the gratification could have been intended, even if the Lad were considered only as an *animal*, & no other final cause existed but that of continuing the species in vigor. But when we say, Providence, we cannot but

remember that man has a moral end – therefore it could not be the
purpose of divine wisdom that men should marry, till their reasonable faculties were developed, & their education finished – 21 years
the earliest – 25 the properest age! – Then it struck me like a flash of
Light – Here is a *proof* indeed from Nature herself, if we only <con-
cede> a moral governor of the World, that Virtue has a *worth* as
virtue – & not merely for its *consequences* – While we yet remain
under subjection & in fear, these disquietudes arise, that we may
form a habit of submitting our desires to *reason*, of which the Parent
& the Tutor are the substitutes. Think now what the consequences
would be, if that impetuous passion should first awake at 25! – What
time for thought! What rash marriages! What violations perhaps!
What an inrush! – A most important, & I Imagine, an original
Suggestion.

In a lecture on Romeo and Juliet *he lays stress on the centrality of marriage in
human culture.*[15]

True it is, that the world and its business may be carried on without
marriage; but it is so evident that Providence intended man (the only
animal of all climates, and whose reason is pre-eminent over instinct) to be the master of the world, that marriage, or the knitting
together of society by the tenderest, yet firmest ties, seems ordained
to render him capable of maintaining his superiority over the brute
creation. Man alone has been privileged to clothe himself, and to do
all things so as to make him, as it were, a secondary creator of
himself, and of his own happiness or misery: in this, as in all, the
image of the Deity is impressed upon him.

Providence, then, has not left us to prudence only; for the power
of calculation, which prudence implies, cannot have existed, but in a
state which pre-supposes marriage. If God has done this, shall we
suppose that he has given us no moral sense, no yearning, which is
something more than animal, to secure that, without which man
might form a herd, but could not be a society? The very idea seems
to breathe absurdity.

From this union arise the paternal, filial, brotherly and sisterly
relations of life; and every state is but a family magnified. All the
operations of mind, in short, all that distinguishes us from brutes,
originate in the more perfect state of domestic life. – One infallible
criterion in forming an opinion of a man is the reverence in which he

holds women. Plato has said, that in this way we rise from sensuality to affection, from affection to love, and from love to the pure intellectual delight by which we become worthy to conceive that infinite in ourselves, without which it is impossible for man to believe in a God. In a word, the grandest and most delightful of all promises has been expressed to us by this practical state – our marriage with the Redeemer of mankind.

Then the question comes to a short crisis: – Is, or is not, our moral nature a part of the end of Providence? or are we, or are we not, beings meant for society? Is that society, or is it not, meant to be progressive? I trust that none of my auditors would endure the putting of the question – Whether, independently of the progression of the race, every individual has it not in his power to be indefinitely progressive? – for, without marriage, without exclusive attachment, there could be no human society; herds, as I said, there might be, but society there could not be: there could be none of that delightful intercourse between father and child; none of the sacred affections; none of the charities of humanity; none of all those many and complex causes, which have raised us to the state we have already reached, could possibly have existence. All these effects are not found among the brutes; neither are they found among savages, whom strange accidents have sunk below the class of human beings, insomuch that a stop seems actually to have been put to their progressiveness.

We may, therefore, safely conclude that there is placed within us some element, if I may so say, of our nature – something which is as peculiar to our moral nature, as any other part can be conceived to be, name it what you will, – name it, I will say for illustration, devotion, – name it friendship, or a sense of duty; but something there is, peculiar to our nature, which answers the moral end; as we find everywhere in the ends of the moral world, that there are proportionate material and bodily means of accomplishing them.

We are born, and it is our nature and lot to be composed of body and mind; but when our heart leaps up on hearing of the victories of our country, or of the rescue of the virtuous, but unhappy, from the hands of an oppressor; when a parent is transported at the restoration of a beloved child from deadly sickness; when the pulse is quickened, from any of these or other causes, do we therefore say, because the body interprets the emotions of the mind and sympathises with them, asserting its claim to participation, that joy is not mental, or that it is not moral? Do we assert, that it was owing merely to fulness of blood that the heart throbbed, and the pulse played? Do we not rather say, that the regent, the mind, being glad, its slave, its willing slave, the body, responded to it, and obeyed the impulse?

• • •

. . . shall it be deemed a sufficient excuse for the materialist to degrade that passion, on which not only many of our virtues depend, but upon which the whole frame, the whole structure of human society rests? Shall we pardon him this debasement of love, because our body has been united to mind by Providence, in order, not to reduce the high to the level of the low, but to elevate the low to the level of the high? We should be guilty of nothing less than an act of moral suicide, if we consented to degrade that which on every account is most noble, by merging it in what is most derogatory: as if an angel were to hold out to us the welcoming hand of brotherhood, and we turned away from it, to wallow, as it were, with the hog in the mire.

In 1819, he outlines to Lancelot Wade the important principles to keep in mind when undertaking a marriage, referring to his own experience and citing his own poems.[16]

I have my very dear — but little to say. That little, however, is of such self-evident Truth, that I could not do other than ascribe wilful infatuation to the person who acted in deliberate opposition to it. I will reduce my thoughts to the form of Principles. –

Principle 1. Our usefulness, & to a great extent even our virtue depend on our happiness, by which word I understand such a general pleasurable state of our Temper, Thoughts, Feelings and Sensations, as is requisite for inward tranquillity and the power of cheerful and active attention to the objects without us.

It follows that whoever wilfully puts to risk his own happiness by a step which once taken is irretrievable, wilfully exposes to a fearful hazard his future usefulness and his own moral Being. He acts *dishonestly*. It avails nothing in excuse that he himself is the greatest sufferer. For in the first place, this is more than he knows or can foreknow: and secondly, to him has God especially entrusted the charge of his own Soul, and at his hands will God principally exact it: and thirdly, no man can injure himself alone – tho' he should have predetermined on living and dying a single man.

Principle 2 – That man wilfully exposes his happiness and therefore compromises his honesty who, in a case in which both happiness & usefulness are irrevocably involved, either will not attend to the indispensable and demonstrable *conditions of chusing wisely*, or who acts in contempt of the same when they have been clearly presented and proved to his own understanding. For instance, now what should we think of a man's honor or even honesty, who being the depository of a secret on which the life or whole Estate of a dear Friend depended, would yet wilfully, and tho' earnestly forewarned of the consequences, get drunk in the company of those who had an especial interest in drawing this secret out of him – nay, tho' he knew from experience, that in a state of intoxication it was constitutional with him to lose all prudence and all power over his tongue? Would you not despise such a man, would you not call his conduct *baseness*? Would you allow it to be an excuse, that all his own Prospects were ruined by the ruin of his friend? Would not this rather aggravate his crime by adding ingratitude to the charge?

Principle 3. In the marriage choice the Happiness (see Principle 1) of a man depends on the fact, whether he can, *after every attempt in his power to ascertain the truth*, answer conscientiously, before God and his own heart, in the *affirmative* to the five following Questions.

α. Moral character and freedom from diseases capable of being entailed on her children? (This I mention for form's sake: for it must be taken for granted by honest men in their right senses.)

β. Has the woman an understanding so far proportionate to your own as to make her capable of being a judicious Friend, an occasional Adviser, & a fire-side Companion? If not, it is impossible that you should have *loved* her, however much the delusion of *animal* desire may have led you to believe it. For Love is a Desire of the whole Being to be united to some object, as necessary to its completion in the most perfect manner that Reason dictates and Nature permits. And herein does Friendship differ from Love, that it is not (or in the case of man and man), cannot be, a union of the *whole* Being – *Perfect* Friendship is only possible between Man and Wife: even as *there* is to be found the bitterest enmity.

γ. Does the woman possess *natural* sensibility, natural disposition to sympathy, a kindliness and lovingness of Nature proportionate to your own, & compared with the *loss* which your happiness would sustain by the want or deficiency of these qualities in the *Half* of your being, whether it prove your better half or your worse? (O that you could feel the wretchness of having your heart *starved* by selfishness and frost-bitten by moral frigidity!)

δ. Supposing the above (γ) Does the woman possess that steadiness of character with that sense of Duty, which can *attach, retain,* and *proportion* her natural sensibility and affection to it's proper objects in their proper order? Take a short illustration of the points aimed at in questions γ and δ in the form of examples. Mrs Y possesses the fourth quality (δ) in *perfection*. Whatever affection she has is all concentered in her husband & family; but so little has she, that it is evidently given to them because they are *her's*. It is but attachment participated between the Face before, and the Image in the Looking-glass of Self-love. In the money or aggrandizement which resulted from her husband's pursuits, she would sympathize *with* him: with his pursuits themselves, with his innocent enjoyments & feelings respecting Nature, Books, Religious Feelings, above all with his old friendships, so far from any fellow feeling, it is well if she be not a thorn in his heart as well as a dead weight upon it – This which I have (overleaf) called *Heart-starving* to a man of any quickness or depth of Feeling, is the one extreme.* Mrs Z on the other side is a woman of overflowing sensibility – her sympathy with others as keen as it is quick – Her heart is always in her hand. But this disposition is so unballasted by Judgment & by that most indispen-

---

* I had *no* Fortune, L — ! and though not in all its features – yet to an extent that cankered in the bud, not my happiness alone, but my health, my genius, and my activity – the Portrait here drawn represents *my* own fate, because it was *my own folly.* – Hence too the gradual weakening and wasting of the Will that brought on an increasing cowardice of mental pain and distressing bodily sensations. – Hence (for THIS is sacred & under the seal of silence between you & me – and I rely on your honor to shew this letter to no one, unless you should yourself wish your Father to see it – to *him,* I, as far as I am concerned, have no wish of concealment, but your Father is the only exception) Hence

> Lur'd by no fond Belief,
> No Hope that flatter'd Grief
> But blank Despair my Plea,
> I borrowed short relief
> At frightful usury!

Do read through my Ode entitled Dejection particularly the stanza beginning with,

> There was a Time &c —

[Note by S. T. C.]

sable steadiness of Nature – her sense of Duty in the *detail of Life* so superficially rooted, so little awake to the *alone-saving* Truth, that a virtuous woman will *not* consciously feel what she ought not, because she is ever on the alert to discountenance & suppress the very embryos of Thoughts not strictly justifiable, so as to prevent them from remaining long enough in their transit over her mind to be even remembered – so deficient I say is Mrs Z in all this inward legislation & secret *police* of the Will & Affections, that every new acquaintance of any shew of Talent, & warmth of manners, every "delightful creature" of a month's, nay, of a week's standing, is her dear, her *very* dear, Mr Fuss-*about* – and then her beloved William or Henry, or whatever his Christian name chances to be – in the mean time, her poor husband is an old piece of House furniture in the Lumber room, or Dormitory of her attachments. She will not indeed (that is if her male acquaintance are *all* honest) she will not suffer herself to be *downright ruined* – and such comfort as a man, whose hopes & happiness are centered in a domestic circle of which he expected to be himself the center, can receive from the conviction, "I have her Body, they (or *he*) her mind" – just that comfort *her* (now soured & home-shunning) Husband enjoys. – Therefore I say, that both the Questions, implied in §§s γ and δ, must be answerable in the affirmative by any Man in his senses, who is not at least sufficiently deranged by his appetites to dip for the one Eel in a bag of Snakes & Vipers. – These are four of the five questions.

The fifth, or ε is: Are we suited to each other? Does she *sincerely* adopt my opinions on all important subjects? Has she at least that known *docility* of nature which, uniting with true wifely love, will dispose her so to do? Do her notions of Happiness point to the same sources as mine – or to Dress, Equipage, Visiting, a fine House &c? Am I sure that I really *love* her? Indeed, indeed, my dear young Friend, I think far too highly of you to believe for a moment that you would marry a woman merely because you felt at that time an *exclusive* appetite for *her* person, [or rather her *body*,] which you could not gratify but by previously making your Concubinage *legal*. No, I do not even suspect the possibility of such self-degradation. But my experience as well as my insight into human Nature (even in the *best* of Men, and not only, tho' doubtless more frequently, in young Men of warm sensibility and new to the sex) authorizes, *compels* me to hold it not merely possible but highly probable that the sexual impulse, acting not openly in the excitement of conscious desire – on a subject of such vital importance, why should I hesitate in adopting the true word, viz. Lust? – but acting covertly & unconsciously in the imagination, and in that form contracting a temporary alliance with the best moral Feelings, may assume and counterfeit the *appearance* of exclusive *Love*. Nothing is more common than for a young man to make up in his own fancy an Ideal representative of all that his Heart yearns after, and then *christen* it by the name of the first pretty or interesting girl that attracts & will receive his attentions. How else could it be that what are called Love-matches are so proverbially unhappy, but that the case here stated is so common in the said Love-matches, and the consequent disappointment acute & alienating in exact proportion to the degree in which the self-deluded Husband is by nature & education susceptible of domestic Bliss, if only he had chosen *wisely* and with his eyes free from Film and Fever? O that you could appreciate by the light of other men's experience the Anguish which prompted the ejaculation

Why was I made for Love, yet Love denied to me?*

or the state of suffering instanced in the following description

> Lingering he raised his Latch at eve,
> Tho' tired in heart and limb:
> He lov'd no other place – and yet
> Home was no Home to *him*!†

Again, then, & again, can this last question be answered in the affirmative, with a full honest conviction of the Reason & the Conscience? I call it question: because tho' it consists of several parts it is in substance but one Question.

Are we suited to each other? Do I *really* love, do I LOVE HER? DOES SHE LOVE me? Mark, I do not demand that prudential motives should have *no* influence on a woman in the acceptance or refusal of a man's addresses. But this, not I but plain good sense and common Delicacy demand, that a woman should be able to say to herself with an approving Conscience – If my favored Lover had had no such fortune, I should not have thought myself justified in marrying him; but I should have grieved that he had not had a sufficient fortune to

---

*The Blossoming of the Solitary Date-tree, line 78; Poems, I. 397.
†The Three Graves, lines 452–55; Poems, I. 282.

have allowed me to marry him. I can say that I do not know any man among those who have expressed any attachment to me, whom I would prefer to my husband elect, were it in my power to *transfer* his fortune to another. I can stand at the altar "before the Almighty's Face" with the full conscience that I am not making a worldly bargain: I feel, that I personally *like*, morally *approve* & ESTEEM and am disposed to love him to the full extent of my marriage vow, and that there are no existing pre-engagements of my affections to prevent it – This is absolutely indispensable, and the man who leads a Woman to the Altar without having used every means in his power to ascertain the truth on this point, courts misery in its worst form – a misery that mixes the *vinegar* and gall of *Regret* with the corrosive poison of *Remorse*. Self-contempt will prepare him to interpret every slight, every shew of coldness in his wife as proofs of her dislike and contempt of him – Jealousy will lour at his door and discord be his constant Table-guest and his Chamber-mate. O God! to have a Wife who in her heart despises you for having been Fool & Coxcomb enough to be duped into the belief that she could marry you for any thing but your money – or because she wanted to be maintained, and who is perhaps too heartless, too conscience-proof, to despise herself for having submitted to be bought. This is a frightful picture – but let Heaven and Earth bear witness! it is a faithful Portrait of more than one in my experience.

This, this tho' it has occupied a whole sheet & a half in its explanation, is my third Principle. And now I have but one other to trouble you with. But before I proceed to it, let me obviate any surprize, that I should not have included the consideration of the TEMPER of the Woman. I did not for two reasons: first, because I believe it scarcely possible for a Man, while he is courting a woman, and before marriage, to discover what a woman's real Temper is or to foresee what it will be. She herself perhaps scarcely knows *it*: secondly, because *such* faults of Temper as are compatible with the good qualities and with the freedom from the ill, at least unsuitable, qualities that are demanded in the four questions, α β γ and δ, may disturb and interrupt, but will not be likely to *subvert*, the happiness of domestic Life. We must not expect Angels, but must minutely bear & forbear, & the best advice that can be given to either Bride or Bridegroom is – Think every instance of bad temper in yourself of serious importance, but pass it over as a trifle in the other. [If the one pouts, the other must kiss, & both make it up.] And now for my fourth & last.

Principle 4. It is our Duty to put ourselves in the place of others, no less when we are solicited than when we solicit, no less when we give, than when we receive, no less when we are about to *offer*, than when the question proposed to our Conscience is – ought I to accept such an offer? It must needs be criminal in a Man to offer to another what (were he in that other's place) he knows that it would be an utter *Baseness* in him to receive – Suppose a case by no means absolutely impossible as far as *you* are concerned. Suppose, that for the last two years you had been domesticated with *me*, and that your Love & Confidence had been doubled or trebled during this time, and my Influence over you, of course, increased in the same proportion; suppose, further, that my Daughter [S. C.], had been living with me, and that (as, if the accounts I hear from all quarters of her Beauty, winning manners, and attractive gentleness are any thing like true, it is more than probable that you would) you had suffered yourself to *fall in Love* (as you striplings phrase it) with her – and that I, knowing the intoxication of mind and the cloud over the natural judgment which more or less will accompany an early passion, did yet avail myself of this circumstance, in addition to my own influence over your Will & actions, to induce you to sign away a large part of your Property to myself or to my Sons, in case my daughter should die before your marriage with her – and to her, singly or conjointly with me or her Brothers, in case you should die after *your* marriage with her! – and all this without the knowledge of your excellent Father & of your best Friend next to your Father – without insisting on your first asking his *advice* at least, or hearing what he might have to offer to the contrary! L —! should I not be a VILLAIN? Can you deny that I should have acted like a BASE Traitor and an Ingrate to the very Love, I was making money of? And if you were told the truth, & yet persevered, would you not be the accessary, the pander, to my Baseness? The estate of a Man of 23 years of age is entailed not by the fallible statutes of fallible men but by the Laws of God himself, in his future years, as many as the divine Decree hath pre-appointed for him. He dare not, except he dare be at once dishonest and unnatural, disinherit this future self – he must not, dare not, if he be in any sense a Christian, alienate his own Will by alienating the sphere of Power within which Providence has enabled him to prove and to exercise it. In this point of view the precept – *Love yourself* as your Neighbor, is no less true & no less imperative than the converse, Love your neighbor as yourself. It is, indeed, one and the same precept as soon as the great supplement "and God

above both" is added – Again, therefore, and yet again, remember –
It is base to *give* what it would be *base to receive* –

Farewell, my dear L —! Whatever happens do not destroy this
Letter – I need not entreat you to give it a serious and meditative
perusal. O it will be, believe me! either a smiling Angel of glad
recollection to you, or an accusing spirit of Self-Reproach –

With the true fervor of a sincere friend, and with the anxiety of
an affectionate Parent, I am, my dear L —,

Yours
S. T. C.

P.S. These are principles, written without any distinct knowledge of
any particulars relative to yourself.

(b) CHILD-REARING

Annotating the *Book of Common Prayer*, Coleridge wrote that the purpose of
marriage was not simply to procreate but to humanise the resulting offspring.[17] His interest in child-rearing, in the best environments for raising
happy children, and in studying the growth of a child's capacity for language use, for conceptualising, and for seeing connections among disparate
things, was revolutionary. In spite of the later often-repeated adage that
Romanticism as a movement was characterised by the discovery of the
child, few Romantic writers paid attention to real children other than the
children they remembered themselves as having been. Coleridge was rare in
involving himself for long periods of time in child-care (even changing
diapers with apparent good humour), in playing joyfully, actively and ener-
getically with his sons, and in careful study of their development. His
observations contributed to his belief in the apprehensiveness of the mind
and in the vital powers of love. At the same time more conventional views
had left their mark, as can be seen from his letters to them about improving
their behaviour.

Despite being a participating, communicative and playful father, Coleridge
left home for long stays in Germany, London, Malta and elsewhere, eventually abandoning his children to the sadness, loss of status and humiliation
entailed at that time by a marital separation. He scarcely saw his daughter
Sara again until she was a grown woman (when her beauty made a great
impression in London society). Parenting, which Coleridge cared deeply
about and understood closely, also brought him heartbreak, intensified by
fears that he was responsible for the subsequent failure and estrangement of
his first born, David Hartley. Wise and subtle theoretic pronouncements
were ironically subverted for him by the events of his life.

In letters to Thomas Poole and to Sara Hutchinson he describes the fascination of his three young children.[18]

Hartley is what he always was – a strange strange Boy – *"exquisitely wild"*! An utter Visionary! like the Moon among thin Clouds, he moves in a circle of Light of his own making – he alone, in a Light of his own. Of all human Beings I never saw one so utterly naked of *Self* – he has no Vanity, no Pride, no Resentment / and tho' *very passionate*, I never yet saw him *angry* with any body. He is, tho' now 7 years old, the merest Child, you can conceive – and yet Southey says, that the Boy keeps him in perpetual Wonderment – his Thoughts are so truly his own. [He is] not generally speaking an *affectionate* Child / but his Dispositions are very sweet. A great Lover of Truth, and of the finest moral nicety of Feeling – apprehension all over – & yet always Dreaming. He said very prettily about half a year ago – on my reproving him for some inattention, & asking him if he did not see something – ["] My Father! ["] quoth he with flute-like Voice – "I see it – I saw it – I see it now – & tomorrow I shall see it when I shut my eyes, and when my eyes are open & I am looking at other Things; but Father! it's a sad pity – but it can't be helped, you know – but I am always being a bad Boy, because I am always *thinking of my Thoughts*." – He is troubled with Worms – & to night has had a clyster of oil & Lime water, which never fails to set him to rights for a month or two –. If God preserve his Life for me, it will be interesting to know what he will be – for it is not my opinion, or the opinion of two or of three – but all who have been with him, talk of him as of a thing that cannot be forgotten / Derwent, & my meek little Sara, the former is just recovering of a very bad epidemic Intermittent Fever, with tearing cough – & the other sweet Baby is even now suffering under it –. He is a fat large lovely Boy – in all things but his Voice very unlike Hartley – very vain, & much more fond & affectionate – none of his Feelings so profound – in short, he is just what a sensible Father ought to wish for – a fine, healthy, strong, beautiful child, with all his senses & faculties as they ought to be – with no chance, as to his person, of being more than a good-looking man, & as to his mind, no prospect of being more or less than a man of good sense & tolerably *quick parts*. – Sara is a remarkably interesting Baby, with the finest possible Skin & large blue eyes – & she smiles, as if she were basking in a sunshine, as mild as moonlight, of her own quiet Happiness. She has had the Cow-pock. Mrs Coleridge enjoys her old state of excellent Health. We go on, as usual – except that tho'

I do not love her a bit better, I quarrel with her much less. We cannot be said to live at all as Husband & Wife / but we are peaceable Housemates.–

Dear little Derwent! he is a sad naughty Boy, but very beautiful. I forgot to tell a sweet anecdote of him, that happened some months before we went into Scotland / He was whirling round & round in the Kitchen, till (and no doubt for the first time in his conscious Life) he made himself compleatly giddy – he turned pale with fear, his pretty Lips began to quiver, and pawing with his two arms as if he was pulling something back, he cries out repeatedly with trembling Voice, The Kisshen is running away from Derwent! The Kishen (Kitchen) is running away from Derwent! – you never saw so pretty a sight. – To this Hour Derwent believes that there are two Derwents, & believes that the Reflection in the Looking-Glass is a real Being / & when I endeavored to convince him of his mistake by shewing him that he could not feel it / ["] Well! ["] says little Cumbria – ["] but you know, the Glass an't broke, & that's the reason, I can't get at *him*." – Dear Hartley is just what he was – if possible, more thought-ful, joyous, and love-worthy than ever. He has afforded me a strik-ing instance of the effect of local association / Since we have moved Houses, Hartley has been 9 times with us where he came once before, & has shewn most manifestly a great increase of affection to me – & to his Mother. – I think of going to Grasmere tomorrow – to stay there a couple of Days, & if possible to take Derwent & leave him there – & thence to London. . . . or Wednesday – . . . thence . . . Bath, & Exeter –

Concern for their welfare in a letter to his wife when he is away.[19]

O my dear Love! I have very much to say respecting our children – indeed, indeed, some very vigorous & persevering measures *must* be taken. Sitting up till 11 o'clock at night – coffee in the morning – &c &c &c – and this for a child whose nerves are as wakeful as the Strings of an Eolian Harp, & as easily put out of Tune! What . . . Trash & general irregularity of Diet! – I know, you will say that you were dieted, & yet had worms. But this is no argument at all – for first it remains to be proved that you were *properly* dieted – secondly, it is as notorious as the Sun in heaven, that bad Diet will & does bring worms – & lastly, Derwent has been manifestly tea-poisoned –

as well as Hartley – & both of them are eat up by worms. Mary would not say, that Derwent had no Tea given him – she only said, that *he had but little*. Good God! what infatuation! – as if a little child could know the difference between Tea, & warm milk & water – & out of mere laziness, because the Tea is in the cup.

The anguish of having children one loves in a loveless marriage.[20]

> My little Children are a Joy, a Love,
>   A good Gift from above!
> But what is Bliss, that still calls up a Woe,
>   And makes it doubly keen
> Compelling me to *feel*, as well as KNOW,
> What a most blessed Lot mine might have been.
> Those little Angel Children (woe is me!)
> There have been hours, when feeling how they bind
> And pluck out the Wing-feathers of my Mind,
> Turning my Error to Necessity,
> I have half-wish'd, they never had been born!
> *That* seldom! But sad Thoughts they always bring,
> And like the Poet's Philomel, I sing
> My Love-song, with my breast against a Thorn.

Notebook entries of 1805 and 1806 describe the resulting hope and despair.[21]

East. Sunday. That beautiful passage in dear and honoured W. Wordsworth's Michael respecting the forward-looking Hope inspired pre-eminently by the birth of a child was brought to my mind most forcibly by my own <independent, tho' in part anticipated,> reflections respecting the [immense] importance of young Children to the keeping up the stock of *Hope* in the human Species / they seem as immediately the secreting-organ of Hope in the great organized Body of the whole Human Race, in all men considered as component Atoms of MAN, as young Leaves are the organs of supplying vital air to the atmosphere.

June 7th 1806. O my Children! – Whether, and which of you are dead, whether any, & which among you, are alive, I know not / and were a Letter to arrive this moment from Keswick (Saturday Night, June

7th, 1806, Leghorn / Gasparini's, or Arms of England Hotel) I fear, that I should be unable to open it, so deep and black is my Despair – O my Children, my Children! I gave you life once, unconscious of the Life I was giving / and you as unconsciously have given Life to me. / Yes! it has been lost – many many months I past I should have essayed whether Death is what I groan for, absorption and transfiguration of Consciousness – for of annihilation I cannot by the nature of my Imagination have any idea / Yet it may be true – O mercy, mercy! – Even this moment I could commit Suicide but for you, my Darlings.

After the separation from his wife, Coleridge tries to keep in touch with six-year-old Derwent.[22]

My dear Derwent!

It will be many times the number of years, you have already lived, before you can know and feel thoroughly, how very much your dear Father wishes and longs to have you on his knees, and in his Arms. Your Brother, Hartley, too whirls about, and wrings his hands at the thought of meeting you again: he counts the days and hours, and makes sums of arithmetic of the time, when he is again to play with you, and your sweet Squirrel of a Sister. He dreams of you, and has more than once hugged me between sleeping and waking, fancying it to be you or Sara: and he talks of you before his eyes are fully open in the morning, and while he is closing them at Night. And this is very right: for nothing can be more pleasing to God Almighty and to all good people, than that Brothers and Sisters should love each other, and try to make each other happy; but it is impossible to be happy without being good – and the beginning and A.B.C. of Goodness is to be dutiful and affectionate to their Parents; to be obedient to them, when they are present; and to pray for [them, and to write] frequent Letters from a thankful and loving [heart], when both or either of them chance to be absent. For you are a big Thought, and take up a great deal of Room in your Father's Heart; and his Eyes are often full of Tears thro' his Love of you, and his Forehead wrinkled from the labor of his Brain, planning to make you good, and wise and happy. And your MOTHER has fed and cloathed and taught you, day after day, all your Life; and has passed many sleepless nights, watching and lulling you, when you were sick and helpless; and she gave *you* nourishment out of her own Breasts for so long a time, that the Moon was at it's least and it's greatest sixteen times, before you lived entirely on any other food, than what came out of her Body; and she brought you into the world with shocking pains, and yet loved you the better for the Pains, which she suffered for you; and before you were born, for eight months together every drop of Blood in your Body, first beat in HER Pulses and throbbed in HER Heart. So it must needs be a horribly wicked Thing ever to forget, or wilfully to vex, a Father or a Mother: especially, a Mother. God is above all: and only good and dutiful Children can say their Lord's Prayer, & say to God, "OUR FATHER", without being wicked even in their Prayers. But after God's name, the name of Mother is the sweetest and most holy. – The next good Thing, and that without which you cannot either honor any person, or be esteemed by any one, is – *always to tell the Truth*. For God gave you a Tongue to tell the Truth; and to tell a Lie with it is as silly, as to try to walk on your Head instead of your Feet; besides, it is such a base, hateful, and wicked Thing, that when good men describe all wickedness put together in one wicked mind, they call it the Devil, which is Greek for a *malicious Liar*; and the Bible names him *a Liar* from the beginning, and the Father of *Lies*. Never, never, tell a Lie – even tho' you should escape a whipping by it: for the Pain of a whipp[ing] does not last above a few minutes; but the Thought of having told a Lie will make you miserable for days – unless, indeed, you are hardened in wickedness, and then you must be miserable for ever! – But you are a dear Boy, and will scorn such a vile thing; and whenever you happen to do any thing amiss, which *will* happen now and then, you will say to yourself – Well! whatever comes of it, I will TELL THE TRUTH; both for it's own sake, and because my dear Father wrote so to me about it."

I am greatly delighted, that you are so desirous to go on with your Greek; and shall finish this Letter with a short Lesson of Greek. But much cannot be done, till we meet; when we will begin anew, and, I trust, not leave off, till you are a good Scholar. And now go, and give a loving Kiss to your little Sister, & tell her, that Papa sent it to her; & will give hundreds in a little Time: for I am, my dear Child!

your affectionate Father,
S. T. Coleridge

He prepares the happy-go-lucky ten-year-old Hartley for a holiday with the family of his strict uncle George.[23]

Coleorton
3 April, 1806 [1807]

My dear Boy

In all human beings good and bad Qualities are not only found together, side by side as it were; but they actually tend to produce each other – at least, they must be considered as twins of a common parent, and the amiable propensities too often sustain and foster their unhandsome *sisters*. (For the old Romans personified Virtues and Vices, both as Women.) This is a sufficient proof, that mere natural qualities, however pleasing and delightful, must not be deemed Virtues, until they are broken in and yoked to the plough of *Reason*. Now to apply this to your own case – I could equally apply it to myself; but you know yourself more accurately than you can know me, and will therefore understand my argument better, when the facts on which it is built, exist in your own consciousness. You are by nature very kind and forgiving, and wholly free from Revenge and Sullenness – you are likewise gifted with a very active & self-gratifying fancy, and such a high tide & flood of pleasurable feelings, that all unpleasant and painful Thoughts and Events are hurried away upon it, and neither remain on the surface of your memory, or sink to the bottom into your Heart. So far all seems right, and matter of thanksgiving to your maker – and so all really *is* so, & will be so, if you exert your reason and free-will. But on the other [hand] the very same disposition makes you less impressible both to the censure of your anxious friends, and to the whispers of your conscience – nothing that gives you pain, dwells long enough upon your mind to do you any good – just as in some diseases the medicines pass so quickly thro' the stomach and bowels, as to be able to exert none of their healing qualities. – In like manner this power, which you possess, of shoving aside all disagreeable reflections, or losing them in a labyrinth of day-dreams, which saves you from some present pain, has on the other hand interwoven into your nature habits of procrastination, which unless you correct them in time (& it will require all your best exertions to do it effectually) – must lead you into lasting Unhappiness.

You are now going with me (if God have not ordered it otherwise) into Devonshire to visit your Uncle, G. Coleridge. He is a very good man, and very kind; but his notions of Right and of Propriety are very strict; & he is therefore exceedingly shocked by any gross Deviations from what is right and proper. I take therefore this mean of warning you against those bad Habits, which I and all your friends here have noticed in you – And be assured, I am not writing in anger, but on the contrary with great Love, and a comfortable Hope, that your Behaviour at Ottery will be such as to do yourself, and me and your dear Mother, *credit*.

First then I conjure you never to do any thing of any kind when out of sight which you would not do in my presence. What is a frail and faulty Father on earth compared with God, your heavenly Father? But God is always present.

Specially, never pick at or snatch up any thing, eatable or not. I know, it is only an idle foolish Trick; but your Ottery Relations would consider you as a little Thief – and in the Church Catechism *picking* and *stealing* are both put together, as two sorts of the same Vice – "and keep my hands from picking and *stealing*." And besides, it is a dirty trick; and people of weak stomachs would turn sick at a dish, which a young FILTH-PAW had been fingering.

Next, when you have done wrong, acknowledge it at once, like a man. Excuses may shew your *ingenuity*, but they make your *honesty* suspected. And a grain of Honesty is better than a pound of Wit. We may admire a man for his cleverness; but we love and esteem him only for his goodness – and a strict attachment to Truth, & to the whole Truth, with openness and frankness and simplicity is at once the foundation-stone of all Goodness, and no small pat of the super-structure. Lastly, to do what you have to do, at once – and put it out of hand. No procrastination – no self-delusion – no "I am sure, I can say it – I need not learn it again" &c &c – which *sures* are such very unsure folks, that 9 times out of ten their Sureships break their word, and disappoint you.

Among the lesser faults I beg you to endeavor to remember, not to stand between the half opened door, either while you are speaking or spoken to. But come *in* – or go out – & always speak & listen with the door shut. – Likewise, not to speak so loud, or abruptly – and never to interrupt your elders while they are speaking – and not to *talk* at all during Meals. –

I pray you, keep this Letter; and read it over every two or three days.

Take but a little Trouble with yourself: and every one will be delighted with you, and try to gratify you in all your reasonable wishes. And above all, you will be at peace with yourself, and a double Blessing

> to me, who am, my / dear, my very dear Hartley, / most anxiously / Your fond Father,

S. T. Coleridge

P.S. I have not spoken about your mad passions, and frantic Looks & pout-mouthing; because I trust, that is all over.

During visits by the children to Coleridge and the Wordsworths in Grasmere in 1808 and 1810 he writes to his wife about them.[24]

My dear Sara

We arrived all three safe. O it was a perfect comedy to see little John on Sara's Entrance – He had screamed with Joy on seeing us come up the Field; but when Sara entered, he ran & crept under the Kitchen-table, then peeped out at her, then all red with Blushes crept back again, laughing half-convulsively yet faintly – at length, he came out, & throwing his pinafore over his face & with both hands upon that, he ran and kissed her thro' the pinafore –. Soon however all was agreed – John has put the Question, & Sara has consented – But (says she) is the Church a far way off? – Nay, replies John – nought but a lile bit – & I'll carry you on my back all the way, & all the way back, after we are married. Sara sleeps with me – She has made the children as happy as happy can be. Every one is delighted with her – indeed, it is absolutely impossible that there can be a sweeter or a sweetlier behaved Child – This is not *my* Speech; but Wordsworth's. – Little John absolutely dotes on her; and she is very fond of him, & very good to all of them. O, she has the sweetest Tongue in the world – she talks by the hour to me in bed – & does not at all disturb me in the night, she lies so very quiet. . . .

Little Sara is gone to bed; but left with me her "loving kind dutiful Love to dear Mama, and to Dervy dear, and Hartley tho' he is sic a wet kisser; and to Edith." She told me, last night, that Edith and she tell each other a deal of knowledge – and verily, Sara is a deal cleverer than I supposed – She is indeed a very sweet unblameable Darling. And what elegance of Form & Motion – her dear Eyes too! as I was telling a most wild Story to her & John, her large Eyes grew almost as large again with wonderment –

Hartley and Derwent came to the Ball on Friday Night, and returned on Saturday Morning, to be at some balloon-sport &c at Mr Lloyd's – They go on better. Mr De Quincey asked Hartley, if they had quarrelled for the last week – "Why, we had one rather violent difference – it was a dispute between Derwent and me on the present state of Agriculture in France. I am very sorry for it – but indeed Derwent is very tyrannical in his arguing." – The stumpy Canary!! – Venerable State-Economists! – What a strange world we live in! And what a quaint Brace of Doglets these Striplings of our's are! – And lile Darran too so childish & simple even *under* his age! – Did you ever tell the story of his grave correcting of me about the Reptiles &c preserved by Noah? – "O yes, indeed, Father! there were – there was a Gra[s]shopper in the ark –I saw it myself very often – I remember it very well." – O there is a treasure in this anecdote for a man disposed to examine into the real state of what is called *Belief* in Religion! –

Hartley looks and behaves all that the fondest Parent could wish. He is really handsome, at least, as handsome as a face so original & intellectual can be. – And Derwent is "a nice little fellow" - and no Lackwit either. – I read to Hartley out of the German a series of very masterly arguments concerning the startling gross improbabilities of the story of Esther (14 improbabilities are stated). It really *surprized* me, the acuteness and steadiness of Judgment with which he answered more than half, weakened many others, and at last determined that two only were not to be got over – I then read for myself and afterwards to him, Eichhorn's Solution of the 14 Im[probabilities,] and the coincidence was surprizing – a[s] Eichhorn after a lame attempt was obliged to give up the two which H. had declared desperate –

Next, I did not like to leave poor Derwent, especially as I was told by Wordsworth, that Hartley's mode of taking leave of him & putting a stop to all thought of *his* walking was too much of a *triumphant* manner – and that Derwent was depressed by it. However, he has been very happy – and you will be pleased to hear, that after repeated examination, I was quite surprized with his process and with the accuracy of his Knowledge in Greek – There lay upon my table a list of words from the original Greek of the Wisdom of Solomon (in the apocrypha) all which were either new-compounds peculiar to that Work, or at least very unusual – the skill, with which Derwent *went about* each word, to analyse it into it's component parts, and the number of them that he made out the meaning of, was truly admirable. – Thus too in a theological work that I was reading, there was a quotation of ten or 12 Hexameter Lines of a Hymn attributed to Orpheus – and Derwent construed nearly one half – that is to say, he knew the meaning of nearly as many of the words, as he was ignorant of – and never made any mistake in the position of the words or in the cases. To day, I pitched on a Chapter in St Paul (i. Corinth. xv) – and having satisfied myself that Hartley [Derwent?] had not read this Epistle at School, I bade him read it to me – and to my surprize he read it as well as I could have done – and not at all in the words of the common translation – But I asked him many ques[tions] of particular words – and he instantly gave the original, & declined it or conjugated it with grammatical fluency. –

To J. J. Morgan in 1812 Coleridge describes his three children, interesting himself particularly in the likenesses of his two boys to himself.[25]

Of course, the first Evening was devot[ed] Laribus domesticis, to Southey & his & my Childre[n. My] own are all, the fondest Father could pray for: & [li]ttle Sara does honor to her Mother's anxieties, reads French tolerably & Italian fluently, and I was astonished at her acquaintance with her native Language. The word "hostile" occurring in what she read to me, I asked her what "hostile" meant? And she answered at once – Why! inimical: only that inimical is more often used for things and measures, and not, as hostile is, to persons & nations. – If I had dared, I should have urged Mrs C. to let me take her to London for 4 or 5 months, to return with Southey – but I feared, it might be inconvenient to you, & I knew, it would be presumptuous in me to bring her to you. But she is such a sweet-tempered, meek, blue-eyed Fairy, & so affectionate, trust-worthy, & really serviceable! Derwent is the self-same fond small Samuel Taylor Coleridge as ever. When I sent for them from Mr Dawes, he came in dancing for joy, while Hartley turned pale & trembled all over – then after he had taken some cold water instantly asked me some questions about the connection of the Greek with the Latin, which latter he has just begun to learn. Poor Derwent, who has by no means strong health, (having inherited his poor father's tenderness of Bowels & Stomach & consequently capriciousness of animal Spirits) has complained to me (having no other possible grievance) that Mr Dawes does not *love* him, because he can't help crying when he is scolded, & because he an't such a genius, as Hartley – and that tho' Hartley should have done the same thing, yet all the others are punished, & Mr Dawes only *looks* at Hartley, & never scolds *him* – & that *all* the boys think it very unfair [– but] he *is* a genius! This was uttered in low spirits & a [bitt]erness brought on by my petting – for he adores his Brother. Indeed, God be praised! they all love each other. I was delighted, that Derwent of his own accord asked me about little Miss Brent that used to play with him at Mr and Mrs Morgan's: adding that he had almost forgot what sort of a Lady she was, only she was littler – *less, I mean* (this he said hastily & laughing at his blunder) than Mama. – A Gentleman who took a third of the Chaise with me from Ambleside & whom I found a well-informed & thinking Man, said after two hours' knowledge of us, that the two boys united would be a perfect representative of myself. –

Coleridge's anxiety about his son Hartley's dismissal from his probationary fellow-ship at Oriel College, Oxford, on the charge of intemperance, obsesses him between 1820 and 1822, particularly when Hartley, increasingly addicted to alcohol, begins to live a negligent and sometimes vagrant life around Grasmere, writing occasional poems. Coleridge's letters, almost frantic at times, show insight not only into Hartley's psychology but also into his own.

Early in July Coleridge learns that Hartley has left Oxford and that his whereabouts are unknown.[26]

My dear Derwent

I were, methinks, to be pardoned if even on my own account I felt it an aggravation of my sore affliction, that your Brother without writing or any other mode of communication should have bent his course to the North as tho' I were not his Father nor he himself bound to Mr and Mrs Gillman by his own knowledge of the affec-tionate & scarcely less than parental anxiety with which they follow him thro' luck and unluck, good report and evil. Or am I to suppose, that having taken his resolutions he found or fancied that it would be less painful to him to imply by his absence than to tell me by word of mouth, that my advice would be to no purpose and my Wishes of the same stuff as my Tears? One thing at least is certain: that had it been his object to make it known and felt, that he considered me as having forfeited the interest and authority of a Father per desuetudinem usûs, & as a Defaulter in the Duties, which I owed his Youth, he could not have chosen a more intelligible (God knows! on his own account too afflictive to be mortifying) way of realizing it.

. . . For O! my dear dear Boy! never forget, that as there is a Self-willedness which drifts away from self-interest to finish it's course in the sucking eddy-pool of Selfishness, so there is a Self-interest which begins in Self-sacrifice, and ends in God. –

. . . O surely if Hartley knew or believed that I love him & linger after him as I do & ever have done, he would have come to me. – . . .

Tuesday Morning, 4 July – I have this moment received your heart-wringing intelligence. I wish that I dared believed that Hartley is bona fide on his road to Keswick – but the same Dread struck at once on Mr G's mind & on mine – that he is wandering on some wild scheme, in no dissimilar mood or chaos of tho[ughts and] feelings to that which possessed his unhappy father at an earlier age during the month that ended in the Army-freak – & that he [may] even be scheming to take passage from Liverpool to America. Again I must say that the venom if not the sharpness of the Pang, which I am suffering, is on account of his own moral being, when I am forced to see that he seems to have had no more reference to *me* than as if no such person had been in existence. My very name appears not to have occurred to him!

Knowing the accusations against him, he writes to Allsop analysing Hartley's character.[27]

I can tell you only that Hartley has so conducted himself as to have given deep offence to the Master and Fellows of Oriel – & that there is the greatest possible danger that he will not be elected at the close his probationary Year, i.e. in October next. He is neither charged with, nor suspected of, any criminal act, nor are any instances of intoxication urged against him – but irregularity & neglect of College Rules & Duties, Carelessness of Dress, low Company in contempt of the exprest warnings as well as wishes of the Master & Fellows, & *fondness for Wine* – the term by which the last Charge is expressed is the only one too mortifying for me to transcribe. I am convinced that this last is owing, *in great part*, to his habit almost constitutional (for it characterized his earliest Childhood) of eagerly *snatching* without knowing what he is doing, & whatever happens to be before him – bread, fruit, or Wine – pouring glass after glass, with a kind of St Vitus' nervousness – not exactly in the same way as my dear & excellent-hearted C.L., but similarly. Alas! both Mr and Mrs Gillman had spoken to him with all the earnestness of the fondest Parents – his cousins had warned him – & I (long ago) had written to him, conjuring him to reflect with what a poisoned dagger it would arm his Father's enemies – yea, and the Phantoms that half-counterfeiting, half-expounding the Conscience, would persecute his Father's Sleep. –

. . . Before God, I have but one voice – Mercy! Mercy! –. Woe is me! – the Root of all Hartley's faults is Self-willedness – this was the Sin of his nature, & this has been fostered by culpable indulgence, at least, non-interference on my part, while in a different quarter, Contempt of the Self-*interest*, he saw, seduced him unconsciously into *Selfishness*.

In a letter to the Provost of Oriel in October he stresses Hartley's habits of acting abstractedly.[28]

When he was not a year old, my Friend & at that time my Neighbor, Mr Poole of Stowey now a justly distinguished Magistrate in the county of Somerset, used to remark, as a curious fact – that the little fellow never shewed any excitement at the *thing*, whatever it was, but afterwards, often when it had been removed, smiled or capered on the arm as at the *thought* of it. – There is another & perhaps more justifying reason for calling this peculiarity his *Nature* – for like all other natural qualities or tendencies, not the result of Reason, Religion, or moral Habits, it has been "a twy-streaming Fount, Whence Good and Ill have flowed, Honey & Gall". –

And to this habit of being absent to the present, often indeed from the reverse extreme, and still oftener from eagerness of reasoning, & exclusive attention to mental acts or impressions, but not seldom from a mere absorption of the active powers, a seeming entire suspension of all distinct Consciousness – I intreat your attention with peculiar anxiety – For it is of the last importance to the just appreciation both of what he is & has been, and of what he is likely to become, that it should be known that this habit so far from having been gradually contracted at School or at the university, & so far from growing on him, was strongest & most glaring from two years old to seven or eight. For the last four years, my Son has been with me twice yearly, from three weeks to two months each time, & for the last three years I have been each visit congratulated by the sincere and enlightened friends whose hospitable roof and regard he shared with me, & at the last time but one, when he accompanied his Brother, Derwent, hither, was most warmly congratulated by all his & my friends in this neighbourhood on his manifest improvement in this point.

. . . When a little child, as soon as he [was] made to sit & had begun to take his food, he used to sink at once from a state of whirling activity into – it is painful to me even to recollect him – for he looked like a little statue of Ideotcy – and even up to the present year no one can have been intimate with him without having occasionally seen him, sometimes in abstraction, but of late more frequently in eagerness of conversation, eating fruit, or bread, or whatever else was before [him], utterly unconscious of what he was doing, or repeatedly filling his glass from the Water-bottle – for his friends were so well aware of this, that they either recalled his attention to what he was doing, or putting the Water by him silently, counted the times, in order to impress him afterwards with the unbecomingness & even danger of these fits of absence –. . . .

Let this fact be taken in combination with his Complexion, the condition of his digestive organs, his disposition to move after meals, &c: and I dare appeal to any medical Man, whether it does not afford more than a presumption against the cruel charge that he had formed a *habit* of intemperance.

Two years later he analyses his own behaviour in search of any failings towards Hartley.[29]

From the hour, he left the Nurse's Arm, Love followed him like his Shadow. All, all, among whom he lived, all who saw him themselves, were delighted with him – in nothing requisite for his age, was he backward – and what was my fault? That I did not, unadvised & without a hint from any one of my friends or acquaintances, interrupt his quiet untroublesome enjoyment by forcing him to *sit still*, and *inventing* occasions of trying his obedience – that I did not without and against all *present* reason, and at the certainty of appearing cruel, and arbitrary not only to the child but to all with whom he lived, interrupt his little comforts, and sting him into a will of resistance to my will, in order that I might *make* opportunities of crushing it? – Whether after all that has occurred, which surely it was no crime not to have fore-seen at a time when a Foreboding of a less sombre character was passionately retracted, as "too [industrious] folly", as "vain and causeless Melancholy" – whether I should act thus, were it all to come over again, I am more than doubtful. Can I help remembering that so far from having fractious, disobedient or *indulged* children, I could count the times on the fingers of one hand, in which I had ever occasion to compel their obedience or punish their disobedience by a *blow* or a harsh sound? If I but lowered my voice, Hartley would say – Pray, don't speak low, Father! – and did or ceased to do as he was told. – Can I forget, how often, when I had expressed myself sorry to see such or such a child so indulged, and referred to the effects on it's Temper, I was told – that I could not expect that all children should be like mine? – . . .

. . . Since the time of Hartley's first arrival at Calne to the present day I am not conscious of having failed in any point of duty, of admonition, persuasion, intreaty, warning, or even (tho' ever reluctantly, I grant) of parental injunction – and of repeating the same whenever it could be done without the almost certain consequence of baffling the end in view. I noticed, and with concern, in Hartley and afterwards in Derwent a pugnacity in self-opinion, which ever had been alien from my own character, the weakness of which consisted in the opposite fault of facility, a readiness to believe others my superiors and to surrender my own judgement to their's – but in part, this appeared to me the fault of the[ir] ages, and in part, I could not refuse an inward assent, tho' I mourned over it in silence, to the complaint made by others – both at Calne and at Highgate – of impressions made on their minds with regard to myself, not more unjust in themselves than unfortunate for them –.

But let it be, that I am rightly reproached for my negligence in withstanding and taming his Self-will – is this the main Root of the Evil? I could almost say – Would to God, it were! for then I should have more Hope. But alas! it is the absence of a Self, it is the want or torpor of Will, that is the mortal Sickness of Hartley's Being, and has been, for good & for evil, his character – his moral *Idiocy* – from his earliest Childhood – Yea, & hard it is for me to determine which is the worse, *morally* considered, I mean: the selfishness from the want or defect of a manly Self-love, or the selfishness that springs out of the excess of a worldly Self-interest. In the eye of a Christian and a Philosopher, it is difficult to say, which of the two appears the greater deformity, the relationless, unconjugated, and intransitive Verb Impersonal with neither Subject nor Object, neither governed or governing, or the narrow proud Egotism, with neither Thou or They except as it's Instruments or Involutes. *Prudentially*, however, and in regard to the supposed good and evil of this Life, the balance is woefully against the former, both because the Individuals so characterized are beyond comparison the smaller number, and because they are sure to meet with their bitterest enemies in the latter. Especially, if the poor dreamy Mortals chance to be amiable in other respects and to be distinguished by more than usual Talents and Acquirements. Now this, my dear Sir! is precisely the case with poor Hartley. He has neither the resentment, the ambition, nor the Self-love of a man – and for this very reason he is too often as selfish as a Beast – and as unwitting of his own selfishness. With this is connected his want of a salient point, a self-acting principle of Volition – and from this, again, arise his shrinking from, *his shurking*, whatever requires and demands the exertion of this inward power, his cowardice as to mental pain, and the procrastination consequent on these. His occasional Wilfulness results from his weakness of will aided indeed, now and then, by the sense of his intellectual superiority and by the sophistry which his ingenuity supplies and which is in fact the brief valiancy of Self-despondence. –

Such is the truth & the fact as to Hartley – a truth, I have neither extenuated nor sought to palliate. But equally true it is, that he is innocent, most kindly natured, exceedingly good-tempered, in the management & instruction of Children excels any young man, I ever knew; and before God I say it, he has not to my knowlege a single vicious inclination – tho' from absence & nervousness he needs to be guarded against filling his wine-glass too often –. But this temptation *at present* besets him only under the stimulus of society and eager conversation – just as was the case with his Grandfather, one of the most temperate men alive in his ordinary practice. – . . .

. . . I have but one other remark to make – that of all the *Waifs*, I ever knew, Hartley is the least likely and the least calculated to lead any human Being astray by his example. He may exhibit a Warning – but assuredly he never will afford an inducement. –

The most agonising moment of all.[30]

It was reserved for the interval between six o'clock and 12 on THAT

SATURDAY Evening to bring a Suffering which, do what I will, I cannot help thinking of & being *affrightened by*, as a terror of itself, a self-subsisting separate Something, detached from the Cause – and when I turn to the Cause, still the solemn Appeals to the Almighty for the falseness of the Charge at Oriel are far, far more terrible to me than the *Habit* charged on him – woeful, and ruinous, and all-*hollow*-making and *future*-dizzying as *that* is! – And then too, I cannot help hearing the sound of my Voice, at the moment when he took me by surprize, and asked for the money to pay a debt to & take leave of Mr Williams – promising to overtake me if possible before I had reached his Aunt Martha's, as I was to stop at Bothe's in York Street by the way – but at latest, before 5 – "Nay, say before *Six. Be*, if you can, by 5 – but *say*, six –." Then, when he had passed a few steps – Hartley! – Six! O my God! think of the *agony*, the *sore agony*, of every moment after six! – And tho' he was not three yards from me, I only saw the color of his Face thro' my Tears! –

. . . a Father's Affection could not exist exempt from a Father's Anxiety.

. . . Sane or insane – a fearful thing it is when a Father could be comforted by an assurance of the latter – but I neither know nor *dare* hear of any *mid* state – of no *vague* necessities dare I hear. Our own wandering Thoughts may be suffered to become Tyrants over the mind, of which they are the Offspring – and the most effective Vice-roys or Substitutes of that dark & dim spiritual Personëity whose whispers & fiery darts Holy Men have supposed them to be – & that these may end in a loss or rather forfeiture of Free-agency, I doubt not – But my dearest Allsop! I have both the Faith of Reason, and the Voice of Conscience and the assurance of Scripture, that "resist the Evil one & he will flee from you." But for self-condemnation H. would never have tampered with Fatalism; and but for Fatalism he would never have had *such* cause to condemn himself. –

Some passages from the late manuscript 'Opus Maximum', in which Coleridge's sensitive and modern theories of child-rearing, and particularly of the mother–child bond, play an important part.[31]

Through all nature there is seen an evolution from within . . . self-unconscious the Man carries on the development of its Animal Being, that organization which places the human in community with the plant and with the mere Animal, and all that arrangement, and that quality of his organs which had been useless, or pernicious for a Being not destined for other & higher & even diverse faculties from those of the mere animal – both these he carries on in the sleep of those faculties, in the passiveness of pure sensation. And yet in vain would these rudiments have been formed, in vain those powers which having formed them, reappear as predispositions & instincts were there not a correspondence prepar'd in the real present. In vain would the conditions, the possibility of the human have been inlaid were not the human in its full development already there to meet & to protect it. Only by disproportion of the means to the ends will the babe abandoned from its birth & suckled in the Forest by the blind & kindly instincts of Nature in the Goat or the Wolf, its eye will remain glazed, its lips the seal of expression, appetite & rage alone. The tongue will utter the sounds of the Ape, the very Ear will be deaf to all but the inarticulate sounds of Nature. Even in its very first week of Being, the holy quiet of its first days must be sustain'd by the warmth of the maternal bosom. The first drawings of its humanity will break forth in the Eye that connects the Mother's face with the warmth of the mother's bosom, the support of the mother's Arms . . . Ere yet a conscient self exists the love begins & the first love is love to another. The Babe acknowledges a self in the Mother's form, years before it can recognize a self in its own –

We have said that Man hath from Birth that which is common with the Animal & that which is especially human. With the Beasts of the Field it possesses the senses & the sensations & the desires of self-preservation and the impulse to pleasure from the pain of its absence. Beyond the beasts yea and above the Nature of which they are the inmates man possesses love & faith & the sense of the perman- ent. As the connexion & the intermedium of both he possesses reflection & foresight, in other words an understanding which is therefore a human understanding, not solely nor chiefly from its greater extent than that which the Dog, the Elephant, & the Ant possess but because it is irradiated by a higher power, the power namely of seeking what it can no where behold & finding that which itself here first transfused the permanent, that which in the endless flux of sensible things can alone be known which is indeed in all but exists for the reason alone for it is Reason.

[The] Understanding [must flow] in one or other of two channels.

It must either develope that which is properly human in Man & the animal Nature, but in subordination nay subjugation to his Humanity or the Animal Nature to which the human is to be made instrumental only & by giving eyes to blind appetite transform selfishness into Self-Love and enrich degradation by consciousness, intention & choice – Thus differing from the Animal in this alone that he hath been made the Animal that he was not born.

[The child in the night cries out] "Touch me, only touch me with your finger." "I am not here, touch me, Mother, that I may be here"! . . . The witness of its own being had been suspended in the loss of the mother's presence by sight or sound or feeling. . . . The child now learns its own alterity, & sooner or later, as if some sudden crisis had taken place in its nature, it forgets hence forward to speak of itself by imitation, that is by the name which it had caught from without. It becomes a person, it is and speaks of itself as I, and from that moment it has acquired what in the following stages it may quarrel with, what it may loosen and deform, but can never eradicate, – a sense of an alterity in itself which no eye can see, neither his own nor other. And this is that which thinks on God.

With the awakening of self-consciousness, the first sign or representative of which is not its own bodily shape, but the gradually dawning presence of the mother's, the conception of life is elevated into that of personeity: and as particular shape is beheld only in the higher and freer conception of form, so again in this form itself this antecedent whole constituent of its parts, is taken up into & becomes one with the yet higher or rather deeper & more inward principle of person. . . . Most noticeable it is and most worthy a wise man's meditation that the notion of objects as altogether objective, begins in the same moment in which the conception is formed that is wholly subjective.

Citing Wordsworth's 'Immortality Ode', Coleridge invokes the fluid behaviour of children as an example for adults, teaching them both how to forget themselves and how to escape the tyranny of fixed images.[32]

. . . "As if their whole vocation / Were endless imitation." Two things we may learn from little children from 3 to 6 years old. 1) that it is a character, an instinct of our human nature, to pass out of our

Self – i.e. the image (or complex cycle or wheel of image, act and sensation, that by its constant presence & rapidity becomes a stationary *unity*, a whole of indistinguishable parts, & is the perpetual *representative* of our Individuum, & hence by all unreflecting minds confounded & identified with it). . . . that it is an instinct of my nature to pass out of myself, and to exist in the form of others. The second is – not to suffer any one form to pass into *me* & to become a usurping Self in the disguise of what the German Pathologists call a *fixed Idea* – Mem. This is always a *Self*-love. . . . As sure as it is cyclical and forms the ruling *Eddy* in our mind, so surely does it become the representative of our Self, and = Self.

(c) EDUCATION

Coleridge's many related thoughts about education had as a common focus the need for development of self rather than for accumulation of information. To quote William Walsh's account of his belief: 'a good education persists not as a collection of information, an arrangement of intellectual bric-à-brac, but as a certain unity of self, more or less coherent, more or less rich, and a certain method of thinking and feeling, more or less complex, more or less sensitive'.[33] He stressed the 'educing' that should go on in education, the drawing out of principles from within, rather than their imposition from without. He advocated Dr Andrew Bell's 'Madras System' of education, as set forth in his *An Experiment in Education made at the Male Asylum of Madras* (1797), and in *The Madras School, or Elements of Tuition* . . . (Chelsea 1808), the aim of which, as Coburn explains, was 'to teach the child, rather than the subject'.[34] By contrast, Coleridge abhorred the system of Joseph Lancaster (even though it was partially adapted from Bell's system) because of the severe punishments it recommended. In a lecture of 1808 Coleridge attacked such systems of punishments – the fool's cap, the rod and, most inhumane of all, 'the yoke and shackles, the cords, and fetters, and cages of Mr Lancaster', as Southey described them in reporting the lecture in his own book on education, *The Origin, Nature, and Object, of the New System of Education*, (1812): 'Mr Coleridge . . . read Mr Lancaster's account of these precious inventions verbatim from his own book, and throwing the book down with a mixture of contempt and indignation, exclaimed, "No boy who has been subject to punishments like these will stand in fear of Newgate, or feel any horror at the thought of a slave ship!" '[35] As Coburn expresses it: 'Coleridge's admiration for Dr Bell was chiefly for his concentration on the child as a person, the vitalist principle congenial to Coleridge's dynamic theories of human experience; his objection to Lancaster was chiefly to his external system of rewards and punishments, a slave system to which Coleridge had very great objections, psychological, moral, and theological.'[36]

Within this wide context of national debate about educational theory,

Coleridge several times proposed setting up his own tutoring programmes for young men, whose fees would defray the Coleridge family's living costs in exchange for intense training in language, philosophy and logic. The first such arrangement, with Charles Lloyd in 1796–7, proved disastrous, but Coleridge continued to experiment with plans that would allow him to talk as he liked to a small group of disciples, to cultivate rather than merely to civilise them, eliciting their inherent power and principles, and to be paid as well: the *Logic* was the result of a later project of this sort. In addition, he noted plans for the education of young women.

Coleridge's ardent lecture on the rival educational systems of Bell and Lancaster culminates in praise of imaginative reading for children and an attack on Malthus (the relevance of which the reporter does not see).[37]

The extraordinary lecture on Education was most excellent, delivered with great animation and *extorting* praise from those whose prejudices he was mercilessly attacking. And he kept his audience on the rack of pleasure and offence two whole hours and 10 minutes, and few went away during the lecture. He began by establishing a commonplace distinction neatly, between the *objects* and the *means* of education, which he observed to be "perhaps almost the only safe way of being useful." Omitting a *tirade* which you can very well supply on the object of E., I come to the means of forming the character, the cardinal rules of early education. These are 1. to work by love and so generate love: 2. to habituate the mind to intellectual accuracy or truth: 3. to excite power.

(1). He enforced a great truth strikingly: "My experience tells me that little is taught or communicated by contest or dispute, but everything by sympathy and love. Collision elicits truth only from the hardest heads." "I hold motives to be of little influence compared with feelings." He apologised for early prejudices with a self-correction – "And yet what nobler judgement is there than that a child should listen with faith, the principle of all good things, to his father or preceptor?" Digressing on Rousseau he told an anecdote pleasantly, *si non vero è ben trovato*. A friend had defended the negative education of R. C. led him into his miserably neglected garden, choked with weeds. "What is this?" said he. "Only a garden," C. replied, "educated according to Rousseau's principles." On punishment he pleaded the cause of humanity eloquently. He noticed the good arising from the corporal inflictions of our great schools – in the Spartan fortitude it excited – in the generous sympathy and friendship it awakened and in the point of honour it enforced: yet on the other hand he shewed this very reference to honour to be a great evil as a substitute for virtue and principle. School boys, he observed, lived in civil war with their masters. They are disgraced by a lie told to their fellows; it is an honour to impose on the common enemy. Thus the mind is prepared for every falsehood and injustice when the interest of the party, when honour requires it. On disgraceful punishments such as fools-caps he spoke with great indignation and declared that even now his life is embittered by the recollection of ignominious punishment he suffered when a child. It comes to him in disease and when his mind is dejected. – This part was delivered with fervour. Could all the pedagogues of the United Kingdom have been before him! 2. On truth, too, he was very judicious. He advised the beginning with enforcing great accuracy of assertion in young children. The parent, he observed, who should hear his child call a round leaf, "long", would do well to fetch it instantly. Thus tutored to render words comfortable with ideas, the child would have the habit of truth without having any notion or thought of *moral truth*. "We should not early begin with impressing ideas of virtue [or] goodness which the child could not comprehend." Then he digressed *à l'Allemagne* – on the distinction between obscure ideas and clear notions. Our notions resemble the index and hand of the Dial; our feelings are the hidden springs which impel the machine, with this difference, that notions and feelings react on each other reciprocally. The veneration for the Supreme Being, sense of mysterious existence, not to be profaned by the intrusion of clear notions. Here he was applauded by those who do not pretend to understanding, while the Socinians of course felt profound contempt for the lecturer. I find from my notes that C. was not very methodical. You will excuse my not being more so. 1. and 2. "Stimulate the heart to love, and the mind to be early accurate, and all other virtues will rise of their own accord and all vices will be thrown out." – When treating of punishments he dared to represent the text, "he that spareth the rod, spoileth the child," as a source of much evil. He feelingly urged the repugnance of infancy to quiet and gloom and the duty of attending to such indications, observing that the severe notions entertained of Religion, etc., were more pernicious than all that had been written by Voltaire and such *"paltry scribblers."* Considering this phrase as the gilding of the pill, I let it pass. Coleridge is in the main right, but Voltaire is no paltry scribbler. *A propos* I could every twenty minutes rap the knuckles of the lectures for little unworthy compliances for occasional conformity. But *n'importe*, he says such a number of things both good and useful at the same time that I can tolerate these draw-backs or rather make-weights. 3. In speaking of Education as a mean of strengthening the character, he opposed our system of "cramming" children. All this you know and feel already, as indeed you do what I have written above. He censured the practice of carrying the notion of making learning easy much too far; and especially satirised the good books in Miss Edgeworth's style. "I infinitely prefer the little books of 'The Seven Champions of Christendom', 'Jack the Giant Killer', etc. – for at least they make the child forget himself – to your moral tales where a good little boy comes in and says, 'Mama, I met a poor beggar man and gave him the sixpence you gave me yesterday. Did I do right?' – 'O, yes, my dear; to be sure you did.' This is not virtue, but vanity; such books and such lessons do not teach goodness, but – if I might venture such a word – goody-ness." What goody he referred to I know not, for he praised Mrs. Trimmer afterwards. He afterwards added, "The lesson to be inculcated should be, let the Child [be good] and know it not. Instructors should be careful not to let the intellect die of plethora." The latter part of the Lecture was taken up in a defence of education for the poor; it was very useful, but very trite. He said nothing worth quotation. He also lugged in most unnecessarily an attack upon Malthus; he was as unfair in his representation as Hazlitt in his answer. He also noticed Cobbett, etc. In conclusion, he eulogised Dr. Bell's plan of education and concluded by a severe attack upon Lancaster for having stolen from Dr. Bell all that is good in his plans. And [he] expatiated [with war]mth on the barbarous ignominious punishments Lancaster introduce[d]. He also accused Lancaster of religious intolerance, but I susp[ect, withou]t knowing the fact, that he on this point did not do justice to the Quaker. He concluded by gratulating himself on living in this age; "for I have seen what infinite good *one* man [can] do by persevering in his efforts to resist evil and spread good over human life. And if I were called upon to say which two men in my own time had been most extensively useful and who had done most for humanity I should say Mr. Clarkson and Dr. Bell."

In the Biographia *Coleridge argues that lack of education hardens the minds of rustics.*[38]

I am convinced, that for the human soul to prosper in rustic life, a certain vantage-ground is pre-requisite. It is not every man that is likely to be improved by a country life or by country labour. Education, or original sensibility, or both, must pre-exist, if the changes, forms, and incidents of nature are to prove a sufficient stimulant. And where these are not sufficient, the mind contracts and hardens by want of stimulants; and the man becomes selfish, sensual, gross, and hard-hearted. Let the management of the POOR LAWS in Liverpool, Manchester, or Bristol be compared with the ordinary dispensation of the poor rates in agricultural villages, where the *farmers* are the overseers and guardians of the poor. If my own experience have not been particularly unfortunate, as well as that of the many respectable country clergymen with whom I have conversed on the subject, the result would engender more than scepticism concerning the desirable influences of low and rustic life in and for itself. Whatever may be concluded on the other side, from the stronger local attachments and enterprizing spirit of the Swiss, and other mountaineers, applies to a particular mode of pastoral life, under forms of property, that permit and beget manners truly republican, not to rustic life in general, or to the absence of artificial cultivation. On the contrary the mountaineers, whose manners have been so often eulogized, are in general better educated and greater readers than men of equal rank elsewhere. But where this is not the case, as among the peasantry of North Wales, the ancient mountains, with all their terrors and all their glories, are pictures to the blind, and music to the deaf.

In the 1818 Friend *Coleridge presents his view that true education does not simply civilise but cultivates, producing 'a well of springing water' from 'deeper and inner sources'.*[39]

We see, that to open anew a well of springing water, not to cleanse the stagnant tank, or fill, bucket by bucket, the leaden cistern; that the EDUCATION of the intellect, by awakening the principle and *method* of self-development, was his proposed object, not any specific information that can be *conveyed into it* from without: not to assist in storing the passive mind with the various sorts of knowledge most in request, as if the human soul were a mere repository or banqueting-room but to place it in such relations of circumstance as should gradually excite the germinal power that craves no knowledge but what it can take up into itself, what it can appropriate, and reproduce in fruits of its own. To shape, to dye, to paint over, and to mechanize the mind, he resigned, as their proper trade, to the sophists, against whom he waged open and unremitting war.

Alas! how many examples are now present to our memory, of young men the most anxiously and expensively be-schoolmastered, be-tutored, be-lectured, any thing but *educated*; who have received arms and ammunition, instead of skill, strength, and courage; varnished rather than polished; perilously over-civilized, and most pitiably uncultivated! And all from inattention to the method dictated by nature herself, to the simple truth, that as the forms in all organized existence, so must all true and living knowledge proceed from within: that it may be trained, supported, fed, excited, but can never be infused or impressed.

• • •

... In the childhood of the human race, its education commenced with the cultivation of the moral sense; the object proposed being such as the mind only could apprehend, and the principle of obedience being placed in the will. The appeal in both was made to the inward man.

... The aim, the method throughout was, in the first place, to awaken, to cultivate, and to mature the truly *human* in human nature, in and through itself, or as independently as possible of the notices derived from sense, and of the motives that had reference to the sensations; till the time should arrive when the senses themselves might be allowed to present symbols and attestations of truths, learnt previously from deeper and inner sources. Thus the first period of the education of our race was evidently assigned to the cultivation of humanity itself; or of that in man, which of all known embodied creatures he alone possesses, the pure reason, as designed to regulate the will.

In the Logic *he argues his case that education is an educing and a drawing forth of the 'instincts of humanity'.*[40]

In the infancy and childhood of individuals (and something analogous may be traced in the history of communities) the first knowledges are acquired promiscuously. – Say rather that the plan is not formed by the selection of the objects presented to the notice of the pupils, but by the impulses and dispositions suited to their age, by the limits of their comprehension, by the volatile and desultory activity of their attention, and by the relative predominance or the earlier development of one or more faculties over the rest. This is the happy delirium, the healthful fever, of the physical, moral, and intellectual being, Nature's kind and providential gift to childhood.

4 In the best good sense of the words, it is the light-headedness and light-heartedness of human life! There is indeed "method in't", – but it is the method of Nature, which thus stores the mind with all the materials for after use, promiscuously indeed, and as it might seem without purpose, while she supplies a gay and motley chaos of facts, and forms, and thousandfold experiences, the origin of which lies beyond memory, traceless as life itself and finally passing into a part of our life more rapidly than would have been compatible with distinct consciousness and with a security beyond the power of choice! Or shall we call this genial impulse a will *within* the will, that forms the basis of choice and the succedaneum of instinct, which the conscious choice will perfect into knowledge? Promiscuously we have said, and seemingly without design, and yet by this seeming confusion alone could Nature (by which we would be always understood to mean the Divine Providence in the creation) have effected her wise purposes, without encroachment on the native freedom of the soul and without either precluding, superseding, or overlaying, the inventive, the experimentative, combinatory, and judicial powers.

But not alone this storing of the mind with the common notices of things, together with those expressions for the same which we acquire by imitation as our mother-tongue, not this alone is necessarily antecedent to all systematic study. The same holds good with regard to the rules and the habits of orderliness or arrangement, regulated by purposes of use and expedience relatively to time and place, to the object and the individuals immediately concerned. And for these likewise ample provision has been made by the necessities that continue the human animal for so long a time under care and governance; in short by the domestic state, and by the social, which is the extension of the domestic; both which, conjointly, are as truly the *natural* state of man, as the wilderness is that of the tiger, and the sea that of the solitary shark.

As far as concerns facts, or the knowledge of things derived immediately from the individual's own observation, enough and even more than the child has distinct places for in its memory, or powers of perception to distinguish, come of their own accord. Man's first effort in his behoof is to render him a *social* being; capable of communication, and consequently capable of understanding and being understood.

The Latin word from which our "educate" is taken is itself a derivative. *Educare ab educere*: "educate" from "educe", that is, "draw forth", "bring out". In its primary sense it is applied to plants, and expresses the process by which man imitates, carries on, and adapts to a determined human purpose, the work of *education* (evolution, development) performed by Nature. What Nature has *educed*, man *educates* or trains up. . . .

. . . The process of *educing* from without is correlative to the *evolving* nature from within, to the intensity of the *power* and the *quid, quale et quantum* of the possible *product*. In other words, the process of *eduction*, or bringing out, is determined by the forms and faculties developing or seeking to develop themselves from within. Still, likewise, education consists of *two* parts, the process of *educing*, and that of *training*: and in the *human* education as in the education of plants, the educing must come first: . . .

If then education be the first stage of education, what is the first step in the eduction? In what way do we first draw or bring out the faculties of the nascent mind? We may reply without hesitation that *in substance* this is found in the question – "What is the *word* for such or such a thing?" Though *formally*, and as a direct *question*, it takes place more frequently in the teaching of a *foreign* language. And what is the form or law in the mind to which this first act of education corresponds? Evidently, that by which we remember things in consequence of their co-presence. The word "table" is sounded at the same time that the eye and the touch are directed to the thing, table. We begin δεικτικῶς, that is, *demonstrando*.

This, however, would barely lead us beyond the precincts of the powers common to men and the higher animals. Not only memory, but even perception, beyond a very limited extent, is impossible otherwise than by the sense of likeness. And here again, we see the beneficent effects of that promiscuous presentation of objects, of which we have before spoken, and which, like a puzzle invented for the purpose of evoking the faculties, at once sustains and relieves the attention by the charms of novelty and continual change, and at the same time by a gentle compulsion solicits the mind to make for itself from the *like* effects of different objects on its own sensibility the links which it *then* seems to *find*, unconscious that both the form, and the light by which it is beheld, are of its own eradiation and but *reflected* from external nature. We may confidently affirm that this catenary curve of likeness is the line in which all the senses evolve themselves and commence their communion with the world, and their *purveyorship* for the understanding.

It is a truth of no mean interest or pregnancy, and which requires only to be reflected on to be found such, though to many minds from want of reflection it will, at the first hearing, sound like a paradox, that of all the *material* elements of knowledge, all that external Nature can furnish as the *stuff* of which our knowledge is composed, the far greater part has been furnished by the time that the child passes into the boy or even at a yet earlier period. Nature has done her part. The needful notices (*notitiae rerum*) have been given; the *tracing* is finished, and she but goes on to refresh and deepen the etching.

Here then the process of artificial education, that is, relative to the *intellectual* powers (and in this relation only it is here spoken of), may be said to commence: so far at least, that at this point the agency of *man*, the scheme of *human schooling*, may be singly and severally contemplated. What it *should* be, and what in the main it *is* and ever has been, among the cultivated portions of mankind, may be easily known from its aim and object: which can be no other than to render the mind of the scholar a fit organ for the continued reception and reproduction, for the elaboration, and finally for the application, of these *notices* supplied by sensation and perception, gradually super-inducing those which the mind obtains, or may be taught and occasioned to obtain, by reflection on its own acts, and which, when formed and matured into distinct thoughts, constitute (and in distinction from the former may be *called*) the mind's "notions" – the word being taken in its best and most proper sense. We take for granted that in order to a full and distinct attention the object to be attended to must be distinctly presented. The contrary position would indeed involve a contradiction in terms.

If then we have rightly stated the *aim* of human education, in its main divisions; and if the latter and that which is more especially the *end* or *final* aim, be the formation of right *notions*, or the mind's knowledge of its own constitution and constituent faculties as far as it is obtained by *reflection*; it is obvious that in order to its realisation the several faculties of the mind should be specially disciplined, and as (if I may be allowed the illustration) the muscles of the leg and thigh are brought out and made prominent in the exercises of the riding school, that *so* should the intellectual powers be called forth from *their* dormant state, so as to become the possible and probable objects of conscious reflection in and for themselves, apart from the particular and contingent *subject matters*, on which they are successively exerted – but, again, in order to this (at least as the best way of securing and facilitating this result) that the *subjects* themselves, on which the faculties are employed, should be in the first instance and as much as is possible the work and (if I may so say) the *reflection* of these faculties, such as owe their own existence to the functions of the human intelligence, and to the laws by which the exercise and application of these functions are governed and determined. But a subject perfectly answering this character is provided for us in the privilege and high instinct of language. . . .

It is sufficient, however, if I have succeeded in unfolding the true character of the education sanctioned by the experience of ages, and its perfect correspondence to the provisions and designs of Nature; if I have shown in what manner its first lessons come in aid of that power of abstraction by which, as the condition and the means of self-knowledge, the reasoning intellect of man is distinguished in *kind* from the mechanical understanding of the dog, the elephant, the bee, the ant, and whatever other animals display an intelligence that we cannot satisfactorily reduce to mere instinct; if, in short, against the caprice of fashion and the pretexts of its pandars and flatterers I have vindicated the old schooling as a scheme eminently entitled to the name of education, inasmuch as by means admirably adapted to the present faculties and the future purposes of the scholar it gradually raises into acts and objects of distinct consciousness what Nature and the alone true *natural* state of man had previously called forth as *instincts* of humanity.

In his Lay Sermons *and* On the Constitution of the Church and State *he asserts the need to humanise the population and develops his plan for a special class of educated people devoted to the task: a 'clerisy', cultivating those qualities in the human being 'that constitute the civilized man in contra-distinction from the barbarian, the savage, and the animal'.*[41]

We suppose the negative ends of a State already attained, viz. its own safety by means of its own strength, and the protection of person and property for all its members, there will then remain its positive ends: – 1. To make the means of subsistence more easy to each individual. 2. To secure to each of its members THE HOPE of bettering his own condition or that of his children. 3. The development of those faculties which are essential to his Humanity, i.e. to his rational and moral Being. Under the last head we do not mean those degrees of intellectual cultivation which distinguish man from man in the same civilized society, but those only that raise the civilized man above the Barbarian, the Savage, and the Animal. We require, however, on the part of the State, in behalf of all its members, not only the outward means of *knowing* their essential duties and dignities as men and free men, but likewise, and more especially, the discouragement of all such Tenures and Relations as must in the very nature of things render this knowledge inert, and cause the good seed to perish as it falls.

But civilization is itself but a mixed good, if not far more a corrupting influence, the hectic of disease, not the bloom of health, and a nation so distinguished more fitly to be called a varnished than a polished people; where this civilization is not grounded in *cultivation*, in the harmonious development of those qualities and faculties that characterise our *humanity*. We must be men in order to be citizens.

The Nationalty, therefore, was reserved for the support and maintenance of a permanent class or order, with the following duties. A certain smaller number were to remain at the fountain heads of the humanities, in cultivating and enlarging the knowledge already possessed, and in watching over the interests of physical and moral science; being, likewise, the instructors of such as constituted, or were to constitute, the remaining more numerous classes of the order. This latter and far more numerous body were to be distributed throughout the country, so as not to leave even the smallest integral part or division without a resident guide, guardian, and instructor; the objects and final intention of the whole order being these – to preserve the stores, to guard the treasures, of past civilization, and thus to bind the present with the past; to perfect and add to the same, and thus to connect the present with the future; but especially to diffuse through the whole community, and to every native entitled to its laws and rights, that quantity and quality of knowledge which was indispensable both for the understanding of those rights, and for the performance of the duties correspondent. Finally, to secure for the nation, if not a superiority over the neighbouring states, yet an equality at least, in that character of general civilization, which equally with, or rather more than, fleets, armies, and revenue, forms the ground of its defensive and offensive power. The object of the two former estates of the realm, which conjointly form the STATE, was to reconcile the interests of permanence with that of progression – law with liberty. The object of the National Church, the third remaining estate of the realm, was to secure and improve that civilization, without which the nation could be neither permanent nor progressive.

That in all ages, individuals who have directed their meditations and their studies to the nobler characters of our nature, to the cultivation of those powers and instincts which constitute the man, at least separate him from the animal, and distinguish the nobler from the animal part of his own being, will be led by the *supernatural* in themselves to the contemplation of a power which is likewise super-*human*; that science, and especially moral science, will lead to religion, and remain blended with it – this, I say, will, in all ages, be the course of things. That in the earlier ages, and in the dawn of civility, there will be a twilight in which science and religion give light, but a light refracted through the dense and the dark, a superstition – this is what we learn from history, and what philosophy would have taught us to expect. But we affirm, that in the spiritual purpose of the word, and as understood in reference to a future state, and to the abiding essential interest of the individual as a person, and not as the citizen, neighbour, or subject, religion may be an indispensable ally, but is not the essential constitutive end of that national institute, which is unfortunately, at least improperly, styled a church – a name which, in its best sense is exclusively appropriate to the church of Christ. If this latter be ecclesia, the communion of such as are called out of the world, *i.e.* in reference to the especial ends and purposes of that communion; this other might more expressively have been entitled *enclesia*, or an order of men, chosen in and of the realm, and constituting an estate of that realm. And in fact, such was the original and proper sense of the more appropriately named CLERGY. It comprehended the learned of all names, and the CLERK was the synonyme of the man of learning. Nor can any fact more strikingly illustrate the conviction entertained by our ancestors, respecting the intimate connexion of this clergy with the peace and weal of the nation, than the privilege formerly recognized by our laws, in the well-known phrase, "benefit of clergy."

Deeply do I feel, for clearly do I see, the importance of my Theme.

And had I equal confidence in my ability to awaken the same interest in the minds of others, I should dismiss as affronting to my readers all apprehension of being charged with prolixity, while I am labouring to compress in two or three brief Chapters, the principal sides and aspects of a subject so large and multilateral as to require a volume for its full exposition. With what success will be seen in what follows, commencing with the Churchmen, or (a far apter and less objectionable designation,) the National CLERISY.

THE CLERISY of the nation, or national church, in its primary acceptation and original intention comprehended the learned of all denominations; – the sages and professors of the law and jurisprudence; of medicine and physiology; of music; of military and civil architecture; of the physical sciences; with the mathematical as the common *organ* of the preceding; in short, all the so called liberal arts and sciences, the possession and application of which constitute the civilization of a country, as well as the Theological. The last was, indeed, placed at the head of all; and of good right did it claim the precedence. But why? Because under the name of Theology, or Divinity, were contained the interpretation of languages: the conservation and tradition of past events: the momentous epochs, and revolutions of the race and nation; the continuation of the records; logic, ethics, and the determination of ethical science, in application to the rights and duties of men in all their various relations, social and civil; and lastly, the ground-knowledge, the prima scientia as it was named, – PHILOSOPHY, or the doctrine and discipline* of *ideas*.

---

* That is, of knowledges immediate, yet real, and herein distinguished *in kind* from logical and mathematical truths, which express not realities, but only the necessary *forms* of conceiving and perceiving, and are therefore named the *formal* or *abstract* sciences. Ideas, on the other hand, or the truths of philosophy, properly so called, correspond to substantial beings, to objects whose actual subsistence is *implied* in their idea, though only *by* the idea revealable. To adopt the language of the great philosophic apostle, they are *"spiritual realities that can only spiritually be discerned,"* and the inherent aptitude and moral *preconfiguration* to which constitutes what we mean by ideas, and by the presence of ideal truth, and of *ideal* power, in the human being. They, in fact, constitute his *humanity*. For try to conceive a *man* without the ideas of God, eternity, freedom, will, absolute truth, of the good, the true, the beautiful, the infinite. An *animal* endowed with a memory of appearances and of facts might remain. But the *man* will have vanished, and you have instead a creature, "more subtle than any beast of the field, but likewise cursed above every beast of the field; upon the belly must it go and dust must it eat all the days of its life." But I recall myself from a train of thoughts, little likely to find favour in this age of sense and selfishness. [note by S. T. C.]

Theology formed only a part of the objects, the Theologians formed only a portion of the clerks or clergy of the national church. The theological order had precedency indeed, and deservedly; but not because its members were priests, whose office was to conciliate the invisible powers, and to superintend the interests that survive the grave; not as being exclusively, or even principally, sacerdotal or templar, which, when it did occur, is to be considered as an accident of the age, a mis-growth of ignorance and oppression, a falsification of the constitutive principle, not a constituent part of the same. No! The Theologians took the lead, because the SCIENCE of Theology was the root and the trunk of the knowledges that civilized man, because it gave unity and the circulating sap of life to all other sciences, by virtue of which alone they could be contemplated as forming, collectively, the living tree of knowledge. It had the precedency, because, under the name theology, were comprised all the main aids, instruments, and materials of NATIONAL EDUCATION, the *nisus formativus* of the body politic, the shaping and informing spirit, which *educing, i.e.* eliciting, the latent *man* in all the natives of the soil, *trains them up* to citizens of the country, free subjects of the realm. And lastly, because to divinity belong those fundamental truths, which are the common ground-work of our civil and our religious duties, not less indispensable to a right view of our temporal concerns, than to a rational faith respecting our immortal well-being. (Not without celestial observations, can even terrestrial charts be accurately constructed.) And of especial importance is it to the objects here contemplated, that only by the vital warmth diffused by these truths throughout the MANY, and by the guiding light from the philosophy, which is the basis of *divinity*, possessed by the FEW, can either the community or its rulers fully comprehend, or rightly appreciate, the permanent *distinction*, and the occasional *contrast*, between cultivation and civilization; or be made to understand this most valuable of the lessons taught by history, and exemplified alike in her oldest and her most recent records – that a nation can never be a too cultivated, but may easily become an over-civilized race.

. . . Our Maker has distinguished man from the brute that perishes, by making hope first an instinct of his nature; and secondly, an indispensable condition of his moral and intellectual progression:

> For every gift of noble origin
> Is breathed upon by Hope's perpetual breath.
>   WORDSWORTH

But a natural instinct constitutes a right, as far as its gratification is compatible with the equal rights of others. And this principle we may expand, and apply to the idea of the National Church.

Among the primary ends of a STATE, (in that highest sense of the word, in which it is equivalent to the nation, considered as one body politic, and therefore includes the National Church), there are two, of which the National Church (according to its idea), is the especial and constitutional organ and means. The one is, to secure to the subjects of the realm generally, the hope, the chance, of bettering their own or their children's condition. And though during the last three or four centuries, the National church has found a most powerful surrogate and ally for the effectuation of this great purpose in her former wards and foster-children, *i.e.* in trade, commerce, free industry, and the arts – yet still the nationality, under all defalcations, continues to feed the higher ranks by drawing up whatever is worthiest from below, and thus maintains the principle of Hope in the humblest families, while it secures the possessions of the rich and noble. This is one of the two ends.

The other is, to develope, in every native of the country, those faculties, and to provide for every native that knowledge and those attainments, which are necessary to qualify him for a member of the state, the free subject of a civilized realm. We do not mean those degrees of moral and intellectual cultivation which distinguish man from man in the same civilized society, much less those that separate the Christian from the this-worldian; but those only that constitute the civilized man in contra-distinction from the barbarian, the savage, and the animal.

In his 'Opus Maximum' manuscript Coleridge laments the false education of his time that transforms human beings into various versions of their animal nature by emphasising objects of sense and material rewards as ends and argues for a mode which will direct the human mind towards the invisible and its powers.[42]

Marvellous indeed is the susceptibility of Man under the forming hands of Art & circumstance. The whole Animal Nature may be made to have each a temporary existence in him, he may be made to exhibit the pride of the Horse, the . . . rage of Turkey, the Vanity of the Peacock, the servility & Docility of the beaten Dog & like the Dog for bread & Meat to learn & practice tricks which are against its nature. Sensual enjoyment can beckon him onward, sensual fear drive him back, & sensual hope re-enliven him. And yet in all this to be indeed an Animal is not permitted to him. The higher part of his Nature remains indissoluble for it is the very Man; but it remains as his avenging Demon. It is not the sensual gratifications themselves as with the Animal who seeks for food when he hungers & when he is satiate sinks to sleep. [I]t is the dream of these, which have obtained a spell like power over powers, aspirations, and impulses disproportionate [and] heterogeneous that sets his whole life in motion. Unnatural usurpers of the imagination, not the things, but the images of the things, no longer his mere objects become his Gods & in their vividness extinguish the self-love in which they commenced. Enslaved by imagination he may be educated to force his way through fire & blood, for one who repays his service, with contempt & injury. Nor can it be otherwise. He must become the victim of those powers beyond Self which he has alienated & estranged from their rightful objects. Not the mere negation of his true human feelings will be seen, (the force & the substance are indestructable & appear in their contraries.) His tendencies upward manifest themselves in idolatry, his sympathies in hatred, the instinct that seeks for correspondences & would fain love itself in another is translated to an impotent craving to verify the possession of power & derives the assurance from the torments which it is capable of exciting. [H]e becomes loveless as the fish, merciless as the snake that kills by poison & cruel as the tiger that indulges its lust of destruction ere yet he appeases his thirst & hunger.

We have thus described the results that are to be expected from the cultivation of the animal being by the early direction of the senses to objects, which having no connexion with the beholder but by their qualities as so many stimulants of the animal sensibility – to objects incapable of being sympathized with, must necessarily reverberate as it were the attention to the beholder's own body as the one object constantly recurring in the constant change of all the rest and thus constitute this body the centre, the proper unity of all else. This image thus potentiated becomes the Self, that namely by which the mind represents its own unity in the imagination. This Self is indeed a mere phantom, and like all other images that recur so constantly as at no one time to attract any distinct and conscious attention is soon bedimmed into a mere blind feeling. . . . The result will best explain, while it proves the nature of the process: for first it is connected with appetites either as craving or as gratified and with such as during the whole earlier period of the mind's growth are incapable of being communicated, in which all is received, nothing in the same moment given in return. What can the fruit or the sweetmeat call to in the individual but that individual's own solitary and incommunicable feelings?

Is it not evident that in the first case there must be soon established a sort of oscillatory movement from the individual to the outward unreceiving object regularly returning back as to its only centre and on the other hand as regular a sallying forth of the Self to the outward & mere object? In all its after life its thoughts and its actions the self i.e. the phantom by which the individual misrepresents the unity of his personal being, instead of being the agent itself becomes the sole motive and the outward objects at once its means and its representatives or proxies. Again by natural reaction as the objects acquire an interest that does not belong to them, by this constant reciprocation with the mind & with the feelings, an interest, a false worth, which is foreign to their nature; and on the other hand the self borrows from the objects a sort of unnatural outwardness. It becomes as it were a thing, and the habit commences of reflecting thereon as on a thing, while the Things are invested, unconsciously indeed, but for that very cause the more intensely, with the attributes of life and power. In this sort of middle & ambiguous state the essence of superstition consists, in the attributing namely of subjective powers & personal agency to the mere objects of the senses, to objects as objects. Alas! we need not travel to the coasts of Africa for Fetisch worshippers – I had been almost tempted to say that the whole constitution of civilized Europe presents the same idolatry and for the greater part in less imaginative forms. It is the dire epidemic of man in the social state to forget the substance in the appearance, the essence in the form. Hence almost every where we behold religion degraded into ceremonies, and then by the reaction before described the ceremonies animated into a strange and unnatural magic. Hence for state-policy we have state-craft and the mockery of expedience; for the fine arts a marketable trade; for philosophy a jargon of materialism, and the study of nature conducted on such principles as to place it in doubtful rivalry with the art & theory of cooking.

A fearful display but a necessary consequence of the first false step in the formation of the human character, and experience is the warrant of its truth. (But does our nature tempt to this process?) No! As sure as ever the heart of man is made tender by the presence of a love that has no self, by a joy in the protection of the helpless,

which is at once impulse[,] motive and reward, so surely is it elevated to the universal Parent. The child on the knee of its mother,
and gazing upward to her countenance marks her eyes averted
heavenward. . . . that which the mother is to her child a someone
unseen and yet ever present is to all. The first introduction to thought
takes place in the transfer of person from the senses to the invisible.
The reverence of the Invisible, substantiated by the feeling of love –
this, which is the essence and proper definition of religion, is the
commencement of the intellectual life, of the humanity. If ye love not
your earthly parent, how can ye love your father in heaven?

5

The Humanity of Human Beings

Coleridge's castigation of those qualities, actions and institutions that debase human beings and transform their actions into the bestial presupposed, throughout, the existence of further potentialities that were inherent in all persons and capable of being brought out by education. Exactly how to define these capacities and impulses was a difficult task; how best to encourage them he saw more clearly. Distinctly human powers required distinctive activities, both as forms for their expression and as testimonies to their existence. Poems, paintings, musical compositions, metaphors in science and art, philosophical systems, religions, all provided clues to the true nature of reason, imagination, conscience and will.

In spite of the downward pull of evil will or inadvertent neglect, these best strivings could still be expressed in worthy qualities and actions, or embodied in created forms, or simply honoured in invented customs. Coleridge believed that the true aim of human institutions should be to nourish and ennoble the person, to develop 'those faculties which are essential to his Humanity, i.e. to his rational and moral Being'.

Within the state, subsidiary institutions such as the family should strive towards the same goal, the encouragement of a 'hungring and thirsting after truth'[1] that would seek out an unknown nourishment to provide its fulfilment.

These positive powers and creations of human beings were fragile and difficult to maintain, however, because individual human beings were constantly in danger of slipping into their brute forms, whether from failures such as weakness of will or (far more dangerously) because once in groups they were readily compromised. Given this fragility, the fact of human creativity or benevolence appeared all the more wonderful.

(a) DISTINCTIVE FACULTIES

In trying to sort out the vexed categories of human mental powers, the terminology for which had been shifting for centuries, Coleridge focused on three pairs: Reason and Understanding; Imagination and Fancy; Conscience and Will. The first two pairs were parallel in presenting powers that functioned at different levels; the third pair differed by presenting equal but sequential aspects of the moral function. With the exception of the lower levels of Understanding, these three kinds of mental powers – cognitive, creative and moral – were exclusive to human beings and indeed helped define human nature at its best: Reason, Imagination and Conscience connected human beings with God.

Reason was the key to Coleridge's philosophy of human freedom. Belonging to no one person as a property, it was a semi-divine power that irradiated the upper reaches of the Understanding, was closely allied with the Imagination, and directed the Conscience. Far from being a merely ratiocinative power, it was an 'organ of inward sense',[2] a universal power, 'a Law in [each person's] own mind . . . at once the cause, the condition, and the measure of his free agency'. Owen Barfield writes of Coleridge's Reason as 'a gift – a gift which the human understanding enjoys, and by virtue of which it is human'.[3]

If understanding is a human, reason is a more-than-human mode of knowledge. Drawing his definitions of Reason from Kant and the Platonic tradition (in a genealogy which can be precisely delineated[4]), Coleridge expressed his belief that reason offers 'direct insight into the universal and transcendent forms', whereas Understanding 'is directed to the concrete world, subsuming and proceeding from the impressions the senses receive from the world of phenomena'.[5] He defined the end of Reason as 'the knowledge of the Whole considered as One'; Understanding, on the other hand, 'concerns itself exclusively with the quantities, qualities, and relations of particulars in time and space. Its functions supply the rules and constitute the possibility of EXPERIENCE'.[6]

In addition to this major distinction, Coleridge believed that Understanding itself had two forms. Barfield describes this twofold operation as both passive and active: ' "mere" understanding – understanding conceived as unirradiated by reason – is a faculty man shares with the higher animals; in whom it is the further development of instinct. . . . But in *man* there is also its polar opposite, active understanding.'[7] These two forms of understanding – one driven by sense, and therefore passive, the other illuminated by Reason and therefore active – can operate simultaneously, but, in the course of their movement downward or upward provide pivotal moments of choice. Understanding is the most human and ambivalent of the mental powers, sometimes choosing to follow the Reason, sometimes responding to impressions of the experiential world, sometimes comprising barely more than the learning skills of the higher animals. It 'generalize[s] and arrange[s] the phænomena of perception', and, by its multitudinous responses, generates individual personality.

In distinguishing these functions, however, Coleridge did not divide them, for 'in every act of Mind the *Man* unites the properties of Sense, Understanding, and Reason'.[8] To unite Reason, or the knowledge of the universal, with Understanding, or the observation of the particular, was for him the supreme task.

By insisting on the various activities of Reason and the higher and lower forms of Understanding, by arguing that Reason was an almost supernatural gift permitting the apprehension of truth and right, and by choosing sources that emphasised the religious and spiritual power of the Reason, Coleridge set out to show that eighteenth-century so-called 'reason' was in fact 'mere understanding', as he put it, that is, an admirable ability to record and arrange sense data, but one differing from animal understanding only in degree. The empiricists' refusal to recognise a higher, more spiritual power in Reason was directly associated with their limited, 'infra-bestial' viewpoint.

In pursuit of a similar strategy, Coleridge also emphasised a quasi-divine activity in his definitions of the two forms of the Imagination, primary and secondary, which, respectively, created coherence passively or actively. While Coleridge's intricate definitions of primary and secondary Imagination in the *Biographia Literaria* have usually been applied to human creativity in literature and art, they also apply on a general level to the human ability to make sense of, or give order and meaning to, the chaos of experience, whether by anticipating or extrapolating the future, or by imagining what is not present to the senses but invisible or unknown, such as possible future states of being.

The Fancy, meanwhile, is relegated to lower levels of creativity, its business being with parts, rather than wholes, local refinements rather than vision. It is a term used largely in a pejorative sense for inferior, uninspired, artistic activities.

Like cognitive operations, imaginative ones are also acts of the whole being. As Michael Cooke puts it: 'the thing to keep in mind in going through [Coleridge's thinking] on imagination is that it directs itself toward the enterprise of being alive and human and of negotiating at once the conditions and contingencies of being. It involves a metaphysical position and an experimental disposition, and it works in terms of responding to what man may make of himself, or grow into, given the ground of being. Taken in this light, the imagination is suffused with a quality of choice, and bears principal responsibility for the shape life (as well as art) takes.'[9]

While the Understanding perceives and integrates the flux of sense experience, the Reason discerns divine truths intuitively; while Fancy arranges the details to correspond within these wholes at a technical rather than inspired level, Imagination creates wholes and infuses them with almost divinely creative life. The subsidiary activities nevertheless are necessary to the total action. Emphasising the integrity in complexity of the whole person, Coleridge writes, 'every intellectual act, however you may distinguish it by name in respect of the originating faculty, is truly the act of the entire man'.[10]

His aim in accentuating these distinctions was to establish a level of mental power undreamed of in empirical psychology and philosophy and so to assert man's ability to originate aesthetically, morally and cognitively, rather than to receive sensations passively as a 'lazy looker-on'.[11] This purpose corresponds to Coleridge's interest in fountains and energies erupting from unknown sources, as in his poem 'Kubla Khan', which may be read in one sense as an account of the levels at which imagination works. Locke's claim that the mind at birth is 'void of characters' was the grain of sand that irritated Coleridge's theory of mind into its lustrous development.

Reason, which does not belong to any one person but illuminates all cognition and creativity, also directs conscience, which 'allows people to be possessed of principles'. By its access to Reason, conscience knows the good and voices it in every person, whether that person acknowledges the voice or not. Coleridge was certain that even in the most determined reprobate it still carries on a hidden existence. The Will, however, must choose whether or not to follow it. There's the rub; for, like Understanding, the Will is human, particular, subject to vicissitudes. 'The Will', wrote Coleridge, 'strictly synonimous with the individualizing Principle, the "I" of every rational Being, [i]s this governing and applying power.'[12] The conscience 'invests us with this "ought" ', but it is there, equally, that problems begin because, as Lockridge puts it, moral judgements 'must be willed and constantly reaffirmed. And they are reaffirmed, Coleridge has said, only in the act of being human.'[13]

Imagination, the higher Understanding, Conscience and Will were the faculties that Coleridge thought of as 'distinctly human'; the activities that resulted were equally so. To set out what was at stake in that characterisation was therefore not only to suggest the nobility of such aspirations and the difficulty of their enactment, but to indicate in the process the uniqueness of human beings themselves.

(i) Reason and Understanding

The relationship between reason and humanity.[14]

This again is the mystery and the dignity of our human nature, that we cannot give up our reason, without giving up at the same time our individual personality. For that must appear to each man to be *his* reason which produces in him the highest sense of certainty; and yet it is *not* reason, except as far as it is of universal validity and obligatory on all mankind. There is one heart for the whole mighty mass of Humanity, and every pulse in each particular vessel strives to beat in concert with it. He who asserts that truth is of no importance except in the sense of sincerity, confounds sense with madness, and the word of God with a dream.

The contrast between Reason and Understanding is set out in a letter to Thomas Clarkson of 1806, and in an 1810 notebook entry.[15]

What is the difference between the Reason, and the Understanding? – I would reply, that that Faculty of the Soul which apprehends and retains the mere notices of Experience, as for instance that such an object has a triangular figure, that it is of such or such a magnitude, and of such and such a color, and consistency, with the anticipation of meeting the same under the same circumstances, in other words, all the mere φαινόμενα of our nature, we may call the *Understand-*

ing. But all such notices, as are characterized by UNIVERSALITY and NECESSITY, as that every Triangle *must* in all places and at all times have it's two sides greater than it's third – and which are evidently not the effect of any Experience, but the condition of all Experience, & that indeed without which Experience itself would be inconceivable, we may call Reason – and this class of knowledge was called by the Ancients Νοούμενα in distinction from the former, or φαινόμενα. Reason is therefore most eminently the Revelation of an immortal soul, and it's best Synonime – it is the forma formans, which contains in itself the law of it's own conceptions. Nay, it is highly probable, that the contemplation of essential Form as remaining the same thro' all varieties of color and magnitude and development, as in the acorn even as in the Oak, first gave to the Mind the ideas, by which it explained to itself those notices of it's Immortality revealed to it by it's conscience.

Your fourth Question appears to me to receive a full answer from the preceding Data / For if God with the Spirit of God created the Soul of Man as far as it was possible according to his own Likeness, and if he be an omnipresent Influence, it necessarily follows, that his action on the Soul of Man must awake in it a conscience of actions within itself analogous to the divine action / and that therefore the Spirit of God truly bears witness to the Spirit of man, even as vice versâ the awakened Spirit will bear witness to the Spirit of God. Suppose a dull impression from a Seal pressed anew by that Seal – it's recovered Characters bear witness to the Seal, even as the Seal has born witness to the latest yet existing Impression. –

Reason indeed & even the incomparably higher degree of our *Understanding*, do distinguish us; but yet not *essentially*. For could we conceive the Principle, I here speak of, with the lowest degree of *Reason*, & as little understanding as the Elephants, it would be still a *human* Soul – But the highest degree of understanding without this even in posse would still be an animal.

In The Friend, *Coleridge finds different ways of defining the Reason as distinctively human.*[16]

It should seem easy to give the definite distinction of the Reason from the Understanding, because we constantly imply it when we speak of the difference between ourselves and the brute creation. No one, except as a figure of speech, ever speaks of an animal *reason*; but that many animals possess a share of Understanding, perfectly distinguishable from mere Instinct, we all allow. Few persons have a favorite dog without making instances of its intelligence an occasional topic of conversation. They call for our admiration of the *individual* animal, and not with exclusive reference to the Wisdom in Nature, as in the case of the storgè or maternal instinct of beasts; or of the hexangular cells of the bees, and the wonderful coincidence of this form with the geometrical demonstration of the largest possible number of rooms in a given space. Likewise, we distinguish various *degrees* of Understanding there, and even discover from inductions supplied by the Zoologists, that the Understanding appears (as a general rule) in an inverse proportion to the Instinct. We hear little or nothing of the instincts of "the half-reasoning elephant," and as little of the Understanding of Caterpillars and Butterflies. (N.B. Though REASONING does not in our language, in the lax use of words natural in conversation or popular writings, imply scientific conclusion, yet the phrase "half-reasoning" is evidently used by Pope as a poetic hyperbole.) But Reason is wholly denied, equally to the highest as to the lowest of the brutes, otherwise it must be wholly attributed to them and with it therefore Self-consciousness, and *personality*, or Moral Being.

Whatever is conscious *Self*-knowledge is Reason; and in this sense it may be safely defined the organ of the Super-sensuous; even as the Understanding wherever it does not possess or use the Reason, as another and inward eye, may be defined the conception of the Sensuous, or the faculty by which we generalize and arrange the phænomena of perception: that faculty, the functions of which contain the rules and constitute the possibility of outward Experience. In short, the Understanding supposes something that is *understood*. This may be merely its own acts or forms, that is, formal Logic; but *real* objects, the materials of *substantial* knowledge, must be furnished, we might safely say *revealed*, to it by Organs of Sense. The understanding of the higher Brutes has only organs of outward sense, and consequently material objects only; but man's understanding has likewise an organ of inward sense, and therefore the power of acquainting itself with invisible realities or spiritual objects. This organ is his Reason. Again, the Understanding and Experience may exist without Reason. But Reason cannot exist without Understanding; nor does it or can it manifest itself but in and through the understanding, which in our elder writers is often called *discourse*, or the discursive faculty, as by Hooker, Lord Bacon, and Hobbes: and an understanding enlightened by reason Shakespear gives as the contra-distinguishing character of man, under the name *discourse of reason*. In short, the human understanding possesses two distinct organs, the outward sense, and "the mind's eye" which is reason: wherever we use that phrase (the mind's eye) in its proper sense, and not as a mere synonyme of the memory or the fancy.

For there is another use of the word, Reason, arising out of the former indeed, but less definite, and more exposed to misconception. In this latter use it means the understanding considered as using the Reason, so far as by the organ of Reason only we possess the ideas of the Necessary and the Universal; and this is the more common use of the word, when it is applied with *any* attempt at clear and distinct conceptions. In this narrower and derivative sense the best definition of Reason, which I can give, will be found in the third member of the following sentence, in which the understanding is described in its three-fold operation, and from each receives an appropriate name. The Sense, (vis sensitiva vel intuitiva) *perceives*: Vis regulatrix (the understanding, in its own peculiar operation) *conceives*: Vis rationalis (the Reason or rationalized understanding) *comprehends*. The first is impressed through the organs of sense; the second combines these multifarious impressions into individual *Notions*, and by reducing these notions to Rules, according to the analogy of all its former notices, constitutes *Experience*: the third subordinates both these notions and the rules of Experience to ABSO-LUTE PRINCIPLES or necessary LAWS: and thus concerning objects, which our experience has proved to have *real* existence, it demonstrates moreover, in what way they are *possible*, and in doing this constitutes *Science*. Reason therefore, in this secondary sense, and used, *not* as a spiritual *Organ* but as a *Faculty* (namely, the Understanding or Soul *enlightened* by that organ) – Reason, I say, or the *scientific* Faculty, is the Intellection of the *possibility* or *essential* properties of things by means of the Laws that constitute them. Thus the *rational* idea of a Circle is that of a figure constituted by the circumvolution of a straight line with its one end fixed.

Under the term SENSE, I comprize whatever is passive in our being, without any reference to the questions of Materialism or Immaterialism, all that Man is in common with animals, in *kind* at least – his sensations, and impressions whether of his outward senses, or the inner sense. This in the language of the Schools, was called the vis receptiva, or *recipient* property of the soul, from the original constitution of which we perceive and imagine all things under the forms of Space and Time. By the Understanding, I mean the faculty of thinking and forming *judgements* on the notices furnished by the Sense, according to certain rules existing in itself, which rules constitute its distinct nature. By the pure Reason, I mean the power by which we become possessed of Principle, (the eternal Verities of Plato and Descartes) and of Ideas, (N.B. not images) as the ideas of a point, a line, a circle, in Mathematics; and of Justice, Holiness, Free-Will, &c. in Morals. Hence in works of pure Science the Definitions of necessity precede the Reasoning, in other works they more aptly form the Conclusion.

Caveats concerning the relationship between Reason and the world.[17]

That Reason should be our Guide and Governor is an undeniable Truth, and all our notion of Right and Wrong is built thereon: for the whole moral Nature of Man originated and subsists in his Reason. From Reason alone can we derive the Principles which our Understandings are to apply, the Ideal to which by means of our Understandings we should endeavour to approximate. This however gives no proof, that Reason alone ought to govern and direct human beings, either as Individuals or as States. It ought not to do this, because it cannot. The Laws of Reason are unable to satisfy the first conditions of Human Society. . . . Geometry holds forth an *Ideal*, which can never be fully realized in Nature, even because it is Nature: because Bodies are more than Extension, and to pure extension of space only the mathematical Theorems wholly correspond. In the same manner the moral Laws of the intellectual World, as far as they are deducible from pure Intellect, are never perfectly applicable to our mixed and sensitive Nature, because Man is something besides Reason; because his Reason never acts by itself, but must cloath itself in the Substance of individual Understanding and specific Inclination, in order to become a Reality and an Object of Consciousness and Experience.

Reason, rightly defined, is seen as ennobling man and providing the basis of good government.[18]

REASON! best and holiest gift of Heaven and bond of union with the Giver! The high title by which the majesty of man claims precedence above all other living creatures! Mysterious faculty, the mother of conscience, of language, of tears, and of smiles. Calm and incorruptible legislator of the soul, without whom all its other powers would "meet in mere oppugnancy." Sole principle of permanence amid endless change! in a world of discordant appetites and imagined self-interests the one only common measure!

•   •   •

. . . Thrice blessed faculty of Reason! all other gifts, though goodly and of celestial origin, health, strength, talents, all the powers and all the means of enjoyment, seem dispensed by chance or sullen caprice – thou alone, more than even the sunshine, more than the common air, art given to all men, and to every man alike! To thee, who being one art the same in all, we owe the privilege, that of all we can become one, a living *whole*! that we have a COUNTRY! Who then shall dare prescribe a law of moral action for any rational Being, which does not flow immediately from that Reason, which is the fountain of all morality? Or how without breach of conscience can we limit or coerce the powers of a free agent, except by coincidence with that law in his own mind, which is at once the cause, the condition, and the measure, of his free agency? Man must be *free*; or to what purpose was he made a Spirit of Reason, and not a Machine of Instinct? Man must *obey*; or wherefore has he a conscience? The powers, which create this difficulty, contain its solution likewise: for *their* service is perfect freedom. And whatever law or system of law compels any other service, disennobles our nature, leagues itself with the animal against the godlike, kills in us the very principle of joyous well-doing, and fights against humanity.

The qualities of intellect are further distinguished.[19]

I define GENIUS, as originality in intellectual construction: the moral accompaniment, and actuating principle of which consists, perhaps, in the carrying on of the freshness and feelings of childhood into the powers of manhood.

By TALENT, on the other hand, I mean the comparative facility of acquiring, arranging, and applying the stock furnished by others and already existing in books or other conservatories of intellect.

By SENSE I understand that just balance of the faculties which is to the judgment what health is to the body. The mind seems to act *en masse*, by a synthetic rather than an analytic process: even as the outward senses, from which the metaphor is taken, perceive immediately, each as it were by a peculiar tact or intuition, without any consciousness of the mechanism by which the perception is realized. This is often exemplified in well-bred, unaffected, and innocent women. I know a lady, on whose judgment, from constant experience of its rectitude, I could rely almost as on an oracle. But when she has sometimes proceeded to a detail of the grounds and reasons for her opinion – then, led by similar experience, I have been tempted to interrupt her with – "I will take your advice," or, "I shall act on your opinion: for I am sure, you are in the right. But as to the *fors* and *becauses*, leave them to me to find out." The general accompaniment of Sense is a disposition to avoid extremes, whether in theory or in practice, with a desire to remain in sympathy with the *general mind* of the age or country, and a feeling of the necessity and utility of *compromise*. If Genius be the initiative, and Talent the administrative, Sense is the *conservative*, branch, in the intellectual republic.

By CLEVERNESS . . . I mean a comparative readiness in the invention and use of means, for the realizing of objects and ideas – often of such ideas, which the man of genius only could have originated, and which the clever man perhaps neither fully comprehends nor adequately appreciates, even at the moment that he is prompting or executing the machinery of their accomplishment. In short, Cleverness is a sort of genius for instrumentality. It is the brain in the hand. In literature Cleverness is more frequently accompanied by wit, Genius and Sense by humour.

(ii) Imagination and Fancy

The difference between Imagination and Fancy.[20]

The IMAGINATION then I consider either as primary, or secondary. The primary IMAGINATION I hold to be the living Power and prime Agent of all human Perception, and as a repetition in the finite mind of the eternal act of creation in the infinite I AM. The secondary I consider as an echo of the former, co-existing with the conscious will, yet still as identical with the primary in the *kind* of its agency, and differing only in *degree*, and in the *mode* of its operation. It dissolves, diffuses, dissipates, in order to re-create; or where this process is rendered impossible, yet still at all events it struggles to idealize and to unify. It is essentially *vital*, even as all objects (*as* objects) are essentially fixed and dead.

FANCY, on the contrary, has no other counters to play with, but fixities and definites. The Fancy is indeed no other than a mode of Memory emancipated from the order of time and space; and blended with, and modified by that empirical phenomenon of the will, which we express by the word CHOICE. But equally with the ordinary memory it must receive all its materials ready made from the law of association.

(iii) Conscience and Will

Conscience is the voice of Reason in each person.[21]

24th March, 1808. In how kind and quiet a manner the *Conscience* talks to us, in general, & at first – how *long-suffering* it is, how delicate, & full of pity – and with what pains when the Dictates of Reason made impulsive by its own Whispers have been obstinately pushed aside, does it utter the sad, judicial, tremendous Sentence after which nothing is left to the Soul but supernatural aid. O what an aweful Being is Conscience! and how infra-bestial the Locks, Priestleys, Humes, Condilliacs and the dehumanizing race of fashionable Metaphysicians. *Metapothecaries*, said one *sportively*, but I *seriously*, should say *Cata*physicians (i.e. *Contra*naturalists) when I spoke of them as *Agents*; but when I regard them merely in *themselves & passive*, I should call them *Hypo*physicians, i.e. *below Nature. Ztwoophytes?* – Nay, there is no contradiction in any thing but degraded man.

I have only to add a few sentences, in completion of this note, on the CONSCIENCE and on the UNDERSTANDING. The conscience is neither reason, religion, or will, but an *experience* (sui generis) of the coincidence of the human will with reason and religion. It might, perhaps, be called a *spiritual sensation*; but that there lurks a contradiction in the terms, and that it is often deceptive to give a common or generic name to that, which being unique, can have no fair analogy. Strictly speaking, therefore, the conscience is neither a sensation or a sense; but a testifying state, best described in the words of our liturgy, as THE PEACE OF GOD THAT PASSETH ALL UNDERSTANDING.

The role of the Will in the state of freedom.[22]

. . . But where a will exists, and Nature determines or controlls the Will, and the Will is in subjection to Nature, that is bondage.

But where again there is no Nature, or (which is the same) the Will constitutes the Nature, there is neither one nor the other. . . . It is a state as much above what we mean by *Freedom* – it is the fulfilment, the end of Freedom. Freedom consummated, which ceases to be Freedom, as a Battle won is no longer a Battle. . . .

But where the Will determines, controlls, and gradually assimilates the Nature – this is Freedom.

(b) DISTINCTIVE ACTIVITIES

Coleridge believed that the two most characteristic directions of human energies, Trade and Literature, were each related to the 'two wants connatural to man'. Trade, the instinct to appropriate the outward world, corresponded to the inherently acquisitive element in man, which was to be condemned for its predatory use of persons as things. He was far more interested in encouraging the creative activities of man,[23] which he saw as spontaneous expressions of the human need to embellish and order life. Even their earliest forms, the ornaments of early people and female dress, indicated that man is 'not to be content with what is necessary or useful'; the same distinctive instinct impelled human beings to the beautiful[24] – which included the orderly, and the rhythmic containment of passion. Coleridge's brilliant statements about language, philosophy, science, poetry, art and music (examined for the most part separately in these volumes under their proper spheres) form when viewed together a larger theory of human culture.

These created structures arose from 'those feelings, convictions, & instincts vital or spiritual, which all men possess as men, which we cannot lose altogether without losing our human nature'.[25] A human being, certainly a human community, was inconceivable without articulate speech, for 'dumb' meant 'brute'. Its absence left human beings without philosophy to counteract 'the chaos of confused knowledge': without science, which might be given pride of place in an acquisitive age of commerce, but was in its true form (as he argued in the 'Essays on Method') another form of human imaginative activity; and without art, which, mediating between nature and man, was, as he wrote in a lecture, 'the power of humanizing nature'.[26]

Without language as a means of communication between the outward and the inward spheres 'human' thought was impossible. Rather than imitating things, words in syntax enacted the movement of the mind: 'the best part of human language, properly so called, is derived from reflection on the acts of the mind itself'.[27] Philosophy and science both expressed a human instinct to find meaning, a craving to humanise the material of the senses, that was deeply within 'the constitution of our nature, as far as it is *human* nature'.[28] Even in a science like botany, which Coleridge believed to be 'little more than an enormous nomenclature',[29] 'some *antecedent* must have been contributed by the mind itself; some *purpose* must be in view; or some question at least must have been proposed to nature, grounded, as all questions are, upon *some* idea of the answer'.[30]

When Coleridge described particular arts, he once again stressed their humanness. Among the fine arts music was the most entirely human, for it borrowed the least from objects, lines or colours to be found in nature. It also expressed a distinctly human yearning: a higher state of existence was 'deeply implied' in music, 'in which there is always something more and beyond the immediate expression'.[31] Poetry, which he frequently described as distinctive of human beings, was at its best when it activated the most faculties. 'The poet . . . brings the whole soul of man into activity';[32] 'poetry is the blossom and the fragrancy of all human knowledge, human thoughts, human passions, emotions, language';[33] the best poetry gratified the largest number of the human faculties in harmony with each other;[34] it resulted from a noble instinct, 'the effort of perfecting ourselves'.[35]

These activities were neither frivolous nor decorative nor irrelevant to the real nature of human beings (as was believed by men of trade and empiricists obsessed by the exclusive importance of science); instead, they expressed that real nature; 'for of all we see, hear, feel, and touch the substance is and must be in ourselves'.[36]

Human voices have expressed their individuality since earliest recorded writing. In his *Confessions of an Inquiring Spirit*,[37] Coleridge included the Bible among these early literary expressions: when he read the Bible he heard not a single dictated voice of God but individual voices, 'utterances of human hearts'. Rather than receiving dictation from a 'superhuman Ventriloquist', Deborah (whom he called a Hebrew Queen Boudicca) and King David sang their own songs: they were not 'instruments' or 'automaton poet[s]' but individual human beings expressing their fundamental human need to excite and to temper their passions, to find order, and to seek beauty. When Coleridge placed the songs of biblical men and women in the context of poetry, he did not intend to diminish the authority of the Bible, but rather to demonstrate how it included the noblest of human activities. As Anthony Harding writes, 'Coleridge tried to define the Imagination, the "mediating power", as a power which was fully human and yet at the same time was the channel of God's communication to humankind.' In insisting on 'the human integrity of the Gospels' originators', he aimed to show that 'Religion, considered subjectively, was therefore "an energy operating in the individual soul" ' and that 'human beings are and always have been free to pass beyond their myths and to participate in the eternal act of creation'.[38]

The distinctive activities of man are described in The Friend.[39]

As there are two wants connatural to man, so are there two main directions of human activity, pervading in modern times the whole civilized world; and constituting and sustaining that nationality which yet it is their tendency, and, more or less, their *effect*, to transcend and to moderate – Trade and Literature.

•　•　•

In the pursuits of commerce the man is called into action from without, in order to appropriate the outward world, as far as he can bring it within his reach, to the purposes of his senses and sensual nature. His ultimate end is – appearance and enjoyment. Where on the other hand the nurture and evolution of humanity is the final aim, there will soon be seen a general tendency toward, an earnest seeking after, some ground common to the world and to man, therein to find the one principle of permanence and identity, the rock of strength and refuge, to which the soul may cling amid the fleeting surge-like objects of the senses.

•　•　•

We have thus delineated the two great directions of man and society with their several objects and ends. Concerning the conditions and principles of method appertaining to each, we have affirmed . . . that in both there must be a mental antecedent; but that in the one it may be an image or conception received through the senses, and originating from without, the inspiriting passion or desire being alone the immediate and proper offspring of the mind; while in the other the initiative thought, the intellectual seed, must itself have its birth-place within, whatever excitement from without may be necessary for its germination.

In a lecture of 1808 Coleridge is heard to speak of dress as an indication of the human desire for embellishment.[40]

I came in late one day and found him in the midst of a deduction of the origin of the fine arts from the necessities of our being, which a friend who accompanied me could make neither head nor tail of, because he had not studied German metaphysics. The first "free art" of man (architecture) arose from the impulse to make his habitation beautiful; 2d. arose from the instinct to provide himself food; the 3d. the love of dress. Here C. atoned for his metaphysics by his gallantry; he declared that the passion for dress in females has been the great cause of the civilisation of mankind. "When I behold the ornaments which adorn a beautiful woman, I see the mirror of that instinct which leads man not to be content with what is necessary or useful, but impels him to the beautiful."

The inborn necessity of philosophising.[41]

What was the origin of philosophy? That I mean which first impelled, rather say, which first impels, the minds of men to philosophize? For those only do indeed philosophize who do so from original impulse or inborn necessity. Is it not to raise the chaos of our confused knowledge & opinion into Science where it moves and at least into clear & distinct conception? <Turn over two leaves> If so, the impulse recognized & understood, i.e. the motive, prescribe the end and aim = den Zweck, of genuine philosophy; and the end furnishes a test. The result of such a philosophy must be its success in this its aim: it must explain to us not only the delusions to which we are subject as individuals, and which betray themselves to suspicion from their mutable, local, and personal character – rising in certain ages and under certain circumstances, as of Despotism, Ignorance, Vice, Disease, or the passions – ~~waxing and waning~~ swelling or ebbing in correspondence with the waxing and waning of these – & in certain others ceasing, or giving place to others – not only these must Philosophy explain to us, which she must do in her preliminary and cathartical discipline, – ~~she must likewise~~ and proving her truth by her power in making these delusions to cease & evanish / for if they be shadows & phantasms of Darkness, & Philosophy be Light, how can they co-exist? – She must likewise explain to us, and bring into distinct and harmonious conceptions all those feelings, ~~living~~ convictions, & instincts vital or spiritual, which all men possess as men, which we cannot lose altogether without losing our human nature, or pretend to despise without introducing a discord & contradiction between the principles of Thought & those of Action, which ought to be in closest harmony – A genuine philosophy will manifest itself therefore by its perfect congruence in *substance* with the catholic creed of Human Nature – quod semper, quod ubique, quod ab omnibus – and by shewing the beauty and rationality of this creed, and thus elevating opinion into surety even where it is not susceptible of certainty, ~~wedding~~ allying faith ~~with~~ to reason, and enabling the describe its own boundary Lines, and itself stand as the Usher in the Portico of the Temple / What then must that Philosophy be, whose final Bond is – to solve nothing of these – but to deny them all! – tho' it gives no assistance to get rid of them! – Why, this is downright swindling & promise-breach!

The philosopher will remain a man in sympathy with his fellow men. The head will not be disjoined from the heart, nor will speculative truth be alienated from practical wisdom. And vainly without the union of both shall we expect an opening of the inward eye to the glorious vision of that existence which admits of no question out of itself, acknowledges no predicate but the I AM IN THAT I AM!

(i) Language

Language as a distinctly human ability.[42]

To trace the if not absolute birth yet the growth & endurancy of Language from the Mother talking to the Child at her Breast – O What a subject for some happy moment of deep feeling, and strong imagination. –

But as words are, themselves, the earliest products of the abstracting power, so do they naturally become the first subject matter of abstraction; and consequently the commencement of human education. Hence it is that civilisation, and the conditions under which a people have become progressive and historical, commences with an alphabet, or with some equivalent discovery imperfectly answering the same purpose.

Language is the sacred Fire in the Temple of Humanity; and the Muses are it's especial & Vestal Priestesses. Tho' I cannot prevent the vile drugs, and counterfeit Frankincense, which render it's flame at once pitchy, glowing, and unsteady, I would yet be no voluntary accomplice in this Sacrilege. With the commencement of a PUBLIC commences the degradation of the GOOD & the BEAUTIFUL – both fade or retire before the accidentally AGREEABLE –.

The best part of human language, properly so called, is derived from reflection on the acts of the mind itself. It is formed by a voluntary appropriation of fixed symbols to internal acts, to processes and results of imagination, the greater part of which have no place in the consciousness of uneducated man.

Every man's language varies, according to the extent of his knowledge, the activity of his faculties, and the depth or quickness of his feelings. Every man's language has, first, its *individualities*; secondly, the common properties of the *class* to which he belongs; and thirdly, words and phrases of *universal* use.

For the nature of a man's words, when he is strongly affected by joy, grief, or anger, must necessarily depend on the number and quality of the general truths, conceptions and images, and of the words expressing them, with which his mind had been previously stored. For the property of passion is not to *create*; but to set in increased activity. At least, whatever new connections of thoughts or images, or (which is equally, if not more than equally, the appropriate effect of strong excitement) whatever generalizations of truth or experience, the heat of passion may produce; yet the terms of their conveyance must have pre-existed in his former conversations, and are only collected and crowded together by the unusual stimulation.

Language supposes Society as the condition of its' Beginning.
    Society or a social State (which is differenced from the gregarious by the Sum of all the differences of Man from Beast, of a Family or Tribe from a Litter or a Herd) supposes Language as the condition of its existence. . . .
    . . . a human Male and Female wholly devoid of Language, whether by Signs or Sounds, could not be the *Parents* of a Family. The female

indeed might for a time, i.e. as long as the helplessness of the Young Ones prevented them from quitting her, be a *Mother*: but an enduring Family requires a Father as well as a Mother. And this again supposes a tacit compact on both sides, and on the part of the Male, who is not assisted by an Instinct, i.e. . . . motherly Yearning; it supposes a *free Act*, a Will determined by Reflection and Forethought. But this, as we have shewn, is not conceivable without language.

(ii) Creative Arts

The information given by art, music and poetry about the structure of the mind and the nature of humanity.[43]

MAN communicates by articulation of sounds, and paramountly by the memory in the ear; nature by the impression of bounds and surfaces on the eye, and through the eye it gives significance and appropriation, and thus the conditions of memory, or the capability of being remembered, to sounds, smells, &c. Now Art, used collectively for painting, sculpture, architecture and music, is the mediatress between, and reconciler of, nature and man. It is, therefore, the power of humanizing nature, of infusing the thoughts and passions of man into every thing which is the object of his contemplation; color, form, motion, and sound, are the elements which it combines, and it stamps them into unity in the mould of a moral idea.

Music is the most entirely human of the fine arts, and has the fewest *analoga* in nature. Its first delightfulness is simple accordance with the ear; but it is an associated thing, and recalls the deep emotions of the past with an intellectual sense of proportion. Every human feeling is greater and larger than the exciting cause, – a proof, I think, that man is designed for a higher state of existence; and this is deeply implied in music, in which there is always something more and beyond the immediate expression.

What is poetry? is so nearly the same question with, what is a poet? that the answer to the one is involved in the solution of the other. For it is a distinction resulting from the poetic genius itself, which sustains and modifies the images, thoughts, and emotions of the poet's own mind. The poet, described in *ideal* perfection, brings the whole soul of man into activity, with the subordination of its faculties to each other, according to their relative worth and dignity. He diffuses a tone, and spirit of unity, that blends, and (as it were) *fuses*, each into each, by that synthetic and magical power, to which we have exclusively appropriated the name of imagination. This power, first put in action by the will and understanding, and retained under their irremissive, though gentle and unnoticed, controul (*laxis effertur habenis*) reveals itself in the balance or reconciliation of opposite or discordant qualities: of sameness, with difference; of the general, with the concrete; the idea, with the image; the individual, with the representative; the sense of novelty and freshness, with old and familiar objects; a more than usual state of emotion, with more than usual order; judgement ever awake and steady self-possession, with enthusiasm and feeling profound or vehement; and while it blends and harmonizes the natural and the artificial, still subordinates art to nature; the manner to the matter; and our admiration of the poet to our sympathy with the poetry.

No man was ever yet a great poet, without being at the same time a profound philosopher. For poetry is the blossom and the fragrancy of all human knowledge, human thoughts, human passions, emotions, language.

   . . . Shakespeare, no mere child of nature; no automaton of genius; no passive vehicle of inspiration[;] possessed by the spirit, not possessing it; first studied patiently, meditated deeply, understood minutely, till knowledge become habitual and intuitive wedded itself to his habitual feelings, and at length gave birth to that stupendous power, by which he stands alone, with no equal or second in his own class; to that power, which seated him on one of the two glory-smitten summits of the poetic mountain, with Milton as his compeer not rival. While the former darts himself forth, and passes into all the forms of human character and passion, the one Proteus of the fire and the flood; the other attracts all forms and things to himself, into the unity of his own IDEAL. All things and modes of action shape themselves anew in the being of MILTON; while SHAKSPEARE becomes all things, yet for ever remaining himself. . . .

Poetry also is purely human; for all its materials are from the mind, and all its products are for the mind. But it is the apotheosis of the former state, in which by excitement of the associative power passion itself imitates order, and the order resulting produces a pleasureable passion, and thus it elevates the mind by making its feelings the object of its reflexion. So likewise, whilst it recalls the sights and sounds that had accompanied the occasions of the original passions, poetry impregnates them with an interest not their own by means of the passions, and yet tempers the passion by the calming power which all distinct images exert on the human soul. In this way poetry is the preparation for art, inasmuch as it avails itself of the forms of nature to recall, to express, and to modify the thoughts and feelings of the mind. Still, however, poetry can only act through the intervention of articulate speech, which is so peculiarly human, that in all languages it constitutes the ordinary phrase by which man and nature are contradistinguished. It is the original force of the word "brute," and even "mute" and "dumb" do not convey the absence of sound, but the absence of articulated sounds.

As soon as the human mind is intelligibly addressed by an outward image exclusively of articulate speech, so soon does art commence. But please to observe that I have laid particular stress on the words "human mind," – meaning to exclude thereby all results common to man and all other sentient creatures, and consequently confining myself to the effect produced by the congruity of the animal impression with the reflective powers of the mind; so that not the thing presented, but that which is re-presented by the thing, shall be the source of the pleasure. In this sense nature itself is to a religious observer the art of God; and for the same cause art itself might be defined as of a middle quality between a thought and a thing, or, as I said before, the union and reconciliation of that which is nature with that which is exclusively human. It is the figured language of thought, and is distinguished from nature by the unity of all the parts in one thought or idea. Hence nature itself would give us the impression of a work of art, if we could see the thought which is present at once in the whole and in every part; and a work of art will be just in proportion as it adequately conveys the thought, and rich in proportion to the variety of parts which it holds in unity.

If, therefore, the term "mute" be taken as opposed not to sound but to articulate speech, the old definition of painting will in fact be the true and best definition of the Fine Arts in general, that is, *muta poesis*, mute poesy, and so of course poesy. And, as all languages perfect themselves by a gradual process of desynonymizing words originally equivalent, I have cherished the wish to use the word "poesy" as the generic or common term, and to distinguish that species of poesy which is not *muta poesis* by its usual name "poetry"; while of all the other species which collectively form the Fine Arts, there would remain this as the common definition, – that they all, like poetry, are to express intellectual purposes, thoughts, concep- tions, and sentiments which have their origin in the human mind, – not, however, as poetry does, by means of articulate speech, but as nature or the divine art does, by form, color, magnitude, proportion, or by sound, that is, silently or musically.

Hence there is in genius itself an unconscious activity; nay, that is the genius in the man of genius. And this is the true exposition of the rule that the artist must first eloign himself from nature in order to return to her with full effect. Why this? Because if he were to begin by mere painful copying, he would produce masks only, not forms breathing life. He must out of his own mind create forms according to the severe laws of the intellect, in order to generate in himself that co-ordination of freedom and law, that involution of obedience in the prescript, and of the prescript in the impulse to obey, which assimilates him to nature, and enables him to understand her. He merely absents himself for a season from her, that his own spirit, which has the same ground with nature, may learn her unspoken language in its main radicals, before he approaches to her endless compositions of them. Yes, not to acquire cold notions – lifeless technical rules – but living and life-producing ideas, which shall contain their own evidence, the certainty that they are essentially one with the germinal causes in nature, – his consciousness being the focus and mirror of both, – for this does the artist for a time abandon the external real in order to return to it with a complete sympathy with its internal and actual. For of all we see, hear, feel and touch the substance is and must be in ourselves.

I wish, I dared used the Brunonian phrase – & define Poetry – the Art of representing Objects in relation to the *excitability* of the human mind, &c – or what if we say – the communication of ~~our~~ Thoughts and feelings so as to produce excitement by sympathy, for the purpose of immediate pleasure, the most pleasure from each part that is compatible with the largest possible sum of pleasure from the whole –?

The art of communicating whatever we wish to communicate so as to express and to produce excitement – or – in the way best fitted to express & to &c – or as applied to all the fine arts

~~The~~ A communication of <mental> excitement for the purposes of immediate pleasure, in which each part is fitted to afford as much pleasure as is compatible with the largest possible Sum from the whole –

Many might be the equally good definitions of Poetry, as metrical Language – I have given the former the preference as comprizing the essential of all the fine Arts, and applying to Raphael & Handel equally as to Milton / But of Poetry commonly so called we might justly ~~say~~ call it – A mode of composition that calls into action & gratifies the largest number of the human Faculties in Harmony with each other, & in just proportions – at least, it would furnish a scale of merit if not a definition of *genus* –

Frame a numeration table of the primary faculties of Man, as Reason, *unified per Ideas*, Mater Legum <Arbitrement, Legibilitatis mater> Judgement, the discriminative, Fancy, the aggregative, Imagination, the modifying & *fusive*, the Senses & Sensations – and from these the different Derivatives of the Agreeable from the Senses, the Beautiful, the Sublime / the Like and the Different – the spontaneous and the receptive – the Free and the Necessary – And whatever calls into consciousness the greatest number of these in due proportion & perfect harmony with each other, is the noblest Poem. –

Thirteenth Lecture, Tuesday, 10 March, 1818.

Man communicates by articulation of Sounds, and paramountly by the memory in the Ear – Nature by the impressions of Surfaces and Bounds on the Eye, and thro' the Eye gives significance and appropriation, and thus the conditions of Memory (or the capability of being remembered) to Sounds, smells, &c. Now *Art* (I use the word collectively for Music, Painting, Statuary and Architecture) is the Mediatress, the reconciliator of Man and Nature. –

The ~~simplest or~~ primary Art is *Writing*, primary if we regard the purpose, abstracted from the different modes of realizing it – the *steps*, of which the instances are still presented to us in the lower degrees of civilization – gesticulation and rosaries or Wampum, in the lowest – picture Language – Hieroglyphics – and finally, Alphabetic / These all alike consist in the *translation*, as it were, of Man into Nature – the use of the visible in place of the Audible. The (so called) Music of Savage Tribes ~~can scarcely~~ as little deserves the name of Art ~~as~~ to the *Under*standing, as the Ear warrants it for Music –. Its lowest step is a mere expression of Passion by the sounds which the Passion itself necessitates – its highest, a voluntary re-production of those Sounds, in the absence of the occasioning Causes, so as to give the pleasure of *Contrast* – ex. gr. the various outcries of Battle in the song of Triumph, & Security.

Poetry likewise is purely *human* – all its materials are *from* the mind, and all the products are *for* the mind. It is the Apotheosis of the former state – viz. Order and Passion – *N.b.* how by excitement of the Associative Power Passion itself imitates Order, and the *order* resulting produces a pleasurable *Passion* (whence Metre) and thus elevates the Mind by making its feelings the Objects of its reflection / and how recalling the Sights and Sounds that had accompanied the occasions of the original passion it impregnates them with an interest not their own by means of the Passions, and yet tempers the passion by the calming power which all *distinct* images exert on the human soul. (This *illustrated*.)

In this way Poetry is the ~~Perp~~ Preparation for Art: inasmuch as it avails itself of the forms of Nature to recall, to express, and to modify the thoughts and feelings of the mind – still however thro' the medium of *articulate Speech*, which is so peculiarly human that in all languages it is the ordinary ~~distinction~~ phrase by which Man and Nature are contra-distinguished – it is the original force of the word *brute* – and even now mute, and dumb do not convey the absence of sound, but the absence of articulate Sounds.

In a lecture of 1811 Coleridge emphasises the supreme role of the poet.[44]

It ~~was~~ is impossible he observed to pay a higher compliment to Poetry than to consider it in the effects which it has in common with ~~Poetry~~ Religion and distinct as far as distinct can be, where there is no division, in those qualities which religion exercises & diffuses over all mankind as far as they are subject to its influence.

He had often thought that Religion (speaking of it only as it accords with Poetry without reference to its more serious effects) is the Poetry of all mankind, so as both have for their object ~~to~~

1. To generalise our notions; to prevent men from confining their attention solely or chiefly to their own narrow sphere of action, to their own individualizing circumstances; but by placing them in aweful relations merges the individual man in the whole & makes it impossible for any one man to think of his ~~present or his~~ future ~~lot~~ or of his present lot in reference to a future without at the same time comprizing all his fellow creatures.

2. That it throws the objects of deepest interest at a distance from us & thereby not only aids our imagination but in a most important way subserves the interest of our virtues for that man is indeed a slave who is a slave to his own senses and whose mind & imagination cannot carry him beyond the narrow sphere which his hand can touch or even his eye can reach.

3. The grandest point of resemblance: that both have for their object (he knew not whether the English language supplied an appropriate word) the perfecting, the pointing out to us the indefinite improvement of our nature & fixing our attention upon that. It bids us while we are sitting in the dark round our little fire still look at the mountain tops struggling with the darkness & which announces that light wch shall be common to us all & in which all individual interests shall dissolve into one common interest and every man find in another more than a brother. –

Such being the case we need not wonder that it has pleased Providence that the divinest truths of religion sho^d be revealed to us in the form of Poetry & that at all times the Poets, tho' not the slaves of any <particular> sectarian opinions, should have joined to support all those delicate sentiments of the heart, (often, when they were most opposite to the reigning philosophy of the day) wch might be called the feeding streams of Religion.

Coleridge had heard it said that "an undevout Astronomer is mad." In the strict sense of the word every being capable of understanding, must be mad, who remains as it were, sunk in the ground on which he treads; ~~any being~~ who gifted with the divine faculties of indefinite hope & fear, born with them, yet fixes his faith on that in wch neither hope nor fear, have any proper field to display themselves. Much more truly however might it be said that an undevout Poet is mad: in other words, an undevout poet in the strict sense of the ~~word~~ term is an impossibility – He had heard of Verse-makers who introduced their work by such questions as these – Whether the world ~~was~~ is made of atoms? Whether [there] ~~was~~ is a Universe, or whether there is a governing mind that supported it: There were verse makers but it should be recollected that Verse makers are not Poets. In the Poet was comprehended the man who carries the feelings of childhood into the powers of manhood: who with a soul unsubdued, unshackled by custom can contemplate all things with the freshness with the wonder of a child & connecting with it the inquisitive powers of his manhood, adds as far as he can find knowledge, admiration & where knowledge no longer permits admiration gladly sinks back again into the childlike feeling of devout wonder.

The Poet is not only the man made to solve the riddle of the Universe, but he is also the man who feels where it is not solved and which continually awakens his feelings being of the same feeling. What is old and worn out, not in itself, but from the dimness of the intellectual eye brought on by worldly passions he makes new: he pours upon it the dew that glistens and blows round us the breeze which cooled us in childhood.

In Confessions of an Inquiring Spirit *he contends that the inspired voices in the* Bible *are human voices.*[45]

But, lastly, you object, . . . " . . . Why should I not believe the Scriptures throughout dictated, in word and thought, by an infallible Intelligence?" – I admit the fairness of the retort; and eagerly and earnestly do I answer: For every reason that makes me prize and revere these Scriptures; – prize them, love them, revere them, beyond all other books! *Why* should I not? Because the Doctrine in question, petrifies at once the whole body of Holy Writ with all its harmonies and symmetrical gradations, – the flexile and the rigid, – the supporting hard and the clothing soft, – the blood *which is the life*, – the intelligencing nerves, and the rudely woven, but soft and springy, cellular substance, in which all are embedded and lightly bound together. This breathing organism, this glorious *panharmonicon*, which I had seen stand on its feet as a man, and with a man's voice given to it, the Doctrine in question turns at once into a colossal Memnon's head, a hollow passage for a voice, a voice that mocks the voices of many men, and speaks in their names, and yet is but one voice and the same; – and no man uttered it, and never in a human heart was it conceived. *Why* should I not? – Because the Doctrine evacuates of all sense and efficacy the sure and constant tradition, that all the several books bound up together in our precious family Bibles were composed in different and widely distant ages, under the greatest diversity of circumstances, and degrees of light and information, and yet that the composers, whether as uttering or as recording what was uttered and what was done, were all actuated by a pure and holy Spirit, one and the same – (for is there any spirit pure and holy, and yet not proceeding from God – and yet not proceeding in and with the Holy Spirit?) – one Spirit, working diversly, – now awakening strength, and now glorifying itself in weakness, now giving power and direction to knowledge, and now taking away the sting from error!

As long as I have the image of Deborah before my eyes, and while I throw myself back into the age, country, circumstances, of this Hebrew Boudicca in the not yet tamed chaos of the spiritual creation; – as long as I contemplate the impassioned, high-souled, heroic woman in all the prominence and individuality of will and character, – I feel as if I were among the first ferments of the great affections – the proplastic waves of the microcosmic chaos, swelling up against – and yet towards – the outspread wings of the Dove that lies brooding on the troubled waters. So long all is well, – all replete with instruction and example. In the fierce and inordinate I am made to know and be grateful for the clearer and purer radiance which shines on a Christian's paths, neither blunted by the preparatory veil, nor crimsoned in its struggle through the all-enwrapping mist of the world's ignorance: whilst in the self-oblivion of these heroes of the Old Testament, their elevation above all low and individual interests, – above all, in the entire and vehement devotion of their total being to the service of their divine Master, I find a lesson of humility, a ground of humiliation, and a shaming, yet rousing, example of faith and fealty. But let me once be persuaded that all these heart-awakening utterances of human hearts – of men of like faculties and passions with myself, mourning, rejoicing, suffering, triumphing – are but as a *Divina Commedia* of a superhuman – Oh bear with me, if I say – Ventriloquist; - that the royal Harper, to whom I have so often submitted myself as a *many-stringed instrument* for his fire-tipt fingers to traverse, while every several nerve of emotion, passion, thought, that thrids the flesh-and-blood of our common humanity, responded to the touch, – that this *sweet Psalmist of Israel* was himself as mere an instrument as his harp, an *automaton* poet, mourner, and supplicant; – all is gone, – all sympathy, at least, and all example. I listen in awe and fear, but likewise in perplexity and confusion of spirit.

(c) DISTINCTIVE EMOTIONS

The three emotions that Coleridge believed to be most distinctively human arose from lack, want, a recognition of the missing. Love, guilt and yearning for immortality, being based on a consciousness of insufficiency and a desire for another self, a better self or a more enduring self, were essential to human nature. The institutions of marriage, law and religion were themselves reifications of such yearnings.

Despite – or because of – his many disappointments as a lover, Coleridge may be considered a major theoretician of love. Although he often cited the Platonic notion of a ladder rising from physical to spiritual love, he experienced and wrote ardently about sensuous love and stressed love's wholeness, rather than its dividedness. In all its forms, as Coleridge saw it, love manifested a yearning for further fulfilment. 'I tremble on the threshold of some Joy, that cannot be entered into while I am embodied – a pain of yearning', he wrote in a notebook[46] and (about his beloved Sara Hutchinson): 'I inevitably by some link or other return to you, or (say rather) bring some fuel of thought to the ceaseless Yearning for you at my Inmost, which like a steady fire attracts constantly the air which constantly feeds it.'[47] When he defined love as 'a perfect Desire of the Whole being to be united to some thing felt necessary to its perfection by the most perfect means',[48] he chose his words carefully. The whole being was included. Whereas Wordsworth could not conceive of love as more than a combination of lust and friendship, Coleridge saw it as a power of a different order. It was 'a passion in itself fit and appropriate to human nature', even 'peculiar to it'.[49] To deny that human beings were capable of feeling these 'passions of justice, charity, and love' was 'moral suicide'; it was to 'wallow like a hog in the mire'.

In *Coleridge and the Power of Love*, J. Robert Barth defines love's three aspects for Coleridge: its 'instinctive nature', its 'essential oneness', and its 'completion of one's self'. He cites a notebook entry that seems to combine these three aspects: 'My nature requires another Nature for its support, & reposes only in another from the necessary indigence of its Being.'[50] Coleridge – like all human beings perhaps – experienced 'this instinctive Sense of Self-insufficingness'; it informed 'the lifelong search for the fullness of love – the permanent. For only man, he went on, was "irradiated by a higher power, the power namely of seeking what it can nowhere behold" '.[51]

If love, in the forms of friendship, marriage, parenting and worship, was at the centre of human life, it was also rooted in the emotions, its self-insufficingness connected with guilt, shame, remorse and other feelings arising from failure, its yearning looking forward to a disembodied future existence. Among English writers, indeed, Coleridge is perhaps the most obsessed by guilt, gnawed, as we have seen in other sections, by a constant anguish at not having fulfilled his promise or lived up to his ideals.

The conviction that a yearning for immortality was innate in human beings was another of his most distinctive beliefs. Ingeniously combining the ontological argument, the teleological argument and recent findings on insect and animal behavior, he argued that this yearning for immortality represented an empty space in the human spirit, a need asking to be met.

A letter of consolation to his wife about the death of their son Berkeley in 1799 had involved a similar argument for the continuity of consciousness. Although the ideas in this letter might be too abstract for a grieving mother, and were developed rather to his friend Poole, to whom he wrote at the same time, they provide one of his most striking meditations on how the human spirit might continue to live after the body dies, on how the very existence of the imagination, which, by creating the vision of unknown, invisible, even improbable worlds, is the faculty that leads human beings to create possible immortal lives for themselves, was evidence in favour of immortality itself. In his later writings analogies with animal and insect metamorphoses sustained the human hope of bursting the chrysalis of bodily existence to assume a freedom like that of the butterfly, or of being prepared in human life as in the womb for behaviour in an unknown prospective world.

These three distinctly human emotions are thus based not on contentment but on dissatisfaction: humans alone can imagine what does not now exist or may never have existed, and this power of projection can be seen as corresponding to their underlying need for a more lasting fulfilment.

(i) Love

From 1806 to 1809, as Coleridge's love for Sara Hutchinson comes to inhabit his whole being, he examines his passions and generalises from them in his notebooks.[52]

I know, you love me! – My reason knows it, my heart feels it / yet still let your eyes, your hands tell me / still say, o often & often say, My beloved! I love you / indeed I love you / for why should not my ears, and all my outward Being share in the Joy – the fuller my inner Being is of the sense, the more my outward organs yearn & crave for it / O bring my whole nature into balance and harmony.

The desire and endeavor to promote the welfare of another equally as our own is Friendship / to prefer it to our own whenever they one or the other must be sacrificed, is the height of Friendship – To do all this and in addition to all this to receive all our happiness by giving it, is *Love*! & when we receive by giving, & give happiness by receiving it, this is mutual Love – the best Emblem & Foretaste of Heaven.

Why then should I fear or blush to say, I *love* you – love you always, and if I sometimes feel desire at the same time, yet Love endures when no such feeling blends with it – yet I desire because I love, & not Imagine that I love because I desire.

Some philosophers have affirmed, that two bodies may be supposed to fill one space, each the whole, without a contradiction in reason. Whether this be true of matter I am as ignorant as whether matter has a being at all – but in the things of Soul and Spirit I am sure it is true. For Love, passionate in its deepest tranquillity, Love unutterable fills my whole Spirit, so that every fibre of my Heart, nay, of my whole frame seems to tremble under its perpetual touch and sweet pressure, like the string of a Lute – with a sense of ~~tremulous~~ vibratory Pain distinct from all other sensations, a Pain that seems to shiver and tremble on the threshhold of some Joy, that cannot be entered into while I am embodied – a pain of yearning which all the Pleasure on earth could not induce me to relinquish, even were it in my power – and yet it *is* a pain, an aking that spreads even into the eyes, ~~and~~ that have a look as if they were asking <a what and a where> even of Vacancy – yea, even when the Beloved is present, seeming to look thro' her and asking for her very Self within or even beyond her apparent Form – And yet full as my Being is of this Love, a sense of Gratitude seems to penetrate and permeate that omnipresent affection / O well may I be grateful – She loves me – *me*, who – O noble dear generous [Asra]! – Herein my Love, which in *degree* cannot be surpassed, is yet in *kind* inferior to yours!

9 Sept. 1808

Something incomprehensible to me in Sara's feelings concerning [Wordsworth] and her <evidently greater pleasure in> gazing on [William], supposing a real preference of Love to me, – But how ~~much~~ much of her Love is Pity? Humane Dread of inflicting Anguish? Dignified Sense of Consistency & Faith? Perchance, I love enough for both.

I appear chearful to my acquaintance, on them bestow my *life* & my lively powers – to you, my friend! am dull & despondent? – O it is too true! but why? – because with those others I can forget myself, what I have been, am, might have been – but with you I cannot do this – You are my better Self – I cannot see, I cannot think of you, without an intense consciousness of what I am: for what I am is only painful, is only delightful to me, by its relations to you.

Unhappy I! – I have loved many more than ever I loved myself, & one beyond myself, & beyond all things, & all persons – but never, never, have I met with any Being who did not love many better than they loved me – Several Women that would have married me because no one whom they better loved, was in their power; but never any one, who would have married me, because, they loved *me* better than any one. This seems the complaint of Selfishness; yet it is in truth the pang most felt by such as have least selfishness & most constancy of nature, such as would revolt from the very thought, that they could cease to love, or love less A to whom they had given their love, because they had found in B or C. greater Beauty, or Wit. – O mercy! O mercy! – In the Anger of agony I could almost bid [Asra] look at herself, & into herself, & then ask whether *she* beloved constantly has a right to compare others with me, & love them better because they are more vigorous, or more this thing or the other / – Love *more*! – O blasphemy! As if in the Love, I am speaking of, there were any *degrees* – as if more than *one* COULD in this sense be LOVED.

O my Heart was transparent to you as a Dewdrop, which you saw thro' & thro', and wherever you fixed your eye, beheld the image of yourself.

So intensely do I feel your absence that sometimes the strange thought forces itself on the sleep of Reason, that it must be for ever – & that you are gone – And O! still oftener, and always after these thoughts your Image is so before [m]e, that it seems impossible that you should ever die – the idea so very vivid, it seems imperishable – and how should I in these trances disconnect the Idea of you, and you. It is truly the Idea, you: even as when present, it is, you, the Idea. Even as when travelling towards a Palace or Mountain, now 20 miles off & now but 3 even such is my feeling when absent & present –

That Love, however, sudden, as affirmed of it – *fall in love* – which is perhaps *always* the case of Love in its highest sense, as defined by me elsewhere, is yet an act of the will – and that too one of the *primary* & therefore unbewusst, & ineffable Acts –. This most important practicable – for if it were not true, either Love itself is all a romantic Hum, a mere connection of Desire with a form appropriated to that form by accident or the mere repetition of a Day-dream – or if it be granted to have a real, distinct, & excellent Being, I know not how we could attach Blame & Immorality to Inconstancy when <it is> confined to the Affections, – <& sense of Preference –> Either therefore we must brutalize our notions with Pope "Loveust thro' some gentle Strainers well refin'd Is gentle Love & charms all woman-kind" – or dissolve & thaw away all bonds of morality by the inevitable Shocks of an irresistible Sensibility with Sterne. This a most important Subject for "The Friend." –

The two sweet Silences – first, in the purpling Dawn of Love-troth, when the Heart of each ripens in the other's looks within the unburst calix – & fear becomes so sweet; it seems but a fear of losing Hope in Certainty – the second, when the Sun is setting in the calm Even of confident Love, and in mute recollection enjoy each other – "I fear to speak, I fear to hear you speak" – So deeply do I now enjoy your presence, so totally possess you in myself, myself in you – The very sound would break the union, and separate *you–me* into you and me. We both, and this sweet Room, ~~are~~ its books, its pictures & the Shadows on the Wall Slumbering with the low quiet Fire are all *our* Thought, ~~one dear~~ a harmonious Imagery of Forms distinct on the still substance of one deep Feeling, Love & Joy – A Lake – or if a stream, yet flowing so softly, so unwrinkled, that its flow is *Life* not Change – / – That state, in which all the individuous nature, the distinction without Division, of a vivid Thought is united with the sense and substance of intensest Reality –.

And do they tell me, there is no such Thing as true *Love*, as a thing of itself? that it is only a domino of Lust? O why then in my noblest, purest hours, when I wander [. . . . thro' the Woods at Bolton] why when I suddenly obtain a clear view of some new Truth, why when I have conquered temptation & performed an arduous Duty – why when ever from nature in her Terrors & in her Fascinations, or from Art in her perfection, or from Science in her ~~most num~~ awfullest Revelations, or from Virtue in the full charm of Disinterestedness, I am raised, ennobled, purified – why, I say, why when ever I am best, & most worthy, most incapable of guilt or folly, do I then feel this yearning, this intense *Love*? – This certain sense of – ah! this is but to know what Heaven is, were Sara here, even the adored here, enjoying it with me – then, then, it would be Heaven possessed!

Love is a perfect Desire of the whole Being to be united to some thing <felt> necessary to its perfection by the most perfect means

That Nature permits & Reason dictates –. <This of finite beings: the converse holds of the Divine Love.>

In a lecture of 1811 on Romeo and Juliet *he sets out to define love.*[53]

When he heard it said that Shakespeare wrote for men but the gentler Fletcher for women, it gave him great pain and when he remembered how much our characters were formed from reading pourtrayed, he could not deem it a slight subject to [be] passed over as if it were a mere amusement like a game at Chess. Coleridge could never tame down his mind to think Poetry a Sport or as a ~~mere~~ amusement for idle hours.

Perhaps there was no one more sure criterion of the degree of refinement in a moral character and the purity of the intellectual intention ~~than~~ & the deep conviction & sense of what our own nature is in all its combinations than the different definitions men would give of love supposing them to be perfectly serious. He would not state the various definitions that had been given: they were probably well known to many & it would be better not to repeat them. He would rather give one of his own equally free from extravagance & pretended Platonism, which like all other things which super-moralize are sure to demoralize and yet he had kept it distinct from the grosser opposite –

Considering himself and his fellow men as it were a link between heaven & earth as composed of the body & of the soul: to reason & to will & the perpetual aspiration which tells us that this is ours for a while but it is not ourselves. Considering man in this twofold character, & yet united in one person he conceived that there could be no <correct> definition of love which did not correspond with the being and with that subordination of one part to another which constitutes our perfection. He w.^d say therefore that

> *"Love is a perfect desire of the whole being to be united to something or some being which is felt necessary to its perfection by the most perfect means that nature permits & reason dictates."*

It is inevitable to every noble mind whether man or woman to feel itself ~~in~~ of itself imperfect and insufficient, not as an animal merely but altogether as a moral being. How wonderfully therefore has providence provided for us to make that which is necessary for us a step of that exaltation to a higher and nobler state. – The Creator had ordained that one should possess what the other does not and the union of both is the most ~~ideal~~ complete ideal of the human character that can be conceived – In everything blending the similar with the dissimilar is the secret of all pure delight – Who should dare then to stand alone and vaunt himself in himself sufficient? In poetry Coleridge had shewn that ~~int~~ it was the blending of passion with order & still more in morals & more than all was it (which woe be to us if we did not at some time contemplate in a moral view solely) the exclusive attachment of the Sexes to each other.

The surest friend of Chastity is love it leads men not to sink the mind in the body but to draw the body to the mind, the immortal part of our nature. Contrast this feeling with the works of those writers who have done the direct contrary even by the ebullitions of comic humour while in other parts of the same work from the vile confusion, great purity is displayed, such as the purity of love which above all other qualities rendered us most lovely.

Love was not like hunger: Love was an associative quality: the hungry savage is a mere animal thinking of nothing but the satisfaction of his appetite. – What was the first effect of love, but to associate the feeling with every object in nature: the trees whisper the roses exhale their perfumes the nightingales sing the very sky seems in unison with the feeling of love: it gives to every object in nature a power of the heart without which it would indeed be spiritless: a mere dead copy.

Shakespeare had described this passion in various states & he had begun as was most natural with love in the young mind. Did he begin with making Romeo & Juliet in love at the first glimpse as a common and ordinary thinker would do? – No – he knew what he was about, he was to develope the whole passion and he takes it in its first elements: that sense of imperfection, that yearning to combine itself with some thing lovely.

In a lecture on poetry and religion, he insists that love is not materialistic or animalistic but essentially human, arguing against the debasement of love and in favour of the Platonic yearning for completeness and going on to discuss its gradations.[54]

I have therefore, said Coleridge, to defend the existence of Love as a passion in itself fit <for> and appropriate to human nature. I say fit for human nature and not only so but peculiar to it: unshared either in degree or kind by any other of our fellow creatures – as a passion which it is impossible for any ~~being~~ creature to feel but a being endowed with reason, with the moral sense & with the strong yearnings, which like all other effects in nature prophesy some future effect.

If he were to address himself to the Materialists, he continued, and with respect to the human kind, (admitting the three great laws which are common to all living beings, viz. the law of self-preservation, that of continuing ~~to rise~~ the race & that of the preservation of the offspring till protection were not needed) & were to ask him whether he thought that the simple necessity of preserving the race [arose] from any motives or prudence or of duty: whether a course of serious reflection such as if it would be better that we should have a posterity, or if there were any sense of duty impelling us to ~~ask~~ seek that as our object: if he were to ask ~~hi~~ a materialist whether such was the real cause of the preservation of the species he would laugh him to scorn: the Materialist would say that nature was too wise to trust any of her great designs to the mere cold calculations of a fallible mortal.

Then the question comes to a short crisis: Is or is not our moral nature a part of the end of Providence? or, are we or are we not beings meant for society? Is that society or is it not meant to be progressive? Not to ask a question which he trusted none of his Auditors would endure: whether independently of the progression of the race each individual had it not in his power to be indefinitely progressive? for without marriage, without exclusive attachment there could be no human society: herds there might be but society there could not be: there could be none of that delightful intercourse between Father & child: none of the sacred affections none of the charities of humanity: none of all those many & complex causes which have raised us to the state we have already reached could possibly have had existence. All these effects do not arise among the brutes: they do not arise among those savages whom strange accidents have sunk below the class of human nature, in as much as a stop seems to have been put to their progressiveness. –

We may therefore fairly conclude that there is placed within us some element if he might so say of our nature: something which is as peculiar to our moral nature as any other part can be conceived to be: name it what you will: name it devotion; name it <friendship or a> sense of duty: that there is something as peculiar to the moral nature wch answers the moral end as we find every where in the ends of the moral world that there are material & bodily means proportioned to them.

We are born & it is our nature & lot to be body & mind but when our hearts leap with joy, ~~when we~~ on hearing of the victories of our country, or the rescue of the unhappy from the hands of an oppressor, or when a parent was transported at the restoration of a beloved child from <a deadly> sickness: when the heart beat and the pulse quickened, do we therefore pretend, because the body interprets the emotions of the mind & as far as it can still strives to maintain its claim to sympathy, that therefore joy is not mental? or that joy is not moral? Do we say that it was owing to a particular degree of fullness of blood that our heart leaped & our pulse beat? or do we not rather say that the regent the mind being glad, its slave the body, its willing slave obeyed it. – Or if we are operated upon by a feeling of having done wrong or by a sense of having had a wrong done to us, & it excites the blush of shame, or the glow of anger on our cheek do we pretend to say that by some accident the blood suffused itself into veins unusually small, & therefore the guilty seemed ashamed or the indignant patriot recoiled from a charge against his honour. We scorn it in all these things and shall it be therefore deemed a sufficient excuse to the materialist to degrade that passion on which not only many of our virtues depend, but upon which the whole frame, the who[le] structure of human society rests, because our body is so united with our mind that the mind has been employed by Providence to raise what is the lower to the higher: we should be guilty of an act of moral suicide to ~~g~~ degrade that which on every account is most noble by merging it in what is most base: as if an Angel held out the welcoming hand of brotherhood & we turned away to wallow with the sow in her stye.

The first feeling that wo.^d strike a reflecting man who wished to see mankind not only in an amiable but in a just light would be that beautiful feeling in the moral world – the brotherly and sisterly affections; the existence of strong affection in the one sex to the other greatly modified by the difference of sex; made more tender more graceful more soothing and conciliatory by that circumstance of the difference of sex, yet still remaining perfectly pure, perfectly spiritual, would be a glorious ~~fact~~ effect of human nature if the instances were only here & there; but how much more glorious when they are so frequent being only not universal: it is the object of religious veneration to all those who love their fellow men or who know themselves.

The power of education is herein exemplified and data ~~of~~ for hope are given of yet unrealized excellences ~~in our~~ perhaps dormant in our nature. When we can see so divine a moral effect spread through all classes what may we not hope of other excellences of yet unknown quality? –

By dividing the sisterly & fraternal from the conjugal affections we have in truth two loves; each of them as strong as any affection can be or ought to be consistently with the performance of our duty and the love we bear to our neighbour. Then by the former preceding the latter, the latter is rendered more pure, more even, & more constant: the wife has already learnt the discipline of pure love in the character of a Sister she has already benefited by the discipline of private life, ~~yi~~ how to yield how to command & how to influence. To all this is to be added the beautiful gradations of attachment which distinguishes human nature: from sister to wife from wife to child, to Uncle, cousin, one of our ~~kind~~, one of our blood, our mere neighbour, our county-man or our countryman –

The bad effects of this want of variety of orders, this graceful subordination in the character of attachment Coleridge had often observed in Italy & other countries where the young were kept secluded from their neighbours & families; all closely imprisoned within the same wall till the time when they are let out of their cages, before they have learnt to fly, without experience ~~and~~ aided by no kind feeling, & detesting the controul which had kept them from enjoying "the full hubbub of ~~life~~ licence." –

The question is how has nature ~~secured~~ & Providence secured these blessings to us? ~~Cu~~ In this way – that the affections in general become those which urge us to leave the paternal nest. We arrive at a definite time of life and feel passions wch invite us to enter into the world and that new feeling assuredly coalesces with a new object. – Suppose we have a vivid feeling which is new to us: that feeling will more assuredly combine with an external object which is likewise vivid from novelty than it would do with a familiar one. –

To this may be added the variation which seems to have acted very strongly in rude ages concerning anything common to us in the animal creation: likewise the desire to keep up the bond of relationship in families which had emigrated from the patriarchal seed.

All these circumstances wo^d render the marriage of brother & sister unfrequent & this would produce in those simple ages an ominous feeling: some tradition might assist this sentiment or for ought we know there might be some law preserved in the Temple of Isis and from thence obtained by the Patriarchs from whence arose the horror attached to such connections. This horror once felt, once propagated the present state of feeling on this subject is easily explained –

Children as early begin to talk of marriage as of death from attending a wedding or following a funeral: a new <young> visitor is introduced to the family and from association they soon think of the conjugal connection – If a child tells his parent that he wishes to marry his sister he is immediately checked by the stern look and he is shewn the impossibility of such a union. The lecturer dwelt some minutes on the effect of the stern eye of reproof not only upon children but upon persons of mature years. – The infant was told that it could not be so and perhaps the best security of moral feeling arises from a supposed necessity – Thus ignorant persons recoil from the thought of anything because it never has been done and has been represented as not to be done –

The individual has by this time learnt the greatest & best knowledge of the human mind that we are in ourselves imperfect and another truth of perhaps equal importance that there exists in nature a possibility of uniting two beings each identified in their nature but distinguished in their separate qualities so that each should retain what distinguishes them & at the same time acquire the qualities of that which is contradistinguished to them. This is perhaps the most beautiful part of our nature: – the man loses not the manly character: he does not become less brave or less determined to go thro' fire & water were it necessary in consequence of love. – Rather say that he becomes far more so. He then begins to feel the beginnings of his moral nature; he then feels the perfectibility of his nature: all the grand & sublime thoughts of a more improved state of being dawn upon him: he can acquire the Patience of woman which in him becomes fortitude: the beauty of the female character which in him will become a desire to display what is noble and dignified – In short he will do what in nature is only done by the blue sky of Heaven: the female will unite the beautiful with the sublime & the male the sublime with the beautiful.

Shakespeare throughout the whole of his Plays has evidently conceived the subject of Love in this dignified light: he has conceived it not only with moral grandeur but with philosophical penetration. The mind of man searches for some of object to assist it in its perfection, which shall assist him, and he also shall give his assistance in completing their moral nature.

A lament in a late notebook over the 'duplicity' of man is followed by the assertion that on its own lust can never rise into love.[55]

Lust can never be transubstantiated into love – it is the lusting Man that gradually depositing the bestial nature, into which he had fallen, under the subliming influences of Affection, Awe of Duty, and Sense of the Beautiful is indeed transubstantiated (= born into) a *loving* Man. . . . The *duplicity* = the double or twofold nature, of the temporary contradiction, Man [must] be known, seen, and understood. Then it will at once appear that Lust and Love are in their essence as contrary as God and Hades, as the self-communicative Fullness and the Self-seeking Emptiness, as the eliciting Light and the dark consuming Fire, as the divine and the bestial. . . .

(ii) Guilt

In two notebook entries of 1805 and 1809 and in a letter to J. J. Morgan of 1811, the larger significance of intense feelings such as those of dread, guilt and regret is explored.[56]

It is a most instructive part of my Life the fact, that I have been always preyed on by some Dread, and perhaps all my faulty actions have been the consequence of some Dread or other on my mind / from fear of Pain, or Shame, not from prospect of Pleasure / – So in my childhood & Boyhood the horror of being detected with a sorehead; afterwards imaginary fears of ~~the~~ having the Itch in my Blood – / then a short-lived Fit of Fears from sex – then horror of DUNS, & a state of struggling with madness from an incapability of hoping that I should be able to marry Mary Evans (and this strange passion of fervent tho' wholly imaginative and imaginary Love uncombinable by my utmost efforts with <any regular> Hope – / possibly from deficiency of bodily feeling, of tactual ideas connected with the image) had all the effects of direct Fear, & I have lain for hours together awake at night, groaning & praying – Then came that stormy time / and for a few months America really inspired Hope, & I became an exalted Being – then came Rob. Southey's alienation / my marriage – constant dread in my mind respecting Mrs Coleridge's Temper, &c – and finally stimulants in the fear & prevention of violent Bowel-attacks from mental agitation / then <almost epileptic> night-horrors in my sleep / & since then every error I have committed, has been the immediate effect of the Dread of these bad most shocking Dreams – any thing to prevent them / – all this interwoven with its minor consequences, that fill up the interspaces – the cherry juice running in between the cherries in a cherry pie / procrastination in dread of this – & something else in consequence of that procrast. &c / – and from the same cause the least languor expressed in a Letter from S. H. drives me wild / & it is most unfortunate that I so fearfully despondent should have concentered my soul thus on one almost as feeble in Hope as myself. 11 Jan. 1805. –

An idea has just occurred to me – it seems important. Is not *Sin*, or Guilt, the first thing that makes the idea of *a* God necessary, instead of τo θειov [the divine] – therefore is not the incarnation a beautiful consequence & revelation of the τo θειov first revealing itself as ὁ Θεoς [God]? – The idea escapes from me as I write it; but purify the mind by humility & self consciousness wholly *retrospective*, & again try to retrace it. To see the Gospel in a new light again – & again read Spinoza – to think vices mere necessitated movements, relative only as stench or roughness, we *know* to be false – but take it in the Kantean idea, as the Anti-type of a moral Law – suppose it like Cohesion – as that simply causing coherence, so this essentialy demanding *morality* – & what becomes of Sinners? I feel the Clouds – yet sure there is something here. –

I dare affirm, that few men have ever felt or regretted their own infirmities, more deeply than myself – they have in truth preyed *too* deeply on my mind, & the hauntings of Regret have injured me more than the things to be regretted – Yet such as I am, such was I, when I was first under your hospitable Roof – and such, unfortunately, when I revisited you at Portland Place. But so it is. Our feelings govern our notions Love a man, & his Talking shall be Eloquence – dislike him, & the same thing becomes Preaching. His quickness of Feeling & the starting Tear, shall be at one time natural sensibility – for the Tears welled into his eye not for his own pains, or misfortunes, but either for others or for some wound from unkindness – the same at another time shall be loathsome maudlin unmanliness. Activity of Thought scattering itself in jests, puns, & sportive nonsense, shall in the bud & blossom of acquaintanceship be amiable playfulness, & met or anticipated by a Laugh or a correspondent Jest –: in the wane . . . of Friendship, an object of Disgust, and a ground of warning to those better-beloved, *not to get into that way*. – Such, however, is Life. Some few may find their happiness out of themselves in the regard & sympathy of others; but most are driven back by repeated disappointments into themselves, there to find tranquillity, or (too often) sottish Despondency. There are not those Beings on earth, who can truly say that having professed affection for them, I ever either did or spoke unkindly or unjustly of them.

(iii) Yearning for Immortality

In a letter to Thomas Poole of 1799, Coleridge describes how his sorrow at the death of his baby son Berkeley is accompanied by an intense feeling that the infant's being cannot die.[57]

My Baby has not lived in vain – this life has been to him what it is to all of us, education & developement! Fling yourself forward into your immortality only a few thousand years, & how small will not the difference between one year old & sixty years appear! – Consciousness –! it is no otherwise necessary to our conceptions of future Continuance than as connecting the present *link* of our Being with the one *immediately* preceding it; & that degree of Consciousness, *that* small portion of *memory*, it would not only be arrogant, but in the highest degree absurd, to deny even to a much younger Infant. – 'Tis a strange assertion, that the Essence of Identity lies in *recollec-*

tive Consciousness – 'twere scarcely less ridiculous to affirm, that the 8 miles from Stowey to Bridgewater consist in the 8 mile stones. Death in a doting old age falls upon my feelings ever as a more hopeless Phænomenon than Death in Infancy / ; but *nothing* is hopeless. – What if the vital force which I sent from my arm into the stone, as I flung it in the air & skimm'd it upon the water – what if even that did not perish! – It was *life* –! it was a particle of *Being* –! it was *Power*! – & how could it perish –? *Life, Power, Being!* – organization may & probably *is*, their *effect*; their *cause* it *cannot* be! – I have indulged very curious fancies concerning that force, that *swarm* of motive Powers which I sent out of my body into that Stone; & which, one by one, left the untractable or already possessed Mass, and – but the German Ocean lies between us. – 'It is all too far to send you such fancies as these! – "Grief" indeed,

> Doth love to dally with fantastic thoughts,
> And smiling, like a sickly Moralist,
> Finds some resemblance to her own Concerns
> In the Straws of Chance, & Things Inanimate!
> *Osorio*, v. i. 11–14.

But I cannot truly say that I grieve – I am perplexed – I am sad – and a little thing, a very trifle would make me weep; but for the death of the Baby I have *not* wept! – Oh! this strange, strange, strange Scene-Shifter, Death! that giddies one with insecurity, & so unsubstantiates the living Things that one has grasped and handled! –

By 1809 he has come to feel a horror at Unitarianism for denying a spiritual world and thus depriving human beings of the grounds of their humanity.[58]

10. Dreadful Religion! which can establish its probability (its Certainty being wholly out of the question, & impossible – quote Priestley's uncertainty how long he might continue a Christian) only on the destruction of all the arguments furnished for our permanent and essential distinction from Brutes – that proves that we have *no grounds*, that on the contrary as wise men, we must reject & declare utterly null, all the commands of the Conscience, all that is implied in these commands, the universal belief from infancy, the utter confusion introduced into our notion of means & ends by the denial of

the Truth &c &c – in order to conduct us over the Mahomet's Bridge of the edge of a Knife, or the breadth of a spear – and if we should discover any new documents, or a more acute logician should make plain the sophistry of the ~~inquiries~~ deductions drawn from the present documents, (and surely a Socinian who has past from Orthodoxy to the loosest Arminianism, thence to Arianism, thence to direct Humanism has no right from his past experience to deny the probability of this) then to fall off into the hopeless abyss of Atheism / for the present Life we know is governed by fixed laws, which the Atheist knows as well as the Theist – and if there be no spiritual world, & no future Life in a spiritual World, what possible Bearing can the Admission or rejection of the *Hypothesis* have on our practice or feelings –

Further notebook entries between 1811 and 1818 concerning the belief in immortality are devoted to the argument that it is 'a necessity inwoven in our Being'. Our passions convince us of their own eternity.[59]

2 April, 1811. – An argument that suggested itself to me against the immortality or rather the usual argument for it (as in Addison's Cato's Soliloquy) turned in its favor – All passions have a tendency to ~~thi~~ make us think them ~~as~~ lasting, & for ever – Love, for instance – but what is the *feeling* of Life, but a feeling which when thought of, involves all others – in giving man therefore *prospective* Thoughts, *any* future at all, Nature compels him to think himself immortal – especially, when to this we add the unimaginability of passing from Something to Nothing, between which there is no medium / sed nusquam in natura Saltus – / or of believing in a negative – & this too, a negative of that Positive which is the perpetual presence of our Being, and the menstruum of all our Thoughts, Feelings, Acts, & Experiences –. Now this is therefore no arbitrary fancy conjured up by our desires – but a necessity inwoven in our Being – just as much reason therefore for affirming the future State as for denying that Nature ever *tells a Lie generically* – never makes animals have milk, when they are never to have sucklings / &c –

Human beings cannot conceive of a discontinuity in their being.[60]

We have had a multitude of books in proof of the immortality of the

Soul – and an equal number for & against the existence of the Soul
itself, as distinct from the Body –.

•   •   •

. . . But the I is not an object; but a self-affirmed act – and if it will
not believe itself, what or whom can it believe?

To me therefore, & I believe to all men, the best proof of immortality is the fact, that the presumption of it is ~~the~~ at the bottom of
every hope, fear, and action. Suppose for a moment an intuitive
certainty that we should cease to be at a given time – the *Whole*
feeling of futurity would be extinguished at the first feeling of such
a certainty – and the mind would have no motive for not dying at
the same moment. –

•   •   •

N.B. The obscurity of this argument consists wholly in the impossibility of actually conceiving a discontinuity in our Being – Eternity
is its Substance.

The belief in immortality is a human instinct.[61]

Either our spiritual Instincts have their correspondent Objects as
well as the animal Instinct, or it is ~~the~~ in the Holiesty ~~Temple~~ Place
of their noblest Temple, the Heart of Man, that Nature tells her first
Lie. Ideas as anticipations are intellectual Instincts – the Future is
their Object, even as Sound to Ear – the Distant is necessary to give
the Direction, the Missing, the Desiderium, the Impulse, – Cause
contains effect – and the effect must be ejusdem generis – yet the
Cause goes before in order and in time / when we understand this,
we shall understand the intellectual & moral Instincts as they must
in part possess (for ~~what~~ how can mere Vacuum *impel?* ~~to)~~ but in part
possess – i.e. they must possess unconsciously, and consciously miss
(ποθεῖν.) – The former the ~~ground,~~ the materia – the *feeling* – the
latter the form, the idea. / Were not man unearthly, unworldly, and
above Time, how could he utter the words earthly, worldly, temporal – they derive their meaning from their opposites. Were there
not Light, Darkness would have no name /

A letter of sympathy after the death of Wordsworth's son Thomas includes the claim that recent studies of the instincts of animals have assisted his belief in immortality.[62]

The words *"religious* fortitude" occasion me to add, that my Faith in our progressive nature, and in all the *doctrinal* parts of Christianity is become habitual in my understanding no less than in my feelings. More cheering illustrations of our survival I have never received, than from a recent Study of the *instincts* of animals, their clear heterogeneity from the reason & moral essence of Man, & yet the beautiful analogy. – Especially, on the death of Children, & of the *mind* in childhood, altogether, many thoughts have accumulated – from which I hope to derive consolation from that most oppressive feeling, which hurries in upon the first anguish of such Tidings, as I have received – the sense of uncertainty, the fear in enjoyment, the pale & deathy Gleam thrown over the countenances of the Living, whom we love – As I saw bef[ore] me the dear little Boy in his Coffin, it *dim*[*med?*] (suddenly & wholly involuntarily & without any conscious connection of Thought preceding) & I beheld Derwent lying beside him! –

But this is bad comforting. Your own virtues, your own Love itself, must give it. –

In a late notebook he reaffirms his hope that his being cannot cease.[63]

That I am, I know. That I can cease to be, I do not know. And if I might, that I shall, I know, & if less be possible, still less. Atheism in its whole treasury of Despair can as little give the one as it can destroy the other certainty. The Power, that can give me Being, or the active Matters that first constituted my Being, must be adequate to continue it: and if there be none such, I am eternal. Perhaps I am dreaming. Perhaps I am awake. N'importe. In either case, I am.

The inbuilt religious instinct of human beings results from their need for a God if they are to be prevented from becoming devils – a need which only those religions that distinguish human beings from animals can satisfy.[64]

Conditions of human Virtue / – That there is a Being, whose will comprizes in itself Goodness, Wisdom, & Power in the plenitude of Perfection – That Man is not that Being – that Man possesses a free

Will separable from perfect Reason, & yet by the very act of separation ceasing to be *free*, and retaining one sole relict of freedom, *Guilt!*
the Guilt of Suicide! – God manifests himself to Man, as a Legislator,
by the Law of Universal Reason, the *obedience* to which is not only
perfect Freedom, but the only possible Freedom: the Law appealing
to the Free Will, i.e. Reason with the consciousness of Will is Conscience – / Where there is no Law, there must be Tyranny – and this
will be either ab extra, or a se – the tyranny of Satanic Pride, or of
bestial Sensuality. Without God Man ceases to be Man, & either
soars into a Devil or sinks into a Beast-Spasm, or Dissolution /
Napoleon "not a man; but a *Cramp!*"

Providence has plac'd for the wisest purposes a religious instinct
in our nature, which leads us to be ever credulous where *religious
feelings* (i.e. the stern precepts & sublime hopes & fears of Morality
are the declared moral of the miracle) but yet as a check to this, has
at the source so constructed our minds, that a miracle as a miracle, as
a work of power without any adequate Object of Doctrine, excites
horror where is it is believed, & *hatred* – & is attributed to Magic
or Devils / and in other minds a disposition to reject without
examination.

*Coleridge's ultimate human philosophy locates true 'Being' in the human heart
that is open to the divine impulse.*[65]

This elevation of the spirit above the semblances of custom and the
senses to a world of spirit, this life in the idea, even in the supreme
and godlike, which alone merits the name of life, and without which
our organic life is but a state of somnambulism; this it is which
affords the sole sure anchorage in the storm, and at the same time the
substantiating principle of all true wisdom, the satisfactory solution
of all the contradictions of human nature, of the whole riddle of the
world. This alone belongs to and speaks intelligibly to all alike, the
learned and the ignorant, if but the *heart* listens. For alike present in
all, it may be awakened, but it cannot be given. But let it not be
supposed, that it is a sort of *knowledge*: No! it is a form of BEING, or
indeed it is the only knowledge that truly *is*, and all other science is
real only as far as it is symbolical of this. . . .
        . . . But as this principle cannot be implanted by the discipline of

logic, so neither can it be excited or evolved by the arts of rhetoric. For it is an immutable truth, that WHAT COMES FROM THE HEART, THAT ALONE GOES TO THE HEART: WHAT PROCEEDS FROM A DIVINE IMPULSE, THAT THE GODLIKE ALONE CAN AWAKEN.

The grounded existence and self-rejoicing of that underlying being.[66]

The ground-work, therefore, of all true philosophy is the full apprehension of the difference between the contemplation of reason, namely, that intuition of things which arises when we possess ourselves, as one with the whole, which is substantial knowledge, and that which presents itself when transferring reality to the negations of reality, to the ever-varying framework of the uniform life, we think of ourselves as separated beings, and place nature in antithesis to the mind, as object to subject, thing to thought, death to life. This is abstract knowledge, or the science of the mere understanding. By the former, we know that existence is its own predicate, self-affirmation, the one attribute in which all others are contained, not as parts, but as manifestations. It is an eternal and infinite self-rejoicing, self-loving, with a joy unfathomable, with a love all comprehensive.

Notes

Introduction

1. *An Essay Concerning Human Understanding* (1690), ed. A. C. Fraser (Oxford, 1894) ch. 1, sect. 2, p. 121.
2. 'The Second Treatise on Civil Government' (1690), in *Two Treatises of Government*, ed. Thomas I. Cooke (New York, 1947) ch. 4, sect 22, p. 132.
3. Letter 383, *CL*, II, 696.
4. *CN*, III, 4180.
5. From a marginal comment on Swift's *Works*, forthcoming in *CM*.
6. *Friend*, II, 82.
7. Alan Bewell, *Wordsworth and the Enlightenment: Nature, Man, and Society in the Experimental Poetry* (New Haven, Conn., and London: 1989) p. 13.
8. See *CN*, III, 3548.
9. Arthur O. Lovejoy, *The Great Chain of Being: A Study of the History of An Idea* (New York, 1936) p. 234.
10. *CL*, III, 513.
11. *CN*, III, 4109.
12. *CN*, III, 3819, 3820, 3860.
13. *PL* (1949), 194–5.
14. *BL*, I, 153–4.
15. *BL*, II, 142.
16. *CL*, I, 86.
17. *CN*, III, 4173.
18. *CN*, III, 4244.
19. Laurence S. Lockridge, *Coleridge the Moralist* (Ithaca, N.Y. and London, 1977) pp. 31–101.
20. *Rasselas*, ch. x.
21. *CL*, III, 513.
22. In philosophical letters to Josiah Wedgewood in 1801 and in his *Biographia Literaria*, chs 5–10.
23. *PL* (1949), 226.
24. *Lects 1795*, 258–318.
25. *Friend*, II, 73.
26. *A Treatise of Human Nature*, ed. Ernest C. Mossner (Harmondsworth, Middx, 1969) pp. 299–300.
27. *CN*, II, 2370.
28. *CL*, II, 948.

Chapter 1   Enquiries into the Nature of Man

1. See, for example, the letter quoted at note 14 below.
2. *CN*, I, 256. The scheme is found in Plato's *Timaeus*.

3. Alice D. Snyder, *Coleridge on Logic and Learning* (New Haven, Conn., 1929) 1 pp. 4–8.
4. *CL*, ɪᴠ, 574–5.
5. *CN*, ɪɪɪ, 3293, 1808–18.
6. See Lockridge, p. 53.
7. *CN*, ɪɪɪ, 3901.
8. See *Friend*, ɪ, 499.
9. *CN*, ɪɪɪ, 4169.
10. *CN*, ɪ, 1304.
11. *CN*, ɪɪɪ, 3320.
12. *CN*, ɪɪɪ, 4186.
13. *CL*, ɪɪ, 1196.
14. Letter 124 to Thomas Poole, 5 May 1796, *CL*, ɪ, 209.
15. Letter 238 to George Coleridge 1798, *CL*, ɪ, 209; letter 504 to Godwin, 4 June 1803, *CL*, ɪɪ, 948.
16. Letter 800 to Lady Beaumont, 21 Jan. 1810, *CL*, ɪɪɪ, 279.
17. *CN*, ɪɪ, 3156, Sept. 1807; *CN*, ɪɪɪ, 3825, May 1810; letter 922 to Joseph Cottle, late April 1814, *CL*, ɪɪɪ, 483.
18. Letter 969 to Wordsworth, 30 May 1814, *CL*, ɪᴠ, 574–5.
19. *Friend*, ɪ, 96, and ɪɪ, 79–81 (1809); Add. Ms. 47, 543, N 48, ff. 19ᵛ–20, and Add. Ms. 47, 529, N 34, after July 1827, ff. 11ᵛ–12.
20. Richard Haven, *Patterns of Consciousness: An Essay on Coleridge* (Amherst, Mass.: 1969) p. 12.
21. *BL*, ɪ, 277, 284, 286.
22. *BL*, ɪ, 124.
23. *BL*, ɪ, 126–7.
24. From a marginal comment by Coleridge in a copy of *Omniana* (1812): see *The Table Table and Omniana*, ed. Coventry Patmore (London, 1917) p. 337.
25. Stephen Bygrave, *Coleridge and the Self: Romantic Egotism* (New York, 1986) p. 3.
26. Laurence S. Lockridge, *Coleridge the Moralist* (Ithaca, N.Y., and London, 1977) pp. 153–5.
27. Bygrave, *Coleridge and the Self*, p. 27.
28. Edward Kessler, *Coleridge's Metaphors of Being* (Princeton, N.J., 1979) pp. 17, 26, 27, 37.
29. *BL*, ɪ, 244; taken in large part from Schelling's *Of Human Freedom* (1809).
30. *CN*, ɪɪɪ, 4007.
31. *CN*, ɪɪ, 3215. See below, p. 41.
32. *CN*, ɪ, 848, 1577 (Oct 1803), 1649 (Nov 1803).
33. *CN*, ɪɪ, 2091.
34. *CN*, ɪɪ, 2944.
35. *CN*, ɪɪɪ, 4409 and 4410.
36. *CN*, ɪɪ, 2399.
37. 'On Poesy or Art', in *Biographia Literaria, with the Aesthetical Essays*, ed. J. Shawcross (London, 1907) ɪɪ, 263.
38. Add. Ms. 47, 542, N 47, Sept. 1830, ff. 17–17ᵛ.
39. *CN*, ɪɪ, 3149; *CN*, ɪɪɪ, 3320.

40. *CN*, ɪ, 921.
41. *CN*, ɪ, 923.
42. *CN*, ɪ, 1597 (var).
43. *CN*, ɪ, 1599.
44. *BL*, ɪ, 124.
45. *CN*, ɪɪɪ, 3632.
46. Ibid.
47. *Lects (1808–19)*, ɪ, 84.
48. *CN*, ɪɪɪ, 4168, Oct. 1812.
49. *CN*, ɪɪɪ, 3559; *CN*, ɪɪɪ, 4186; *BL*, ɪ, 272–5 and 276–85.
50. Letter 845 to unknown correspondent, 15–21 Dec. 1811, *CL*, ɪɪɪ, 355.
51. *CN*, ɪɪɪ, 3242, 1808–11.
52. *LS*, 24.
53. *CN*, ɪɪɪ, 3593.
54. *BL*, ɪ, 244.
55. *CN*, ɪɪ, 3215. Cf. *PW* (EHC) ɪɪ, 797.
56. *AR*, 135–6.
57. Add Ms. 47, 531, N 36, 27 Nov 1827, f 4.
58. Ibid., ff. 2–3.
59. Add. Ms 47, 533, N 38 (1829) ff. 6ᵛ–7.
60. Letter 170 to John Thelwall, 31 Dec. 1796, *CL*, ɪ, 294–5.
61. *CN*, ɪɪ, 2317, Dec. 1804.
62. *CN*, ɪɪ, 2402, Jan. 1805.
63. Letter 634, 13 Oct. 1806, *CL*, ɪɪ, 1196–8.
64. Letter 909 to Thomas Roberts, 19 Dec. 1813, *CL*, ɪɪɪ, 463.
65. *BL*, ɪ, 116–21 (quoting Paradise Lost, ɪᴠ 18).
66. *PL* (1949), 362–3.
67. Add. Ms. 47, 533 N 38 (1829), f. 33ᵛ.
68. Letter 762 to Thomas W. Smith, 22 June 1809, *CL*, ɪɪɪ, 216.
69. In I. Kant, *Fundamental Principles of the Metaphysics of Morals*, trans. Thomas K. Abbott (Indianapolis, Indiana, 1979) pp. 45–6.
70. *BL*, ɪ, 205.
71. Add. Ms. 47, 541, N 46, August 1830, ff. 9ᵛ–10ᵛ.
72. *Friend*, ɪ, 189–90.

Chapter 2   Questions of Species and Gender

1. *Friend*, ɪ, 154–6.
2. Cited in In 'The Wild Man Comes to Tea', in *The Wild Man Within: An Image in Western Thought from the Renaissance to Romanticism*, ed. Edward Dudley and Maximillian E. Novak (Pittsburg, Pa., 1972) pp. 189–200.
3. Ibid., p. 231.
4. In 'The Wild Man's Pedigree', ibid., p. 266.
5. John Beer, *Coleridge's Poetic Intelligence* (London and Basingstoke, 1977) p. 55.
6. *CL*, ᴠ, 574.
7. Letter 448 to Sara Hutchinson, *CL*, ɪɪ, 827.
8. *CN*, ɪɪɪ, 3586, July–Sept. 1809.

9. *CN*, III, 4022 (1810).
10. *Friend*, II, 296–7.
11. *CN*, II, 2555, April 1805.
12. *Lects 1795*, 10–12, 39–40.
13. *Lects 1808–19*, II, 270.
14. *LS*, 183 note.
15. *TT*, I, 235; Add. Ms. 47, 547, N 52, f. 21.
16. *CN*, III, 4109, 1811–16.
17. *CN*, III, 4088, May–July 1811.
18. Letter 1038 to unknown correspondent, 1816, *CL*, IV, 697–8.
19. *LS*, 18–19.
20. See Fruman, 'Coleridge's Rejection of Nature', in *Coleridge's Imagination*, ed. Richard Gravil *et al.* (Cambridge, 1985) pp. 69–77.
21. *EOT*, I, 255.
22. *Friend*, I, 443.
23. *CN*, III, 4060, April 1811.
24. *AR*, 80 and 267–8 note.
25. *TL*, 33, 42, 44, 44–5, 48, 70, 84–5, 86.
26. *Friend*, I, 497.
27. Letter 1488 to James Gillman, 9 Oct. 1825, *CL*, V, 496–7.
28. Add. Ms. 47, 529, N 34, 1827, ff. 8–11^v.
29. Add. Ms. 47, 541, N 46, ff. 13^v–14, 14^v–15.
30. Alan Bewell, *Wordsworth and the Enlightenment: Nature, Man, and Society in the Experimental Poetry* (New Haven, Conn. and London: 1989) p. 41.
31. See Anya Taylor, *Magic and English Romanticism* (Athens, Georgia, 1979) pp. 99–133.
32. *CN*, III, 3339; *CN*, III, 3538; *CN*, III, 3770.
33. *CN*, I, 1637; part of a longer discussion of incest, less concerned with the animals, but also referring to the Temple of Isis than the one quoted below, pp. 253–4.
34. *CN*, III, 3921.
35. 'On Poesy or Art', *Biographia Literaria, with the Aesthetical Essays*, ed. J. Shawcross (London, 1907) II, 253.
36. *BL*, II, 52–4.
37. *Friend*, I, 501–2.
38. *TT*, II, 133n.
39. *CL*, III, 474–5; 24 April 1814.
40. Letters 65, 66, 68 to Southey, 21 Oct., 24 Oct. and 3 Nov. 1794, *CL*, I, 114–5, 119–20, 122–3.
41. Letter 112 to the Rev. John Edwards, 20 March 1796, *CL*, I, 192; *EOT*, I, 239–40, *The Morning Post*, 16 April 1800; *EOT*, II, 140–1, *The Courier*, 13 May 1811; *TT*, 21 Nov 1830, I, 216–17; 14 Aug. 1833, I, 420 (cf. 216–7).
42. Letter 50 to Southey, 6 July 1794, *CL*, I, 83; letter 102 to the Rev. John Edwards, 4 Feb. 1796, *CL*, I, 182; letter 314 to Southey, 25 Jan. 1800, *CL*, I, 562–3; letter 333 to William Godwin, 21 May 1800, *CL*, II, 589; letter 597 to Southey, 16 April 1804, *CL*, II, 1127–8; letter 595 to Sir George Beaumont, 16 April 1804, *CL*, II, 1123; *CN*, III, 4172, Dec. 1812.
43. Letter 855 to J. J. Morgan, 18 Feb. 1812, *CL*, III, 370–1.
44. *Lects 1808–19*, II, 269–70.

45. *CN*, II, 2556, April 1805.
46. Letter 904 to Mrs J. J. Morgan, 20 Nov. 1813, *CL*, III, 459.
47. *CN*, II, 2310, Dec. 1804; *CN*, III, 4277, 1815–16; *CN*, II, 3316, May 1808; *CN*, II, 3345, May–June 1808; *CN*, III, 4250, May 1815.
48. *CN*, III 4272, Dec. 1815; *TT*, 3 May 1830, 26 Sept. 1830, I, 117, 206, 207, 208, and Allsop's Recollections, *TT*, II, 388.

Chapter 3   The Difficulty of Sustaining Humanity

1. Add. Ms. 47, 529, *N* 34, f. 11^v.
2. *Op Max ms*, II, 71.
3. *PL* (1949), 150.
4. *Friend*, I, 100–6.
5. Letter 927 to J. J. Morgan, 14 May 1814, *CL*, V, 489–91.
6. Add. Ms. 47, 537, *N* 42, f. 2^v.
7. See Roy Porter, *Mind Forg'd Manacles: A History of Madness in England from the Restoration to the Regency* (Cambridge, Mass., 1987).
8. *CN*, III, 3431, 1808–9.
9. Letter 513 to Robert Southey, 14 Aug. 1803, *CL*, II, 974.
10. *CN*, II, 2078, May 1804.
11. *CN*, II, 2237, 22 Oct. 1804.
12. *CN*, III, 3322 2nd n, 18 May 1808. Cf. *Remorse*, IV, i, 68–73: *PW*, II, 861.
13. Letter 805 to Lady Beaumont, 15 April 1810, *CL*, III, 287.
14. *Friend*, II, 68.
15. *CN*, II, 2368, Dec. 1804.
16. *CN*, II, 2557, April 1805; *CN*, II, 2860, June 1806.
17. Letter 717 to T. G. Street, 12 Sept. 1808, *CL*, III, 124.
18. Letter 719 to John Prior Estlin, 3 Dec. 1808, *CL*, III, 127–8; letter 721 to Thomas Poole, 4 Dec. 1808, *CL*, III, 131.
19. Letters 920 and 921 to Joseph Cottle, 6 and 27 April 1814, *CL*, III, 478 and 479.
20. Letters 927 and 928 to J. J. Morgan, 14 and 15 May, 1814, *CL*, III, 489–91.
21. Letter 936 to Josiah Wade, 26 June, 1814, *CL*, III, 511.
22. 'Spirits', *EOT*, II, 174–6. *The Courier*, 30 May 1811; *Friend*, II, 71.
23. Letter 1249A, *CL*, V, 106–7.
24. Letter 1765, *CL*, VI, 933–5.
25. Add. Ms. 47, 545, *N* 50, 22 Feb. 1832, ff. 38^v–9^v.
26. *Lects 1795*, 6, 38.
27. *CN*, II, 2955, Nov.–Dec. 1806; *CN*, III, 4311, April 1816; letter 1048 to T. G. Street, 22 March 1817, *CL*, IV, 711.
28. *Friend*, II, 128–9.
29. *CN*, III 4244 (1815).
30. *Op Max ms*, II, 72–8.
31. Add. Ms. 47, 541, *N* 46, ff. 9^v–10^v. See above, pp. 52–3.
32. *Lects 1795*, pp. 11–12, 45, 38–9, 68–70.
33. *Lects 1795*, 236–51. From Thomas Clarkson, *An Essay on the Impolicy of the African Slave-Trade* (2nd edn, 1788) and from Anthony Benezet, *Some*

Historical Account of Guinea . . . with an Inquiry into the Rise and Progress of the Slave-Trade . . ., 2 vols (Philadelphia, 1781).

34. *EOT*, I, 230, *The Morning Post*, 25 March 1800.
35. *LS*, 219–20.
36. *The Table Talk and Omniana*, ed. Coventry Patmore (London, 1917) p. 342.
37. Ibid., 356.
38. *Lects 1795*, 56–7.
39. *PW (EHC)*, I, 258–60.
40. *EOT*, III, 144–5.
41. *CN*, II, 2873.
42. *EOT*, III, 145–6,*The Courier*, 3 Oct. 1816.
43. Letter 1181 to J. H. Bohte, 27 Feb. 1819, *CL*, V, 922.
44. *EOT*, II, 484–9, *The Courier*, 31 March 1818.
45. Bygrave, 150–64.
46. *Lects 1808–19*, II, 315.
47. Ibid., 327
48. Mary Midgley, *Wickedness: A Philosophical Essay* (London and New York, 1984) pp. 115, 116, 122, 135, 138.
49. Laurence S. Lockridge, *Coleridge the Moralist* (Ithaca, N.Y., and London, 1977) pp. 63–5.
50. Ibid., p. 66.
51. *LS*, 65.
52. *AR*, 276–7.
53. *EOT*, I, 226.
54. *CN*, III, 3304, 1808–10.
55. Letter 80 to Southey, 19 Jan. 1795, *CL* I, 150; letter 819 to William Godwin, 29 March 1811, *CL* III, 316–17; *TL*, 58.
56. *Lects 1795*, 74, 139–40.
57. *EOT*, II, 199.
58. *CN*, I, 1770; *CN*, II, 2090, May 1804; *CN*, II, 2271, Nov. 1804; *CN*, III, 3294, 1808–18; *CN*, III, 3341, May 1808; *CN*, III, 3510, April–August 1809; *CN*, III, 4273, Dec. 1815.
59. Letter 238, 10 March 1798, *CL*, I, 396.
60. From 'Confessio Fidei', Nov 1810: *CN*, III, 4005; *AR*, 139–40.
61. Letter 959, *CL*, IV, 553.
62. *PL* (1949), 150–1.
63. *Friend*, II, 83–4.
64. *Friend*, II, 175–6.
65. *AR*, 138–9, 266–70, 271, 273.
66. *LS*, 65–6.
67. *CN*, III, 3293 and 3298, 1808–18; ibid., 3875, June 1810.
68. *Friend*, II, 85.

Chapter 4   Transmitting Humanity

1. *CN*, III, 3729.
2. *CN*, III, 3648.

3. *CN*, III, 4110.
4. Letter 77, *CL*, I, 145.
5. Letter 269, 14 Jan. 1799, *CL*, I, 458.
6. Letter 417, *CL*, II, 767.
7. Letter 438, *CL*, II, 796–7.
8. Letter 449, *CL*, II, 832–3; letter 464, *CL*, II, 875–6.
9. Letters 467 (see also above, section 2b), 470, and 481, *CL*, II, 881–2, 887–8, and 908–9.
10. Letter 635, 19 Nov. 1806, *CL*, II, 1200.
11. Letter 642 to George Coleridge, 2 April 1807, *CL*, III, 7.
12. Letter 677, *CL*, III, 65–6.
13. Letter 682, *CL*, III, 76.
14. Letter 696 to Daniel Stuart, 18 April 1808, *CL*, III, 92–3; *CN*, III, 3530, July–Sept. 1809; *CN*, III, 3648, Nov.–Dec. 1809; *CN*, III, 3729, March 1810; *CN*, III, 4110, 1811–16; *CN*, III, 3908, June 1810.
15. *Lects 1808–19*, II, 498–9, 505–6.
16. Letter 1169, *CL*, IV, 903–9.
17. *CM*, I, 704.
18. Letters 525 and 530, 14 Oct. 1803 and 19 Dec. 1803, *CL*, II, 1014–15 and 1024.
19. Letter 481 to Mrs S. T. Coleridge, *CL*, II, 909–10.
20. *CL*, II, 797.
21. *CN*, II, 2549 and 2860.
22. Letter 639, 7 Feb. 1807, *CL*, III, 1–3.
23. Letter 643, 13 April 1807, *CL*, III, 9–10.
24. Letter 713, 9 Sept. 1808, *CL*, III, 120–1; letter 802, 19 Feb. 1810, *CL*, III, 284; letter 804, 14 April 1810, *CL*, III, 286; letter 807, 29 April 1810, *CL*, III, 289.
25. Letter 856, *CL*, III, 375–6.
26. Letter 1242 to Derwent Coleridge, 3 July 1820, *CL*, V, 81–3.
27. Letter 1241 to Thomas Allsop, 31 July 1820, *CL*, V, 79–80.
28. Letter 1250 to Edward Copleston, Provost of Oriel College, 11 Oct. 1820, *CL*, V, 113–5. The letter for Hartley to send is on pp. 112–13 above.
29. Letter 1303 to John Dawes, late May 1822, *CL*, V, 229–33.
30. Letter 1317 to Thomas Allsop, 8 Oct. 1822, *CL*, V, 251–2.
31. *Op Max ms*, II, 64–6; 67–8; 69; 90–2; 98.
32. Add. Ms. 47, 542, N 47, 19 Oct. 1830, ff. 19^v–20^v.
33. William Walsh, *The Use of Imagination: Educational Thought and the Literary Mind* (London and New York, 1959) p. 54.
34. *CN*, III, 3291n.
35. Cited K. Coburn, *CN*, I, 291n.
36. *CN*, III, 4181n.
37. 'The Education of Children', *Lects 1808–19*, I, 105–9.
38. *BL*, II, 44–5.
39. *Friend*, I, 472–3 and 500–1.
40. *Logic*, 7–13 and 19, citing *Hamlet* II, ii, 204.
41. LS, 216–7; C&S, 42–9 and 73–4.
42. Selected passages from *Op Max ms*, II, 71–9.

Chapter 5 The Humanity of Human Beings

1. *Friend*, I, 495.
2. *Friend*, I, 156.
3. Owen Barfield, *What Coleridge Thought* (Middletown, Conn., 1971) p. 95.
4. As by Bate and Engell in *BL*, I, lxxiii–civ.
5. Walter Jackson Bate, *Coleridge* (London, 1969) p. 158.
6. *LS*, 18–19.
7. Barfield, *What Coleridge Thought*, pp. 98–9.
8. *Friend*, II, 104.
9. Michael G. Cooke *The Romantic Will* (New Haven, Conn., and London, 1976) p. 17.
10. *Friend*, I, 158.
11. *CL*, II, 709.
12. *CN*, III, 3708.
13. Laurence S. Lockridge *Coleridge the Moralist* (Ithaca, N.Y., and London, 1977) pp. 258–60.
14. *Friend*, I, 97.
15. *CL*, II, 1198–9; *CN*, III, 3911.
16. *Friend*, I, 154–5; 156–7 (citing *Hamlet*, I.ii.150, 185); II, 104.
17. *Friend*, II, 131, 132.
18. *Friend*, I, 190–1.
19. *Friend*, I, 419–20.
20. *BL*, I, 304–5. This topic will be covered more fully in a later volume of *Coleridge's Writings*.
21. *CN*,III, 3281, 24 March 1808; *LS*, 66–7.
22. Add. Ms. 47, 529, N 34, 31 July 1827, ff. 7–7ᵛ.
23. *Friend*, I, 507, 508, 513.
24. *Lects 1808–19*, I, 115.
25. *CN*, III, 3824.
26. *Biographia Literaria, with the Aesthetical Essays*, ed. J. Shawcross (London, 1907) II, 253.
27. *BL*, II, 39–40; see James C. McKusick, *Coleridge's Philosophy of Language* (New Haven, Conn., and London, 1986) pp. 65–7, and A. C. Goodson, *Verbal Imagination: Coleridge and the Language of Modern Criticism* (New York, 1988) pp. 88–90, for the development of Coleridge's ideas about language, often in opposition to Wordsworth's.
28. *Friend*, I, 439.
20. *Friend*, I, 469.
30. *Friend*, I, 466.
31. *Biographia Literaria*, ed. J. Shawcross, II, 261.
32. *BL*, II, 15.
33. *BL*, II, 25–6.
34. *CN*, III, 3827.
35. *Lects 1808–19*, I, 224.
36. *Biographia Literaria*, ed. J. Shawcross, II, 259.
37. S. T. Coleridge, *Confessions of an Inquiring Spirit* (reprinted Palo Alto, Cal., 1956) pp. 51–3.

38. Anthony John Harding, *Coleridge and the Inspired Word* (Kingston and Montreal, 1985) pp. 79, 87, 94.
39. *Friend*, I, 507, 508, 513.
40. *Lects 1808–19*, I, 115.
41. *CN*, III, 3824, May 1810; *Friend*, I, 519.
42. *CN*, II, 2352; *Logic*, 15; letter 946 to John Murray, 23 Aug. 1814, *CL*, III, 55; *BL*, II, 54, 55, 56–7; Add. Ms. 47, 528, N 33, 1827, ff. 2–2ᵛ.
43. 'On Poesy or Art', *Biographia Literaria*, ed. J. Shawcross, II, 253 and 261; *BL*, II, 15–17, 25–6, 26–8; 'On Poesy or Art', *BL* (1907), II, 254–5 and 258–9; *CN*, III, 3827, May 1810; *CN*, III, 4397, March 1818.
44. *Lects 1808–19*, I, 325–6.
45. 'Confessions of an Inquiring Spirit', Letter III, 51–3.
46. *CN*, III, 3370.
47. *CN*, III, 3708.
48. *CN*, III, 3514.
49. *Lects 1808–19*, I, 329.
50. J. Robert Barth, S. J., *Coleridge and the Power of Love* (Columbia, Missouri, 1988) p. 3; *CN*, I, 1679.
51. Barth, *Coleridge and the Power of Love*, pp. 7, 9.
52. *CN*, II, 2938; *CN*, III, 3284, 3370, 3386, 3430, 3442, 3626; 3512, 3562, 3705, 3989 and 3514 (after Cartwright; see also next entry).
53. *Lects 1808–19*, I, 313–14, 315–16.
54. *Lects 1808–19*, I, 329–34 (cf. II, 507–8). See also above, pp. 78–9.
55. Add. Ms. 47, 543, N 48, ff. 8ᵛ–9.
56. *CN*, II, 2398 and III, 3510; letter 831, *CL*, III, 337. Many of Coleridge's expressions of his own feelings of guilt will be found in other sections of the present volume.
57. Letter 274, *CL*, I, 479.
58. *CN*, III, 3581, section 10, July–Sept. 1809.
59. *CN*, III, 4061, April 1811.
60. *CN*, III, 4356, August 1817.
61. *CN*, III, 4438, Aug.–Sept. 1818.
62. Letter 881, 7 Dec. 1812, *CL*, III, 424–5.
63. Add. Ms. 47, 532, N 37, f. 85ᵛ.
64. *CN*, III, 3866 and 3894, June 1810.
65. *Friend*, I, 524.
66. *Friend*, I, 520–1.

Select Bibliography

This bibliography is intended to provide a guide to editions of Coleridge's writings, and to some of the more important secondary works dealing with his writings about human nature, human behaviour, human institutions and human faculties and emotions. For editions referred to by abbreviations, consult the List of Abbreviations (p. xi).

Primary Works

The definitive edition of Coleridge's writings is the Princeton *Collected Works* (CC). Coleridge's multifarious thoughts about the nature of humanity appear in all the volumes, but especially in *Lectures 1795, The Friend, The Lay Sermons, Biographia Literaria, Lectures 1808–19* and *Aids to Reflection*. See also the *Collected Letters* and the *Notebooks*.

Earlier volumes containing useful material include: *Biographia Literaria, with the Aesthetical Essays*, ed. J. Shawcross (London, 1907); *Inquiring Spirit: A Coleridge Reader*, ed. K. Coburn (New York, 1951); and *The Table Talk and Omniana of Samuel Taylor Coleridge*, ed. Coventry Patmore (London, 1917).

Secondary Works

The introductions to the various volumes of *The Collected Works* contain excellent scholarly studies. The works listed below may also prove useful.

Barfield, Owen, *What Coleridge Thought* (Middletown, Conn., 1971).
Barth, J. Robert, S. J., *Coleridge and Christian Doctrine* (Cambridge, Mass., 1969).
——, *Coleridge and the Power of Love* (Columbia, Missouri, 1988).
Beer, John B. (ed.), *Coleridge's Variety* (London and Pittsburg, Pa., 1974).
——, *Coleridge's Poetic Intelligence* (London and New York, 1977).
——, *Coleridge the Visionary* (London and New York, 1959).
Boulger, James D., *Coleridge as Religious Thinker* (New Haven, Conn., 1961).
Butler, Marilyn, *Romantics, Rebels and Reactionaries: English Literature and its Background, 1760–1830* (Oxford, 1981).
Bygrave, Stephen, *Coleridge and the Self: Romantic Egotism* (London and New York, 1986).
Calleo, David, P. *Coleridge and the Idea of the Modern State* (London and New Haven, Conn., 1966).
Coburn, Kathleen, *The Self-conscious Imagination* (London, 1974).
Colmer, John, *Coleridge: Critic of Society* (Oxford, 1959).
Cooke, Michael G., *The Romantic Will* (New Haven, Conn., and London, 1976).
Davidson, Graham, *Coleridge's Career* (London and New York, 1990).

Fruman, Norman, 'Coleridge's Rejection of Nature and the Natural Man," in Richard Gravil *et al.* (eds), *Coleridge's Imagination* (Cambridge, 1985).

Fulford, Tim, ' "Living Words": Coleridge, Christianity, and National Renewal', *Prose Studies: History, Theory, Criticism*, 15(2) (Aug. 1992) 187–207.

Goodson, A. C. *Verbal Imagination: Coleridge and the Language of Modern Criticism* (New York, 1988).

Harding, Anthony John, *Coleridge and the Idea of Love: Aspects of Relationship in Coleridge's Thought and Writing* (London, 1974).

——, *Coleridge and the Inspired Word* (Kingston and Montreal, 1985).

Jackson, J. R. de J., *Method and Imagination in Coleridge's Criticism* (London and Cambridge, Mass., 1969).

Jasper, David, *Coleridge as Poet and Religious Thinker: Inspiration and Revelation* (London and Basingstoke, 1985).

Kessler, Edward, *Coleridge's Metaphors of Being* (Princeton, N.J., 1979).

Lefebure, Molly, *Samuel Taylor Coleridge: A Bondage of Opium* (London and New York, 1975).

——, *The Bondage of Love: A Life of Mrs Samuel Taylor Coleridge* (London and New York, 1986).

Lockridge, Laurence S., *Coleridge the Moralist* (Ithaca, N.Y., and London, 1977).

——, *The Ethics of Romanticism* (Cambridge, 1989).

McKusick, James C. *Coleridge's Philosophy of Language* (New Haven, Conn., and London, 1986).

McFarland, Thomas, *Coleridge and the Pantheist Tradition* (Oxford, 1969).

——, *Romanticism and the Forms of Ruin: Wordsworth, Coleridge and Modalities of Fragmentation* (Princeton, N.J., 1981).

Muirhead, J. H. *Coleridge as Philosopher* (London, 1930).

Perkins, Mary Anne, *Coleridge's Philosophy: The Logos as Underlying Principle* (Oxford, forthcoming).

Plotz, Judith, 'Childhood Lost, Childhood Regained: Hartley Coleridge's Fable of Defeat', *Children's Literature*, 14 (1986) 133–61.

Rajan, Tilottama, *Dark Interpreter: The Discourse of Romanticism* (Ithaca, N.Y., and London, 1980).

Taylor, Anya, *Coleridge's Defense of the Human* (Columbus, Ohio, 1986).

——, *Magic and English Romanticism* (Athens, Georgia, 1979).

——, ' "A Father's Tale": Coleridge Foretells the Life of Hartley', *Studies in Romanticism*, 30 (Spring 1991) 37–56.

——, 'Coleridge and Alcohol', *Texas Studies in Literature and Language*, 33 (3) (Fall 1991) 355–72.

——, 'Coleridge on Persons and Things', *European Romantic Review*, 1 (2) (Winter 1991) 163–80.

——, 'Coleridge on Persons in Dialogue', *Modern Language Quarterly*, 50 (4) (Dec. 1989) 357–74.

Walsh, William, *The Use of Imagination: Educational Thought and the Literary Mind* (London and New York, 1959).

Wheeler, K. M., *The Creative Mind in Coleridge's Poetry* (London, 1981).

Woodring, Carl R., *Politics in the Poetry of Coleridge* (Madison, Wis., 1961).

——, *Nature into Art: Cultural Transformations in Nineteenth-century Britain* (Cambridge, Mass., 1989).

Willey, Basil, *Samuel Taylor Coleridge* (London and New York, 1972).

Wilson, Douglas B., 'Two Modes of Apprehending Nature: a Gloss on the Coleridgean Symbol', *PMLA*, 87 (1) (Jan. 1972) 42–52.

Index

addiction, 98–9
adultery, 86, 157
affection, men's need for, 97
agency, 3, 11, 16–17, 24, 33–4, 42,
    47–51, 151, 226; denied by
    associationists, 48–9, in moral
    acts, 50–1; compromised, 98;
    annihilation of, 107–8; in
    labouring children, 138; loss of,
    197
Africa, 124
alterity, 199
Allston, Washington, 47–9
America, 131
animals, 4, 43, 55–9, 61, 63–5, 76;
    distinguished from humans, 50,
    65–6, 72; images of, 72, 98, 110,
    117, 120, 122, 130; self as, 103;
    analogies to, 214–15, 245, 259–61
anthropology, 13; early theories of,
    77–8
ants, 55
Arabian Nights Entertainments, 73
aristocracy, 117, 119, 125–6
art, 229, 235, 237–8
astronomers, 241
atheism, 259, 261
Aveyron, Savage Boy of, 78
Ayer, A. J., 52

Bacon, Francis, Lord Verulam, 155
Barfield, Owen, 219
Barth, J. Robert, S. J., 244
Beer, John, x, 56
Beethoven, Ludwig von, 74
being, 79, 244–5, 262–3
Bell, Dr Andrew, 200, 203
benevolence, 60, 128
Bewell, Alan, 4, 77
Bible, voices in, 9, 230, 242–3
Blumenbach, J. F., 55
body, as dungeon, 42; as sheath,
    42; as caterpillar, 44–5
body/mind problems, 17–18, 23–4,

29–30, 42, 44, 66, 68, 104, 106,
    172–3, 249–50, 252
Boehme, Jacob, 8, 140
Boudicca, 243
Brent, Charlotte and Mary, 90, 91
Buffon, Georges-Louis Leclerc,
    Comte de, 55
Burk, John G., 55–6
Burton, Robert, 99
butterflies, 64
Bygrave, Stephen, 23, 140
Byron, George Gordon Noel, 6th
    Baron Byron, 47–9

cannibals, 127–8, 131
chasm, 5, 56, 59, 70
children, 5, 29, 31, 33, 57–8, 84,
    117–18, 158, 160, 162–3, 165,
    180–200; in industry, 134–9;
    cruelty to his own, 109; in Italy,
    253
choices, 5–6, 10–11, 24, 62–3, 154,
    162, 173–4, 199, 219–20
Christianity, 9, 65–6, 85, 114–15,
    127, 134, 146, 150, 258–61
circumstances, 5–7, 62–3, 151
Clarkson, Thomas, 122–31, 203
class, labouring, 110–11, 114,
    119–22, 128
clerisy, 210–12
cleverness, 227
Cobbett, William, 116–17, 203
Coburn, Kathleen, x, 200
Coleridge, Berkeley, 257–8
Coleridge, David Hartley, 31, 56–7,
    112–13, 165–6, 181–8, 190–7; and
    Oriel College, 191–5, 197;
    similarities to his father, 191–2,
    195–6; responsibility for, 194–6
Coleridge, Derwent, 165, 181–4,
    189–92, 194–5, 261
Coleridge, George, 165, 186–7
Coleridge, Samuel Taylor, poems
    cited and referred to: 'The

Blossoming of the Solitary Date-tree', 177; 'Christabel', 55, 74, 139; 'The Eolian Harp', 44; 'Fears in Solitude', 132–3; 'Frost at Midnight', 22; 'Letter to Sara Hutchinson' (revised as 'Dejection: an Ode'), 158, 160, 175, 183; 'Osorio' (later *Remorse*), 101, 258; 'The Rime of the Ancient Mariner', 55, 74, 139; 'The Three Graves', 177; 'To a Young Ass . . .', 55
Coleridge, Sara (daughter), 179, 181, 184, 188, 190
Coleridge, Sara (wife), 83–4, 86, 156–7, 159–67, 181–5, 188, 256
colonialism, 79–80, 123–4, 132
community, 210
Condillac, Étienne Bonnot de, 12, 228
conscience, 32, 47, 105–6, 113, 115, 117, 143, 146, 150, 153, 155, 169, 177, 186, 258; throwing off restraint of, 148, law of, 150; defined, 220–1, 226, 228–9
consciousness, 16–17, 23, 30, 257–8; as act, 35; gradations of, 45–7; suspended, 193
contempt, 178
continuity, in nature, 69, 71
Cooke, Michael, 220
crime, 107, 122–6, 131; distinguished from vice, 146–9
cultivation, 204–5; of humanity, 210; compared to civilisation, 204–5, 210, 213

Darwin, Charles, 1, 5
Darwin, Erasmus, 56
Davy, Sir Humphry, 13, 89
death, 46–7, 68, 104, 257–8, 261
dehumanisation, 119–23, 131
depravity, 145
De Quincey, Thomas, 189
differences of kind and degree, 20, 59, 64, 65, 118, 246–7
discontinuity in species, 56; in being, 259–60
divorce bill, 86

dread, 255–6
dreams, 23–9, 100–1, 256
drinking, 101, 103–4, 108, 110–11, 147–8, 192–4, 196–7, 257; among Irish, 110–12; kinds of, 112–15
Dudley, Edward, 77
duplicity, of man, 255
duty, 16, 157, 162, 172, 175, 179, 192, 252

economists, political, 135
education, 60, 202–5, 208, 210; of women, 83; lack of, 110, 119–20, 122; false, 214–15
educing, 200
egotism, 23
emotions, distinctly human, 244–63
Evans, Mary, 157, 256
evil, 109, 139–55; origins of, 139–41, 143; in individual, 150–2; like insects in the heart, 145; as sign of freedom, 9–10
evolution, 5; early theories of, 13, 19, 20, 56, 197–8; in nature below man, 69–70

faculties, distinctly human, 218–21
faith, as instinct, 65
Fall, the, 22, 34, 139, 146
fancy, defined, 228
fatalism, 197
fatherhood, 181–97
federative being, man as, 22
feeling, 30–1
fetishism, 119, 141, 216
Ficino, Marsilio, 7
freedom, 10–13, 24, 40–1, 74, 162, 226, 229; suspension of, 115–18, 132–3
French Revolution, 115
Freud, Sigmund, 23
friendship, 162–4, 256

genius, 73, 169; defined, 226–7, 238; commanding, 153
German philosophers of human nature, 8
Gibbon, Edward, 114
Gillman, James and Anne, 191–3

god, need for, 261–2; image of, 21, 65–6, 72, 103
Godwin, William, 11
Grattan, Henry, 110
guilt, 106, 108, 131, 140, 244–5, 255–7, 262; as self-forfeiture, 53; and belief in God, 145–6, 256

Harding, Anthony J., 230
Hartley, David, 48, 99
Haven, Richard, 23
Hazlitt, William, 203
Hobbes, Thomas, 4–5, 13, 77
Huber, Jean Pierre, 55
human culture, 209–12, 218, 229
human nature, 16, 18, 76
Hume, David, 2–3, 4, 12, 14–16, 49, 51, 52, 119, 228
husbands, unhappy, 101, 169–70
Hutcheson, Francis, 56
Hutchinson, Sara, 57–8, 91, 154, 156, 158, 164, 166, 181, 244–7, 256

I, two-fold, 43; poor worthless, 49; unhappy, 247; as act, 260
I am, 36, 37
Ideas, 21, 39, 225; constituting humanity, 212
identity, 33, 257–8
imagination, 23; defined, 220, 227–8; 236, 241, 245; diseased, 100
imbrutement, 78
immortality, 3, 11, 46, 245, 257–63; as inwoven, 259; as instinct, 260–1
Inchbald, Elizabeth, 89
incest, 78–9, 254
Indians, 131
individuality, 5–7, 10, 22, 62–3
individuation, 70–3
industrialism, 119, 136–8
innate ideas, 3
insects, 3, 72
instinct, 56, 73; of butterfly, 64; for immortality, 3, 11, 260–1; human, 209, 213–14, 229, 231–2, 230, 232, 260, 262
insufficiency, 244, 250
invisible, 204, 217, 245

Isis, Temple of, 79, 254
Islam, 114–15

Jacobi, Frederic H., 9, 21, 52
Jesus, 47, 52, 115
Jews, 133–4
Johnson, Samuel, 10–11
joy, 244–6, 248, 252, 263
Jung, Carl, 23

Kafka, Franz, 57
Kant, Immanuel, 8–9, 11, 52, 119, 219, 256
Keats, John, 7

Labour, 134–8
Lamb, Charles, 7, 8, 193
Lamb, Mary, 7, 134
Lancaster, Joseph, 200
language, of rustics, 80–1; in children, 180–2, 189–91, 199, 207, 209; distinctly human, 229–35
law, indwelling, 81, 154
Linnaeus, Carolus, 56
Locke, John, 2–3, 12, 19, 77, 99, 220, 228
Lockridge, Laurence, 10, 23, 140, 221
love, 4, 45, 92–3, 96, 154, 156, 159–60, 162, 170–3; as desire of the whole being, 174, 249–50; in teaching, 201; as yearning, 244–6; defined, 250; as human, 251–3, 263
Lovejoy, A. O., 5
Luddism, 139
lust, 170–1, 176–7, 248, 255

Machiavelli, Niccolo, 155
machines, 75–6, 138–9
madness, 10, 57–8, 107, 118, 143, 147–8, 151–2, 256; 18th-century study of, 99; of heart, 150
magic, 73–4, 77–8, 216
Malthus, Thomas, 201, 203
man, distinguished from animals, 171–2, 198–200; *see also* animals
marginal beings, 4, 59, 77–8
marriage, 83, 141, 156–80, 244, 251–2; contract in, 162–3;

friendship in, 174; his own, analysed, 158–66, 175, 178; advice for, 167–80
materialism, 141–2, 214–15
Maupertuis, P.-L. M. de, 55
McCormick, Peter J., 52
medicine, 99
metamorphoses, 55–6, 64–5, 74, 76–7
Midgley, Mary, 140
Milton, John, 38, 128, 131, 140, 142, 153, 169
mind, 23, 230; theories of, 2–5, 7, 16, 24, as water-insect, 32; powers of, defined, 218–21
mobs, 115–17
Monboddo, James Burnett, Lord, 55
Montaigne, Michel de, 77
moral sense, 60–1
morality, and persons, 51–4, 79; and reason, 225–6
Moses, 79
mothering, 184–5, 187, 197–9
mothers, 83, 91, 163, 166; and language, 233, 235
Mozart, W. A., 77
music, 58, 80, 230, 235, 240

Napoleon, 13, 117, 130, 140, 153, 262
nature, as non-human, 50, 66–7, 75–6; as ladder, 71; as pyramid, 72; as witch, 74; as chain, 151–2; not slave of, 68; as bondage, 228–9; not lying, 259–60
Nimrod, 153
Novak, Maximillian E., 77

object, 34, 36; tyranny of, 214–17
ontological argument, 245
opium, 24–6, 29, 96, 103–9, 115
orang-utan, 20, 55, 56, 77
original sin, 139–40, 150–2
origination, 68–70, 220
origins of human civilisation, 77–9
ouran outang, see orang-utan

pain, 102–4, 109
Paley, William, 51, 153
pantheism, 66

Pantisocracy, 83–5
parenting, 180–200; anxieties of, 182–97
Parfit, Derek, 52
Patriarchs, 79, 294
Peel, Sir Robert, 139
Penn, William, 168
persons, 7, 53–4, 67, 82, 129–30, 199, 211, 216, 220; defined, 51–2; as ends, 52–3; as things, 119–39, 144, 154; fractured, 98–9; 'bundle theory' of, 14–15
philosophy, aim of, 232–3
Pico della Mirandola, G., 7–8
Pindaric Odes, 74
Pitt, William, 141
Plato, 29, 44, 152, 172, 225
Platonists, 7, 8, 249, 251
poems, see S. T. Coleridge and W. Wordsworth
poet, 233, 241–2
poetry, as human, 230, 237–8, 240–2; defined, 235–6, 239; and mind, 237; and pleasure, 239; not a sport, 249
Poole, Thomas, 181, 193
poor laws, 137, 204
Pope, Alexander, 2, 20, 92, 96, 223, 248
population, 137
poverty, 60, 88, 111–22, 136–7
prayers, 25–6, 47, 106, 109, 185
pregnancy, 86
pride, 159; satanic, 152–3, 262
Priestley, Joseph, 228, 258
primitivism, 77
principle, 21, 39–40, 149, 153–5; absence of, 103
procrastination, 102, 256; in Hartley, 186–7
property, 53
prostitution, 111, 121
prudence, 51, 153–5, 170–1; defined, 141–2
psychology, flux of terms, 24
punishments, 137, 200–2

rank, 161, 164–6
readers, kinds of, 38–9

reason, 21, 33, 59, 66, 117–18, 186, 198, 205, 262–3; defined, 219, 220–6; compared to understanding, 209, 221–5; occultation of, 151–2
reform, 139
Reimarus, Johann A., 55
religion, and persons, 51; and poetry, 241–4; and yearning, 244
remorse, distinguished from regret, 151, 178
Renaissance, 7
restlessness, 112, 153
Reynolds, Sir Joshua, 8
Robespierre, I. M. de, 140
Robinson, Mary, 88–9, 156
Rousseau, Jean-Jacques, 2, 4, 13, 55, 77, 201
rum, 126–7

sailors, cruelty to, 122–4
savages, 79–80, 117, 172, 252
scalping, 131
Schelling, F. W. J. von, 8, 9, 23–4, 34–8, 70, 140
self, 23, 33–5, 246–7; divided, 104, 107–8, 147; absence of, 195; usurping, 200; unity of, 200; as phantom, 215–16
self-affirmation, 263
self-analysis, 159, 161
self-consciousness, 20, 23, 30–4, 37–8, 199, 223
self-disgust, 100–1, 104–9
self-insufficiency, 244
self-love, 200
self-willedness, 192–5
selfishness, 51, 67, 82, 142, 175, 192–3, 212, 247
sense, 49, 64, 224–5, 227; slave to, 241
sensibility, 128, 142
Shakespeare, 13, 23, 41, 55, 60–1, 77–9, 92, 96, 140, 171–3, 236; compared to Milton, 236, 249–51; on love, 255
Shelley, Percy Bysshe, 7
sin, 10, 43, 144–5, 151–2
slave-trade, 122–31, 142, 150; mothers in, 125

slavery, 122–31, 200
Smeathman, Henry, 55
Smith, Adam, 67, 119
Smith, Charlotte, 89
Socinians, 61, 259
Socrates, 98, 147–8
song, human, 58
soul, 9, 24, 30, 39–49, 60, 70, 72, 103–5, 149, 155, 173; and nature, 68; sick, 102; of iron, 116; enslaved, 120–2, 130; prostration before power, 143; and reason, 221–3, 249–50, 260
Southey, Edith, 167
Southey, Robert, 47–9, 79, 83–5, 103, 108, 141, 157, 165, 168, 190, 200, 256
speech, 229–30, 237, 240
Spinoza, Baruch, 19, 256
spirit, 24, 34–9, 40–3, 65, 68–9, 262; and evil, 152
state, 12; purposes of, 209–10, 213–14
subjectivity, 23–4, 34–8, 52
sugar, boycott of, 126, 142
suicide, 104, 108, 124–5, 184, 244
Swedenborg, Emmanuel, 27
Swift, Jonathan, 3–4, 13–14
Symcox, Geoffrey, 55

talent, 227
teaching, schemes for, 17, 201
temperance societies, 113–14
Tetens, J. N., 8
thing, 31, 52–3, 141, 161, 216
thing-seekers, 53; as idolators, 215–16
thinking, 23, 31–2
touch, 4, 28, 41, 199; double touch, 28
trade, 122, 127, 129–30, 132, 135, 138, 229, 231
transportation, 121
tygers, 6–7, 46, 62–3, 76, 78, 131
Tyson, Edward, 55

Understanding, 66, 198–9; Universe, riddle of, 242; defined, 219–20, 228–9

ventriloquist, 243
vice, 112, 143, 146–7, 157; of slaves, 130
villainy, 149, 179
virtue, fragility of, 147–9
volition, 107, 196
Voltaire, 13, 77, 114, 202

Walsh, William, 200
war, 121, 131–3, 148–50; heart-hardening effects of, 141–2
Washington, George, 129
Wedgwood, Josiah, 2
Weil, Simone, 140
wickedness, 148–9
wild children, 77–8, 198
will, 23, 34, 41–2, 49, 68–70, 76, 98, 103–4, 107–8, 111, 150, 152, 186; failures of, 98, 140; idiocy of, 114; diseased, 146, 148; secret police of, 176; within the will, 206; defined, 221; and freedom, 229, 261–2
will-wantonness, 99
Williams, Bernard, 52
wives, 156, 157, 159–67, 174–6;

rights of, 163; ideal, 167–8; bad, 169–70
women, 82, 118, 121; petty concerns of, 83–4, 93–5; suffrage, 87–8, 118; and property, 87–8; and character, 96–7; and Reason, 87; scourging of, 86–7; as workers, 134; ideal, 91, 157; proposed novel about, 95; and dress, 232; heroic, 243; differences from men, 247, 254–5
Wordsworth, Dorothy, 10, 82, 154
Wordsworth, John, 166
Wordsworth, Mary, 154, 166, 169
Wordsworth, William, 10, 16, 19–20, 56, 66, 77, 78, 80, 94, 96, 141, 153–4, 163–4, 213, 244, 246, 261; 'Lines written . . . above Tintern Abbey', 21, 30; 'Michael', 183; 'The Recluse', 16, 19–20, 78; 'These times . . .', 213

yearning, 118, 230, 235, 244–5; pain of, 246, 249, 251

Zola, Emile, 57
zoology, 3, 55, 223